How America Became Capitalist

How America Became Capitalist

Imperial Expansion and the Conquest of the West

James Parisot

First published 2019 by Pluto Press
345 Archway Road, London N6 5AA

www.plutobooks.com

British Library Cataloguing in Publication Data
A catalogue record for this book is available from the British Library

ISBN 978 0 7453 3788 3 Hardback
ISBN 978 0 7453 3787 6 Paperback
ISBN 978 1 7868 0386 3 PDF eBook
ISBN 978 1 7868 0388 7 Kindle eBook
ISBN 978 1 7868 0387 0 EPUB eBook

This book is printed on paper suitable for recycling and made from fully managed and sustained forest sources. Logging, pulping and manufacturing processes are expected to conform to the environmental standards of the country of origin.

Typeset by Stanford DTP Services, Northampton, England

Simultaneously printed in the United Kingdom and United States of America

Contents

Acknowledgements

During the time this book was written, from its inception as a graduate school paper, to a dissertation, to its completed form, I worked as an adjunct instructor at five different universities. Writing a book while working as a precarious adjunct university employee can be an awkward and difficult experience. While many books contain statements of all the institutional support the scholar received, for an adjunct struggling to write while surviving by juggling whatever teaching positions they may find, and without a stable response to the question asked at conferences "what school are you affiliated with?" it is a complicated task to write a list of those who helped you through the process. This is due to the fact that adjunct instructors are generally treated as economic calculations on a spreadsheet, names to fill classes, and faceless figures floating in and out of departments. More broadly, the adjunctification of university teachers has reached a crisis point as well over two-thirds of faculty, in the US case, are some form of precarious labor. This is the result of the adoption of the business model of the university which puts money and "impact factor" over the education of students. And the dominance of precarious work in academic life has hit instructors in socially marginalized positions the hardest, whether it be due to structural discrimination based upon gender or race, class discrimination against those who could not afford elite universities, or simply the pushing aside of scholars working outside of the mainstream.

That being said, I would like to thank the Filson Historical Society for providing me with funding to dig through their archives. Working with Pluto Press has also been a refreshing experience in what can be an alienated world of publishing, and David Castle and Neda Tehrani have been especially helpful in supporting this book to see the light of day.

This work could not have been written without the support of my dissertation adviser, Fred Deyo, who took the time to figure out what I was trying to argue, even in messy and incipient forms, and understood the relationship between the research itself and the material conditions under which it was written. I could not have survived those difficult years at Binghamton University without the help and guidance of Linda

Zanrucha and Denise Spadine, two of the most hard working and important members of the sociology department, and everyone else who expressed solidarity over the years in which this book was written. During this time, Walden Bello also supported my pre-dissertation work, and Ana Candela went out of her way to support my progress. It is sometimes difficult to draw a line between intellectual and emotional support, and in this regard, Ege Özen, Sinem Silay Özen, and Alper Ecevit worked to make sure I did not lose my cıvık-ness (humor) after spending countless hours studying the depressing history of the United States. Babyrani Yumnam also contributed to this project in untold ways, often resulting in a large pile of books on the dinner table. I am thankful to the many other people who helped make this work possible. These include, in no particular order: Bengü Kurtege-Sefer, Akın Sefer, Deepan Ghimiray, Raju Huidrom, Katie Drouin, Nilufer Akalin, Kai Yang, Busra Ferligul, Mushahid Hussain, Alvin Camba, Nilay Ozok- Gündoğan, Azat Zana Gündoğan, and everyone else who expressed solidarity through those years of collective suffering.

From my days at York University in Toronto, Sean Starrs always kept me motivated with his unrestrained enthusiasm, as he continues to do so. Geoff McCormack's patience, thoughtfulness, and honesty has also served as a model for how to be both a thorough scholar and a decent human being, something that often gets lost in the world of academic egoism. Thanks also to Leo Panitch who supervised my master's thesis all those years ago, and has continued to support my progress through the academic world. I am also indebted to Brad Bauerly who took the time to read the project in its dissertation form in its entirety.

Going back to my undergraduate days at The Evergreen State College, thanks to Ellis Scharfenaker and Thomas Herndon for our jam sessions and discussions of Marxism and political economy, and to Philip Spencer for his unusual patience in reading and discussing. Adam Kohut also left a lasting political imprint on me, and remains a motivating force in pushing me to consider different ways of organizing work and social life. Special thanks to Alan Nasser for introducing me to the labor theory of value and opening my eyes as a young undergraduate.

Santino Regilme's practical wisdom has also guided me through the challenges of the publishing industry, and his good humor, combined with his sharp mind, helped to keep me moving forward. Sam Allingham has also served as a model writer-activist due to his unrelenting optimism and faith in the face of the uphill battle to organize contingent faculty.

My bartender, Nice Guy Nate, also deserves gratitude for keeping our glasses full and our minds just soggy enough to sprout new ideas.

Ken Baker's humility was an inspiration for what a researcher and teacher should be. Tynesha Davis introduced me to new ideas and exemplified the passion necessary to make social change happen. Neither are here to read this book, but I hope you both would have liked it.

Thank you to my Turkish family, Ayşe, Ilker, and Cem Tanır, Sirin Ozgun, and most importantly Yasemin and Leyla. And of course to my American family, too many to name, so I will leave it at "you know who you are." Finally, this project would not exist were it not for my grandparents, to whom I am grateful: Betty and Bob Jones, Ron and Virginia Parisot, J.P. and Sue Quinn, and Bob and Alice Glasgow.

Most importantly of all, I thank Canan Tanır, whose ever critical mind has pushed me to take this book further than I would have been able to otherwise. Her presence pushes me to be a better scholar and a better person in ways words fail to capture.

On the Prospect of
Planting Arts and Learning in America

The Muse, disgusted at an age and clime
Barren of every glorious theme,
In distant lands now waits a better time,
Producing subjects worthy fame.

In happy climes, where from the genial sun
And virgin earth such scenes ensue,
The force of art by nature seems outdone,
And fancied beauties by the true;

In happy climes, the seat of innocence,
Where nature guides and virtue rules,
Where men shall not impose for truth and sense
The pedantry of courts and schools:

There shall be sung another golden age,
The rise of empire and of arts,
The good and great inspiring epic rage,
The wisest heads and noblest hearts.

Not such as Europe breeds in her decay;
Such as she bred when fresh and young,
When heavenly flame did animate her clay,
By future poets shall be sung.

Westward the course of empire takes its way;
The four first Acts already past,
A fifth shall close the Drama with the day;
Time's noblest offspring is the last.

George Berkeley, 1728[1]

Introduction: The Embrace of Empire

The phrase "westward the course of empire takes its way" originated in a poem by George Berkeley, who lived in Rhode Island from the late 1720s to early 1730s. The poem celebrated colonization as the advancement of human civilization and as the next step in the intellectual and geographical progress of western society. By the time of the Civil War, northerners had embraced the motto as part of their struggle against southern secession. In 1862, for example, Emanuel Gottlieb Leutze completed his painting *Westward the Course of Empire Takes its Way* for the US Capitol.[1] In many respects, his painting represents the typical image of American expansion: masculine pioneers, chopping down trees, charting the territory of future empire, while their wives and children follow to tame and populate the virginally gendered ecology. At the top a man stands reconnoitering the mountainous terrain while another climbs to hoist the American flag, forging the path of empire. In the middle of the painting is a black man—liberated from the chains of slavery—who can find freedom through empire, yet is subordinate to the white men charting the course.[2] And the pro-union newspaper out of Marysville, Kansas, *The Big Blue Union*, for instance, announced each issue with "westward the course of empire takes its way!" directly below the title of the paper itself. Its editor for a time, Edwin Manning, future member of the Kansas State House of Representatives, was personally invested in both empire and capitalism. Among other exploits, he founded the town of Winfield, Kansas with the hopes of selling land to make a profit. Like many of the white settlers who built the west, Manning was someone whose life reflected both profit and empire.[3]

The idea and imagery of empire was historically embraced by Americans from the founding of the post-Revolutionary state through the nineteenth century.[4] The unprecedented pace of human expansion underlying this was observed by travelers such as Joseph John Gurney who explored Ohio in the early 1840s, noticing "undoubtedly the most interesting and surprising circumstance which engaged my attention, during this journey on the main route to the westward, was the unparalleled scene of movement—all in one direction—of which we were witness. 'Westward, westward speed thy way,' seemed to be the common motto."[5] And as another commentator put it, regarding expansion past the Alleghenies, "so rapid has been the emigration into that section of the Union, and so sudden its transformation from barbarism to refinement, that it seems rather the effect of magical power, than of human exertions, operating in the ordinary way."[6]

But this seemingly magic-fueled empire was not always guided by the power of profit-seeking capitalists. While capitalist interests were involved in colonial adventures in North America from the start, as joint-stock companies funded the transportation of populations across the ocean with hopes to profit from white-settler colonization, the history of American expansion is not simply a linear story of a transition from a non-capitalist to a capitalist society. Rather, the first two and a half centuries of American expansion are a circuitous tale, in which historically specific and unique social relations were built which often defy strict binary notions of "capitalism" or "non-capitalism." While land speculators and fur trappers and traders may have moved west seeking profits, other settlers relocated in order to escape the pressures of capitalism which pulled them from their freedom and autonomy and forced them into a system of dependence, revolutionizing their mode of production and habits of social life.

This book tells the story of how a *society with capitalism* became a *capitalist society*.[7] On the one hand, capitalist aspects existed from the earliest colonial days and continued to develop so that, by the 1830s, one traveler could write, "there is probably no people on earth with whom business constitutes pleasure, and industry amusement, in an equal degree with the inhabitants of the United States of America … business is the very soul of an American."[8] On the other hand, this same author could also say "an American prefers cultivating the smallest patch of his own to working on the largest farm of his neighbors, and rather emigrates further to the west than consent to become, in any manner or degree, dependent on his fellow-beings."[9] While part of the soul of an American may have been business, for many settlers, westward movement was a way to escape rising relations of capitalist dependence in the east. These settlers were not opposed to participating in market relations but they were reluctant to embrace a lifestyle of *absolute* market dependence. In the long run, though, capitalism did come to dominate and control the American population as the accumulation of capital penetrated into each and every aspect of daily life and the concept of what it meant to be a free American shifted to accommodate wage labor dependency as a life-long, normalized condition.

Overall, if there has been one constant in this messy history of social change, from the colonization of Jamestown to the global corporate, banking, and military empire the United States sustains today, it was what William Appleman Williams called "empire as a way of life."[10] Historically, *empire* was thought of as something to celebrate. And at certain moments in US history debate over the term has reappeared. Talk of American imperialism, for instance, was rekindled during the Vietnam War and during the US-led invasions of Afghanistan and Iraq.[11] But more commonly today "imperialism" is replaced with "intervention" as the United States "spreads democracy," just as European colonialists supposedly spread "civilization" at the expense of the lives of millions of victims of colonialism. In other cases, "empire" is replaced with "hegemony" and "leadership" or, at best, "informal empire," as soft-power and consent building are seen as the central characteristics of American power domestically and internationally. But, if anything, the idea of American power as hegemonic in a sense similar to Antonio Gramsci's definition—a dominant power engaging in consent building by presenting its interests as the universal interest—historically underemphasizes both the role of violence in the last seven decades of American global domination, and, as significantly, the centrality of empire as a central social and cultural aspect of American life from the start.[12]

From Western films depicting "cowboys versus Indians" and the continual reproduction of an image of "the west" as a harsh and volatile—yet mostly empty—space claimed triumphantly by white frontiersmen, to today's reproduction of imperial tropes through video games such as *Call of Duty*, films including *American Sniper*, or television ads recruiting young men to join the military as a way of fulfilling their masculine fantasies, Americans have always celebrated empire either directly, or in a fetishized, obscured form. To be an American patriot is to support the spread of freedom. This freedom was found through Andrew Jackson's use of violence to tame the supposed uncivilized indigenous peoples and through practically countless foreign interventions, from the invasion of the Philippines at the end of the nineteenth century to the Bush Administration's Iraq War to Obama's drone strikes, and beyond. To, say, live in the United States and not support American imperialism, albeit often clothed as a sheep, is to be un-American and a traitor to the nation. To criticize American power and society, at its roots, is supposedly to miss the point of freedom. And, after all, if you don't like it in America, its defenders chant, you can leave. And for those outside the highly policed borders of the United States, well, you are just jealous of "our" freedom.

Although its forms and meanings have changed—from Washington and Jefferson to Obama and Trump—imperialism has maintained its position as a mainstay of American life and US power. American consent building, domestically and abroad, has always rested on American military and police might, and, most centrally, the fact that imperialism is deeply embedded in the culture of society. Imperialism is not simply a political practice, it is a practice of daily life within American society, reaching down into the deepest roots of what it means to be "an American."

The purpose of this book is to partially excavate the historical depth of this. To this day, many studies of American imperialism tend to focus on the top down—as if imperialism is a political-economic practice—rather than a pattern of daily life. And while some work has been done over the last two decades examining the culture of imperialism, the question of the relationship between capitalism and empire building from below has been left relatively open.[13] In this context, the specific goal of this book is to examine the history of capitalism and empire in (what became) the United States and, in that, to locate how capitalist imperialism became a dominant factor in the structure of American power.

My method to accomplish this is to present an interpretation of the US' 250-year transition to capitalism. By showing the uneven social forms involved in the history of American expansion I aim to document how, from the early colonies through the Civil War and Reconstruction, the social relations underlying and driving empire building shifted. My focus on western expansion also allows the narrative to investigate the way empire formed as a racialized and gendered project. The American transition to capitalism as the dominant force organizing social life and the incorporation of further western territories into the American Empire were part of the same historical process. This is not to say empire simply "caused" capitalism or capitalism "caused" empire, exactly, in a general sense, although by the last phase of continental expansion capital did play the leading role shaping empire's form. Rather, the shape of each developed through an internal historical relation with the other. The goal in this book is to show the complexity of how these relations took shape. By the 1870s empire was essentially, although perhaps not completely, driven by capitalist interests. The logics and patterns of capitalism and empire had fully merged. Capital subsumed empire to its own historically specific imperial forms as the west became a space for capital to remake its own image with the labor of a multiracial working class.

The broad aim of this project comes out of an attempt to draw from the legacy of historical sociology going back to Marx and Weber and their struggles to understand what might be unique about capitalism by studying how it came into being. But to develop a relatively comprehensive interpretation of a two and a half century-long story would take a lifetime or two. Therefore, to organize a project of such historical scope but, at the same time, manageable focus, this book highlights particular states (in the making) as, in a way, case studies to demonstrate aspects of the larger thesis the book develops. The result may be a book that raises as many questions as it solves, and leaves open avenues for future research as much as it fills them in.

Additionally, while much of the narrative is based upon a state by state analysis, I do not mean to claim, by any means, that history happens "in" states. Capitalism emerged as an international system, just as the history of even, say, the Missouri frontier was shaped through broadly interconnected social processes linked on a world scale. Organizing the book this way was primarily a method to make a complex and huge story manageable to write, and to help focus the narrative on the interrelations of white settlers and empire. The interpretation of history presented here may also come across as messy and circuitous and that is, simply, because history is more often than not a disorganized and chaotic process. Capitalism in the United States did not emerge because of its incorporation into the world market, nor was solely it the product, exactly, of the unintended consequences of a clearly delineated class struggle. Locating class positions on the American frontier and expanding west, alone, tends to be complicated by the problem of class fluidity. The stories of individual settlers were often stories of class mobility, or overlapping and continually shifting class positions wherein families were squeezed between clear-cut class lines. White settlers' day-to-day decisions over several decades often found them, at the end of this, in a position in which capitalism had a greater degree of control over their life than before this process.

The argument presented here may also challenge currently existing disciplinary boundaries. Here I want to suggest a critique of some of what might fall into the contemporary structure of academic "professionalism." As Marx famously demonstrated, knowledge is never separate from material power relations, and reflects the ideology of the social power relations underlying its production. Historical knowledge is produced for different reasons—more often than not as nationalist knowledge to legitimate state power—and is generally divided, periodized, and compartmentalized by the ways that historians segment, regulate, police, and professionalize their division of labor. In other words, research does not just fill gaps in a literature, but is shaped by the power relations that shape the social sciences in themselves. For a scholar to find their place in "the discipline," then, means to follow the boundaries of a particular specialization or, at best, engage in "interdisciplinary" research which in most cases does not actually challenge these divides but simply combines them into countless sub-areas. Particularly in the age of neoliberalism, social scientific research is organized by the ways researchers brand and market themselves as a specific type of commodity, say, an "early American historian" or a "southern historian" or a "constitutional historian" or a "social historian," and so on. And this professionalized compartmentalization, reinforced by the elitist, prestige and status-based culture of the academy, tends to obscure the long and complex history of capitalism.

But as Fernand Braudel discussed many decades ago, historical time has many layers, from the day-to-day events we read about in the newspaper to the deep, long-standing structures of history that shape our lives in ways we are often not aware of or, in the case of capitalism, tend to naturalize.[14] Overly fragmenting history can block the advancement of our understanding of the history of capitalism as a deeply embedded social order that does not necessarily fit into clearly delineated conceptual and temporal boxes. In this way, the methodology and temporal scale of this book may hope to act as a call to problematize and rethink these divisions and the material power and status relations which underlie them.[15]

In this context, the overarching theme of this book is one of multi-linear complexity. If we draw our patterns and frameworks too tightly upon history's turbulent and tumultuous randomness and irrationality, then we end up creating neat looking abstractions *against* history's complex layers, as can sometimes be the tendency of sociologists. But if we take history as a disorganized jumble, as is sometimes the case with historians, then the connections between past and present, and, most significantly, the story of capitalism, can become lost. This book presents one way to address this problem, albeit not necessarily the "best" way if ever such a thing might exist.

Imperialism: the birth of a concept

For the so-called founding fathers, who built a state on the backs of African slaves and working class immigrants, *empire* was seen as something positive. For South Carolina Chief Justice William Henry Drayton, writing a case for American independence in 1776, all empires, from Rome to Britain, were destined to rise and fall. The next step in history was the rise of American Empire; a space of freedom and independence from the tyranny of Britain's cage. As he put it, "the Almighty setteth up; and he casteth down: He breaks the Sceptre, and transfers the Dominion: He has made Choice of the present Generation to erect the American Empire."[16] The idea and imagery of empire, drawing from influences heralding back to ancient Greece and Rome, shaped the physical and intellectual architecture of the country: Manifest Destiny, it would later be called. And even by the middle of the nineteenth century empire was still seen through a positive lens. It was, essentially, through the advancement of civilization that native populations were destroyed, replaced by the bright white light of American Empire so that:

> whatever colour poetry may lend to the removal of the Indians, it is, nevertheless, but the removal of a sick bed from a place where death is certain, to one from which it is more remote. Neither is it the death of youth or of manhood, but that of old age and decrepitude, which the Indian is doomed to die; and in his mouldering ashes germinates the seed of empires, destined to change the world.[17]

But something changed. Over time the categories of imperialism and empire shifted meaning. Through the 1800s the word imperialism began to take on negative connotations, so that empire became seen as a thing of the past: something nation-states advanced beyond, even if, in reality, the practice of empire remained.

In what remains the most detailed study of the history of the concept of imperialism by Richard Koebner it was argued that "the word *imperialism* was introduced into the English language as a gloss on a regime which had been established in France. It indicated the various—and in English eyes often dubious—ways by which the *Empire* of Napoleon maintained its hold on the French during the period 1852–1870."[18] It is said this is when "imperial" became an *ism*.[19] But in fact references to imperialism in the case of American history go back further than this. The term can be found in American newspapers as far back as the 1830s, if not earlier. In 1837, for example, the *Morning Herald*, a short-lived New York City newspaper, contains a column with a letter which states, "if these lines meet the eye of one now enthroned in American imperialism of political power, he may bid you beware of further publications."[20] While in the American context "imperial" itself was a term regularly used, often in reference to China and various other world powers, imperial*ism* also appears in the mid-1840s not in reference to France, but the Mexican Empire. As an 1844 piece in the *New-York Daily Tribune* says,

> Mexico, newly emancipated, and too inexperienced to use her wealth discreetly, was reeling to and fro in the intoxication of Freedom, and lavishing her resources on every hand with blind and careless profusion. She was making her experiment in Imperialism, when Austin appeared in the Capitol, and he found Iturbide on the throne.[21]

For the author, imperialism refers to the reign of Iturbide who was emperor of Mexico after its independence. The concept, in other words, describes a concentration of power.

Following this, imperialism would become used in reference to Napoleon III's centralization of power. As one Washington, DC newspaper reported regarding France in 1848, "the chief subject of discussion in political circles, and the source of serious alarm to the republican parties, is the diffusion of the spirit of imperialism throughout the country, but more especially in the army."[22] And the *Evansville Daily Journal* reported "since his election Imperialism had spread to an alarming extent throughout the country."[23] References to Napoleon's imperialism continued through the next several decades. In 1859, for example, several newspapers including Louisiana's *The Sentinel* printed an article by Italian political figure Giuseppe Mazzini. In it he warned against the spread of imperialism throughout Europe, stating, "the life of the Empire in France requires the triumph of imperialism in Europe."[24] And in 1865 another paper reports, "they know that the Emperor Napoleon is, by choice, both in literature and the more earnest world of fact, the great defender of imperialism in Europe."[25] Continuing, in June of 1869 *The Daily Evening Telegraph* of Philadelphia carried an article on the tension between imperialism and liberalism in the Bonaparte regime. It argued "imperialism is assailable on every side, and the Emperor will ever feel the ground sinking from under his feet, and the fruits of his policy turn to ashes in his grasp. In attempting to reconcile Liberalism and Imperialism, he has not succeeded on either side."[26] In these contexts, imperialism still tends to refer not to, say, colonization or expansion, so much as the tendency of a political leader to centralize power upward.

From here, the category began to develop its own American characteristics. Imperialism, it was now believed, was not simply a European phenomenon: Americans risked becoming dominated by an imperialist state at home. Specifically, Reconstruction was seen as a form of Republican Party imperialism against a defeated south, with President Ulysses Grant representing the American version of Napoleon. As one newspaper reports in 1874,

> this is an outgrowth of Republican rule, and of Grantism, which controls the party organization. It is a step in the direction of Imperialism, which Louis Napoleon illustrated when he threw off the mask of simplicity as a republican president and seized absolute power by a corrupt conspiracy of adventurers not unlike some who are now flourishing in Washington.[27]

And another paper goes so far as to title an article "The Fifteenth Amendment. A Blow at the Organic Structure of the States and in the Interests of Imperialism."[28] The Fifteenth Amendment, giving former slaves the right to vote, was seen as an imperialist policy because it destroyed the federal character of the American government and replaced it with a centralized form of imperialism as the north forced its policies upon the rest of the country. Anti-Republican papers would continue to equate Grant with imperialism through the 1870s and start of the 1880s. The *Nashville Union and American*, for instance, titled an article "Imperialism of the Grant Administration," suggesting "some of the Republican journals are growing somewhat restive and excited under the demonstration of the imperialism of the Grant administration."[29] And in 1880 one report stated, "General Hancock stands prominently forward as a man upon whom all true lovers of law and constitutional liberty can unite, as against centralism, imperialism, Grantism."[30] Joseph Pulitzer also wrote on the topic in this era, suggesting imperialism is "injustice, inequality, class distinctions, privileges to the few, wrong to the many, corruption and venality, but above all—fraudulent one-man power."[31] Thus, imperialism continued to refer to the concentration of corrupt political power.

In the 1890s the meaning of the term continued to transform as American expansion culminated in the Spanish-American War. Imperialism no longer referred to the tendency of governmental power to centralize, but American expansion abroad and the domination of colonized populations. As J.H. Tyndale wrote in 1899, "for all practical purposes imperialism and militarism are synonymous terms. Imperialism means to conquer with … sword and militarism to hold by brutal force."[32] This definition signifies what imperialism came to mean: to dominate another population and overpower them with violence. Or as *The Commoner* put it, "imperialism is the polite term used to describe wholesale killing and grand larceny."[33]

Some commentators also began to link imperialism with commercialism and trusts. As Norman Etherington points out, this may also be due to the fact that American newspapers such as Boston's *United States Investor* were actually calling for expansion and imperialism as a way to solve domestic problems of overproduction at the turn of the century.[34] And as Walter LaFeber famously discussed, the closing of the frontier at the end of the 1800s created a panic among some American intellectuals and political leaders who called for expansion as a way to solve the country's economic problems.[35] In many ways those critical of imperialism took their arguments from politicians and capitalists who, themselves, were advocating expansion as a way to solve problems of overproduction and economic slowdown domestically. These arguments were given form clearly by Charles Conant who stated,

> the writer is not an advocate of "imperialism" from sentiment, but does not fear the name if it means only that the United States shall assert their right to free markets in all the old countries which are being opened to the surplus resources of the capitalistic countries and thereby given the benefits of modern civilization.[36]

In other words, the United States needed to expand internationally and invest abroad to prevent its own crisis of over-savings. Imperialism was not necessarily an evil. Against this, by 1900 H. Gaylord Wilshire created an early socialist theory of capitalist imperialism.[37] He argued that the root of imperialism was American trusts damming up the domestic economy in the search for profits.[38] He developed this idea further over the next year, soon after writing, "'imperialism' is a means of diverting to foreign shores this threatening deluge of domestic 'savings.'"[39]

By the turn of the century the political embrace of American imperialism had started to go out of fashion, as even those who positively employed the concept tended to do so with reservation. And gradually in this context Americans would no longer present their "democratic experiment" as an empire. Imperialism led to the thirty years' war of 1914–45. Post-colonial movements emerged globally in the ashes of Europe's implosion and the collapse of aggressive Japanese nationalism. Following this, the United States supposedly became a leader ruling through consent rather than coercion, and supporting decolonization at the expense of the European empires. We are said to have moved from a world of empires into a world of nation-states. Globalization would integrate the world and, at least in theory, as liberal perspectives on international power suggest, states that are incorporated into dense market networks lose the motivation to go to war. With China's transition to capitalism, the collapse of the Soviet Union, and the spread of global neoliberalism, the poor of the world were to be elevated while the rich also succeeded: everyone would supposedly be a winner in the eyes of capital. Of course, following 2008 the global economy was driven to the precipice of collapse and a decade later a new leader has emerged, President Donald Trump, with a plan to "make America great again." Acceptance of racial equality and the embrace of gender diversity are threats to white Americans, who see their historical privilege under threat. A new president, driven by popular support for xenophobia and racism, has come to power, claiming to be able to protect the American way of life by closing the border to immigrants. But while the ideology of imperialism may have shifted, hiding its form, the practice of imperialism remains.

Defining capitalism

Central to this book is the concept of capitalism. Capitalism is a sticky term. On the one hand, it is necessary to define it as clearly and succinctly as possible. After all, if scholars and activists claim to be studying, or even fighting, capitalism, it must be possible that there is some general agreement on what it is, exactly. On the other hand, many greatly differing definitions exist, giving way to seemingly endless dispute. In a sense it may be the case that, while it is necessary to define capitalism, at the same time, no definition or abstract analysis of the system's inner logic or "laws of motion" will be able to capture the complexity—and most importantly great diversity—of its historical forms.

For the purposes of this book, though, I define capitalism as a social order in which practically all aspects of social life are organized around capital accumulation and the extraction of surplus value from a variety of labor forms. Capital, as Marx pointed out, is value in motion generated through the exploitation of workers.[40] The heart of capitalism lies in the relations of production, in essence, the organization of labor and ways in which value in produced. The approach used here, though, differs somewhat from Marx's work in *Capital* in that it suggests, historically, capitalists have always utilized a wide variety of labor forms that defy the abstract binary of "free" and "unfree" labor.[41] The making of capitalist labor relations, additionally, went along with the invention of race and remaking of gender relations.[42] In this regard, one of the themes of this book is to uncover the complexities of the ways that ever-changing constructs of gender—both within and beyond the household—transformed with the rise of capitalism.

Methodologically, the book is grounded in a historical materialist perspective in which "levels of abstraction" are continually expanded to move towards a broader whole. Conceptually, I also keep in mind the problem of reification, that is, the replacement of historical data with theoretical constructs. Marxist historiography contains a tendency to build models and impose them upon history, in so doing violence to history itself.[43] Many years ago Jean-Paul Sartre pointed this out when he suggested many variants of Marxism have engaged in apriorism. This means that "it [vulgar Marxism] has already formed its concepts; it is already certain of their truth; it will assign to them the role of constitutive schemata. Its sole purpose is to force the events, the persons, or the acts considered into pre-fabricated molds."[44] Or as E.P. Thompson phrased it another way, capitalism does not necessarily have any timeless or essential laws or rules of reproduction: "in my view, subsequent historical materialism has *not* found this kind of 'organism', working out its own self-fulfillment with inexorable idealist logic, nor has it found any society which can simply be described as 'capital in the totality of its relations.'"[45] My approach follows Jairus Banaji's call for historical materialism to stay continually open to the complexities of history against the tendency to box history in as, for example, perspectives that locate capitalism's origins in the sixteenth-century English countryside or, in another way, the view of capitalism as a strictly defined "world-system" tend to.[46] I do not claim the definition of capitalism as used here as a universal definition that potentially captures *all* of capitalism's history; in a sense, Marx's process of abstraction calls for the continual redefinition of categories as the analysis proceeds, and suggests staying open to further refined category clarification. But it does provide a particular working lens through which the history of the remaking of social relations towards dominance by capital from below as well as above may be seen.

This book also goes against the dominant "market revolution" approach in early American historiography in that it sees the social dynamics of particular market relations constituted by the social relations which underlie them.[47] Thus, "the market" is not something that has a life of its own, but is built through human labor and takes different historical forms depending upon the way the class relations underlying and structuring market relations are organized. In other words, the market revolution, and the ways in which social life became incorporated into relations of exchange, in the American case, has an overlapping but not necessarily simultaneous history with the *capitalist* revolution in which the logic of accumulation—rooted in social relations of production—became the dominant force guiding social development and colonial and imperial expansion.

My argument also goes against the idea that plantation slavery was not capitalist.[48] Southern American capitalist slavery was characterized by increasing productivity and technological advancement, from the cotton gin to the cross breeding of seeds, rational accounting, the hiring out of slaves if it proved more profitable than holding them—to keep capital in motion—a large-scale interstate slave trade, and a constant push to expand geographically: imperialism in pursuit of profit.[49] The primary difference with wage labor-based capitalism is that, instead of purchasing the temporary labor power of a worker, the capitalist purchases the entire life of the worker themselves. In addition to slavery, the narrative constructed here also attempts to locate the wide variety of labor forms capital subordinated historically including plantation slaves, hired slaves, tenant farmers, indentured servants, wage workers, and so on.

In conclusion, in this book capitalism is seen as theoretically definable at a particular level of abstraction as the point thereafter when capital restructures relations of production themselves. But capitalism is only truly definable through historical interpretation itself. Simply put, capitalism is not a definition but the concrete history, the complexities of which, and the labor forms and, more broadly, forms of power involved, defy closely knit, tight sounding definitions imposed upon history. This does not mean that *no* definition is necessary, or history can be told without theory. But it simply means that the goal of this book is *not* to develop a universal conception of capitalism or make a complete theoretical typology of its features, but to show how it historically came into being in its messiness and complexity and changed the lives of those who were gradually subsumed to its logic. In other words, my goal is to locate and bring out the grey areas in the history of capitalism which defy easy classification in order to challenge existing narratives as well as provide an alternative to them.

Defining empire

I define a capitalist empire as a structure of power overdetermined by the power of capital accumulation in which an often but not necessarily centralized political-economic system with diffuse, relatively autonomous arms, and containing expansive formal and informal tendencies along a continuum, controls, regulates, and dominates diverse populations and polities through a wide variety of methods of social control including the hegemonic construction of consent, creation and reproduction of racial hierarchy, regulation of patriarchal gender norms, and support for class inequality and exploitation. Capitalist empires differ from states in that states tend to be the central regulating political bodies of empires, but empires are generally broader structures than states in themselves. For example, the global British Empire was something larger than the British national state, just as in the American Empire the state plays a role of regulator of national and global capitalism, but corporations and banks contain their own co-constitutive logics and expansionary tendencies.[50] In other words, just as the British East India Company was initially part of the British Empire but not necessarily a part of the British "state" per se, so Walmart's global presence is supported by the American state, but is also a part of the broader American Empire as a whole. This perspective also differs from the majority of works on the history of empires in that it aims to radically historicize the concept of empire beyond transhistorical generalizations which take "empire" out of the context of "capitalism."[51]

Empire is expressed in the form of capitalist imperialism; the expansion of the power of capital usually against the wills of those who are forced under the weight of its violence. Marxists have tended to view imperialism as, with variation, the result of the push of capital to expand outside of national boundaries.[52] From this angle, imperialism is essentially caused by the interactions between banks and financial firms, industrial companies, states, and so on; in other words, imperialism is imposed from the top down. In this, the ways that gender and race are embedded in imperialism tend to be downplayed. But in contrast to the list of names more usually associated with sociological advancement of the theory of imperialism—Hobson, Hilferding, Lenin, Bukharin, Luxemburg, Kautsky—one key thinker developed another perspective which is often overlooked.[53] More than any of the other classical thinkers, W.E.B. Du Bois saw that imperialism was about more than states and capital: it was an experience of life traversing relations of class, gender, and race. His work *Darkwater*, for example, first published in 1920, featured a systematic analysis of the role of race and its relation to gender in European imperialism in the context of an anti-capitalist politics.[54]

For Du Bois, race and gender were built relationally and historically constructed through the history of European imperialism and colonialism. In inventing whiteness, Europeans claimed a higher level of self-perfection than any peoples in world history before them, asserting, essentially, a monopoly on civilization and nobility, and the right to spread through means deemed necessary in their own terms. Violence against other races, both in the United States and internationally, was done in the name of white morality, justice, and "motherhood"; as white Europeans also claimed to be authorities on proper gender roles, and whites also self-proclaimed their own visions of "masculinity" and "femininity" as hegemonic.

For Du Bois, while other commentators may have analyzed aspects of imperialism and capitalism, their analysis was incomplete without including the ways in which racialized capitalist states and their capitalist firms battled to divide the world up to create profits through the exploitation and value extraction of racialized labor forces on a world scale. And this racial imperialism was also gendered. European imperialism itself was rooted in the actions of men, and, in defining their own masculinity, they defined the masculinity of other races as lesser than their own. As he puts it, "they are not simply dark white men. They are not "men" in the sense that Europeans are men."[55] In addition, black womanhood was viewed as unclean and immoral. From the perspective of white supremacy, black women were inherently unable to reach the levels of high civilization of white motherhood. In a broader sense, then, he begins to show that white conceptions of femininity and motherhood were generated through the history of colonialism and imperialism as the ideal image of what a woman was "supposed" to be was built through processes in which white European femininity was seen as the standard and other racialized populations were viewed as deviations from this. This, at the same time, was used as a way to reinforce masculinity and patriarchy amongst European men.

Drawing from this legacy, this study aims to explain capitalism, imperialism, and empire as processes reaching down into daily life and stretching back to broad historical structures which they in turn co-shape. Western expansion on the frontier, for instance, was driven by the ways in which white masculinity was formed through the regeneration of empire. Race and gender were never peripheral to capitalist imperialism, but central to its history. By linking the saga of empire and capitalism with an analysis of gender and race, overall, this book aims to move past more limited abstractions and frameworks towards painting a broader picture of the history of American Empire.

Outline of the chapters

Chapter 1 examines the early colonization of British North America in the context of the broader international origins of capitalism. The development of late-medieval European capitalism formed through Europe's relations with the rest of the world, from the Italian city-states drawing from Arab commercial innovations to Northern Europe's connections with the Mediterranean, and beyond. Even England, which became the supposed national model of capitalism par excellence and the supposed ideal of the first fully developed capitalist society, advanced economically through its international linkages. Resulting from this world historical process, yet taking on specific characteristics due to the political economy of England's own unique capitalist pathway, the colonies of Virginia and New England formed their own historically specific characteristics. While capitalist interests and social relations played a large role in the Virginia colony from the start, albeit with some challenges and alternatives, in New England social relations formed that in many regards were not necessarily capitalist. From the start, the colonies were characterized by an unevenness of a variety of modes of social reproduction which would play out over the north-south patterns of development as empire expanded west. This chapter also highlights the complexities of gender in the history of empire. Most importantly, it suggests a less binary approach to the question of capitalist transition than has tended to be the case, and provides an outline of what this might look like. Here, I also introduce the category of patriarchal household mode of social reproduction as an ideal type to explain the role of gender relations in colonial and early American history.

Chapter 2 continues to trace the history of white-settler colonialism through Massachusetts, New York, and Pennsylvania. Here, my aim is to highlight the uneven distinctiveness of each region in the context of the transition towards a capitalist society. In so doing, the aim is to problematize the complexity of colonial and early American history itself, as much as explain the history of capitalist development in these particular states-in-the-making. While in Massachusetts, the township model provided an early method of settlement, and westward movement was driven in large part due to the expansion of patriarchal household relations, western New York, for example, was very much a project of capital-led development by the Holland Land Company, albeit in a way which articulated with petty-commodity relations of production. And Pennsylvania's proprietary history under the Penn family, religious experiments, and racialized patterns of squatter settlement and Native American removal also led the region to have a relatively distinct social history.

The third chapter brings the story together by examining the history of Kentucky, Ohio, and the borderland between. Here, settlers and squatters both cooperated and conflicted with American military forces which, in some cases, attacked their homes. These frontier settlers were also racialized as at times they were considered "white Indians." While light-skinned, these vagabonds did not fit the supposedly civilized norms which white Americans further east identified as the key component of their race. This chapter also examines the space between slavery in Kentucky and so-called freedom in Ohio, to examine the complex grey area between wage labor and slavery, and bring out the ways that capitalist development, from the start, exploited a variety of interchangeable labor forms between the states that defy economistic categories of "free" or "unfree" labor.

Chapters 4 and 5 switch the lens to the American south. As much as the United States was an empire of small farmers and laboring artisans, it was also an empire of racialized chattel slavery. I argue in Chapter 4 that the form of plantation slavery which developed across the Americas was unique in that it meant that the bodies of slaves were wholly commodified. In contrast to the argument that plantation slavery was not capitalist, or a hybrid form of capitalist and non-capitalist relations, I suggest that it was a form of capitalism in which plantation capitalists extracted surplus value from slave labor. But I also suggest that not all American slavery was plantation slavery, and necessarily capitalist. Particularly in the upper south, many households acquired small amounts of slaves to incorporate into the patriarchal household mode of production, similarly to the non-capitalist form of frontier production in the north. This chapter also discusses the "poor white trash" and "plain folk" of the old south to outline the general social structure and, in this, the articulation of capitalist and non-capitalist agrarian relations.

The fifth chapter applies this interpretation to the history of the territories which became the states of Missouri, Arkansas, and Texas. Here, I examine the first white settlers into these territories, and the slaves they brought, as up through the Civil War, slavery, in its uneven forms, drove much of southern empire building. For instance, it was not unusual for a planter to send slaves and an overseer to the frontier of empire, wait for the slaves to establish the infrastructure of colonialism, then follow after. These particular territories I have selected highlight the unevenness of slave relations of production. Too often, slavery is equated with the deep south, but by telling the stories of slave relations on the expanding western edge of empire, this chapter also aims to emphasize the complexity of capitalism, slavery, and empire in the south.

Chapter 6 brings the narrative together in the context of the Civil War and Reconstruction. I argue that the war was rooted in the complex interactions and contradictions between two forms of imperialism: one increasingly normalizing wage labor in the north and the other slave based in the south. Each major conflict escalating in the war was essentially about what the legal and social characteristics of newly incorporated territories would be, and whether slavery was to be legal or not. From the Missouri Crisis of the 1820s to the "Bleeding Kansas" conflict of the mid-1850s, to several attempts by southerners to take control of states in the Caribbean and Central America in the decade before the war, the slave system pushed a logic of empire building through extensive geographical expansion which could only be solved through the continual incorporation of new land into the empire of slavery. It was this tension which led to the war, and the result, Reconstruction, would play a key role in consolidating American capitalism. While by the 1850s the new Republican Party began to normalize wage labor as compatible with freedom, after the war the Democrats would as well. Meanwhile, "Slave Power" reorganized by defeating the attempts of free blacks to develop autonomous relations of production throughout the south and re-subjugating them with new forms of work including sharecropping.

The book concludes by briefly outlining the last phase of continental expansion. Instead of frontier households organizing in a patriarchal household mode of social reproduction, the last phase of western expansion was driven primarily by railroad and mining interests, agribusiness, and, fundamentally, the logic of capital. This is symbolized by, for instance, the Gadsden Purchase, as the last piece of continental territory was acquired for the purposes of profit through railroad building. Although the Homestead Act of 1862 did, for instance, allow the small farmer to persist in the newly incorporated territories, the convergence of capitalism and empire was, on the whole, complete.

1

The Origins of Colonial Society

The colonial exploit that became the United States emerged as a product of the European, and most significantly British, empire-building process. And while the community patterns of the colonial power were transplanted to the colonies, these were not necessarily reproduced identically. English aristocrats—or want-to-be aristocrats—indentured servants, African slaves, and other classes of settlers who migrated out of choice or force, found themselves in alien conditions with a foreign ecology to grapple with and living upon land already settled by native populations. In their new surroundings the white-settler societies of New England and Virginia did not simply emulate the habits they brought but adapted to their conditions to build something unique.

In this context, this chapter has two goals. First, it examines the ways that the Virginia and New England colonies emerged out of the international history of capitalism. In a broad sense, European global colonial expansion developed in an era in which Europe itself was going through a slow and uneven transition to capitalism, and patterns of colonialism reflected this. Each colony echoed a different aspect of European migration, and distinct intentions, which led to a less capitalist social structure in the north and social formation that was initially more capitalist in the south. Secondly, the chapter presents an overview of how gender relations were made in the colonial era and provides a framework for understanding some of the ways in which gender was recreated with the rise of American capitalism. In particular, I emphasize the concept of a patriarchal household mode of social reproduction, but also aim to move past binary conceptions of gender roles in the transition(s) to capitalism.

While in today's world many people assume capitalism is the "natural" outcome of human nature, in fact, as generations of social scientists have discussed, this is not the case. Rather, on a world-historical scale, it is relatively new as the dominant form of social life. Historically, in northern European cities such as Ghent and Bruges capitalism began to sprout as early as the twelfth century.[1] Textile production in Flanders was stimulated through relations with the international market as wool was sourced from England and finished goods made their way south to the Mediterranean through the Champagne fairs.[2] And, as capitalism was international from its origins, fluctuations in the Flemish textile industry stood directly in relation to economic movements elsewhere. From Flemish traders traveling to England in the thirteenth century to establish an interdependence between English wool production and the textile industry back home, to the first Genoese sea voyage to Flanders in 1277 bypassing the Champagne fairs, economic movements in the textile industry were linked to fluctuations in the international market.[3] Wage labor and class struggle were also present in both rural and urban Flanders. Many of the textiles produced were created by the labor power of workers who went on large-scale strikes several times, the greatest being in 1280.[4]

Connected from England to Italy, to the Baltic through the Hanseatic League, Bruges became the entrepôt of northern Europe and developed a sophisticated financial system to accompany its commercial growth.[5] Within the region, capital also flowed towards maximizing profitable investments and managing risk. In fourteenth-century Ghent, for instance, capital shifted towards the countryside to search for lower labor costs.[6] Capital also invested in infrastructure, specifically in the form of water management and flood prevention technologies. These projects generally used temporary laborers paid relatively low wages and were organized by contractors who expected to profit from taxes that water boards collected. Water boards also sold annuities to investors, who hoped to profit from the infrastructure projects.[7] And while some labor was organized into guilds, this did not necessarily preclude capitalist development. While guilds regulated prices, supply and demand, and regulated class conflict and compromise within production processes and between producers and merchants, many apprentices and journeymen never themselves became masters as the apprentice system partially functioned to create a working class of labor for masters to use.[8] Overall, as Bas van Bavel notes, in the Netherlands, by the eleventh and twelfth centuries market relations were well established and by the thirteenth and fourteenth centuries, land was commodified and marketized and capital-wage labor relations took off, as, by the sixteenth century, in the Netherlands as a whole, perhaps one-third to half of all labor was wage labor, with higher rates in some parts of the countryside.[9]

Further south the development of capitalism in the Italian city-states was shaped by international relations and appropriations, especially from Islamic societies. The Crusades spurred the growth of Italian wealth as capital sought profits through violence. Venice supplied ships and in return for transporting soldiers and weapons Venetians would demand partial control over captured cities, which they could then profit from through taxation and control of licenses for productive enterprises. And Venetian capital, perhaps in part emulating the Arab *qirad*, was regularly pooled into *commendas*, partnerships in which investors could merge their capital to manage risk.[10] Many other aspects of what would become early capitalism in the Italian city-states seemingly derived in part from Arab ideas and institutions. Commercial terms such as *sakk* which became translated into *check*, an instrument of monetary exchange, among many other concepts, came from Arabic words. The adoption of Arabic numerals made calculations much easier than using Roman numerals and, along with algebra, made the Italian "invention" of double-entry book keeping possible.[11] And leading mathematical thinkers such as Leonardo Fibonacci, who grew up in Algeria, developed commercial mathematics after learning from Arabs.[12] Europeans also modeled their coins after Islamic currencies.[13]

Additionally, through the latter part of the thirteenth century, Florence developed a capitalist economy in which wool produced in England, Spain, and Portugal was shipped through the Low Countries and France into Florence to be worked by the Florentine proletariat to sell to traders in the Levant for Asian goods. By the 1330s a significant proportion of Florence's population lived on wages from the textile industry.[14] Overall, by the thirteenth and fourteenth centuries, many aspects of capitalism unevenly developed throughout Europe. Capitalists pooled their capital in associations to manage risk, complex credit and financial tools were developed, workers sold their labor power to capital for wages, and merchant capitalists made great profits, and sometimes losses, from international trade.

Slave labor also played a key role in the rise of capitalism. Initially, Portuguese expansion set up the pattern for the European conquest and colonization that followed. This included creating the model of plantation slavery that spread across the Atlantic to the West Indies and North American colonies. Settling on Madeira in 1419, the Azores in 1427, and the Cape Verde Islands in 1450, and later Sao Tome and Fernando Po in the 1470s and 1480s, Portuguese merchants soon found, first, profits from intercepting the already existing African slave trade and, secondly, that slave labor could be put to profitable use. They found slaves could be a useful source of labor to work on and strengthen their trading posts.[15] Thus, Sao Tome and Fernando Po were settled and quickly became centers of the slave trade based on the use of slaves to build fortifications, churches, and so on. And Lisbon responded to the rise of the slave trade by introducing licenses and taxes on slave traders with the goal not of capitalist development, but financing the monarchy as taxing merchant capital became a major source of wealth for the Crown, by 1560 perhaps half of its revenue.[16]

By the middle of the fifteenth century, all the components for the rise of a plantation sugar industry on islands off the coast of West Africa were in place. The Portuguese brought sugar cane and processing equipment from Sicily (as islands such as Cyprus, historically, had plantation sugar production in the fourteenth century) and Spain to Madeira in 1446. Beginning as a way to finance exploration, colonization and plantation building brought together territorial empire building, capital, and market relations stretching from Italy to Africa, and beyond. By 1500 Madeira had become a large center of sugar production, with about 2,000 slaves working in a total population of 15,000–18,000. Slavery then spread across the Atlantic to the Americas. As the native populations were wiped out by the millions and indigenous labor proved difficult to sustain and control, the Spanish and Portuguese soon resorted to African slave labor, and by the middle of the fifteenth century, dozens of sugar plantations were set up in the Americas, some of which had more than a hundred slaves. By 1570, it is estimated that there were perhaps 2,000 to 3,000 African slaves in Portuguese Brazil, and perhaps ten to fifteen as many native slaves. But by 1600, there were perhaps 12,000 to 15,000 Africans in the colonies, and between 1600 and 1650, it is estimated at least 200,000 Africans were brought across the ocean.[17]

In this emerging world order, by the time capitalism developed in England, its international formation had been in motion in fits and starts for several centuries. England's contribution to the origins of capitalism, then, was not, as some have argued, that capitalism was essentially invented there.[18] Rather, England took this uneven history several steps forward as the enclosures dispossessed the agrarian population, a wage labor class with nothing to sell but labor power formed, and capitalism gradually took hold, setting the stage for the British to build a global empire.

From England to Virginia

Out of this historical process the colonies of North America were founded. From one angle, it might appear the colonies were capitalist from their inception. They arose interconnected with the developing Atlantic world market, held together by ships sailing for profit. Yet social historians have argued that the social relations that formed within the first two centuries of colonization may have not been capitalist. So we seem to have two different possibilities: either (what became) the United States was capitalist from the start, and never went through a transition in the first place, or else at some point the country became capitalist.[19]

In the case of Virginia, capitalist interests tended to prevail from the start. The first British merchants, gentlemen, and adventurers began to explore the coast of North America in the last quarter of the sixteenth century. And the first substantial attempt at colonization was the lost colony of Roanoke. The reasons for the creation of the colony were manifold, from interimperial rivalry with Spain to privateering.[20] While dreams of the profits of empire may have guided the Roanoke adventurers, resulting in failure after three expeditions, following in the path of the Spanish and Portuguese, some English investors continued to see North American colonization as a path towards profits. They dreamed of locating precious metals, or finding a Northwest Passage, or producing wine and silk for the English market. Thomas Hariot, for example, wrote a guide in 1588 describing commodities which could be produced in Virginia to stir up excitement for colonization among English investors.[21] And adventurers and investors such as Richard Hakluyt believed that a colony could produce basic commodities such as oil, wine, and sugar, moving England away from dependence on foreign sources. It would additionally create an outlet for the English poor, dispossessed by the rise of capitalism. The colony would likewise provide an impetus to expand English naval power, particularly as natural resources such as timber could be used to develop a shipbuilding industry.[22] But this capitalist fantasy eventually clashed with reality as early settlers instead found a country populated by native peoples who resisted their expansion, in which precious metals were scarce and silk and wine difficult to produce, no evidence of a Northwest Passage, and a climate in which tobacco, partially to the consternation of the ruling political elite of the Virginia Company of London, became the staple of local farming.

From the start, Virginia was built on a combination of capital and colonization. But the dream of an independent American Empire was yet to be conceived for almost two centuries. Rather, settlers were part of the emerging British Empire. The colony was born at a time in which England was going through its own transition to capitalism, and the political economy of colonial Virginia reflected this, as it was not the British Crown that initially governed the colony, but the Virginia Company. For investors in the Virginia Company, the colony was a potential source of primary resource extraction and hopes existed that gold and silver might be found. It was also a way to break England's dependence on foreign imports by producing basic agricultural commodities for the English market. And it was believed that a route to China could be found through America. In any case, for investors in the Virginia Company colonization was seen as a potential route towards profit.[23]

The first settlers reached Virginia in late April of 1607 and explored the area until, in mid-May, they choose the site to build Jamestown. From the start, tensions arose with the natives. First, the Native Americans found a group of two or three dozen explorers in Cape Henry, and chased them back to their ships. And after spending a week constructing a fort, the colonists, under Captain Christopher Newport, headed up river to explore and begin diplomatic relations with the natives. They learned that local native groups were linked together through the leader Powhatan, and on returning to Jamestown three days later, found Powhatan's warriors had attacked the fort.[24] Of course, relations with the natives were not always so violent, and the settlers quickly became dependent on their food. This was in large part due to the poor planning of the English. Rather than sending over potentially self-reproducing families, or laborers and farmers who could work the land, a disproportionate number of settlers were gentlemen. In the first three shiploads, for example, 293 men and two women came, and 110 of these were gentlemen. Only fifty-one were laborers (in some cases servants of the gentlemen) and twenty-seven craftsmen.[25] The fundamental problem was that "gentlemen, by definition, had no manual skill, nor could they be expected to work at ordinary labor."[26] Instead, their role was supposed to be "force of knowledge" and "exercise of council"; in other words, organizational planning and governance. But a colony cannot be built on brains alone, and the inability of Virginia to become self-sustaining in its early years meant that, by the cruel winter of 1609–10, it has been said that colonists were possibly going so far as to resort to cannibalism.[27]

The social forces that drove the colonization of Virginia were also very much a masculine infused form of capitalism. Men risked their lives, and often died, traveling across the ocean seeking profit and prestige. Given that the majority of settlers were men, the Company also sent over shiploads of women, "Tobacco Brides," to marry them. For example, the Company's notes of 1619 record they sent over ninety "young maids to make wiues for so many of the former Tenants."[28] And in 1621 the Company sent over fifty women as "they require one hundredth and fiftie of the best leafe tobacco for each of them; and if any of them dye there must be a proportionable addition vppon the rest."[29] A social logic of patriarchal expansion was also quickly established in the colony. The 1619 Proceedings of the Virginia Assembly contain, for example, a petition to assign land to the male children of planters.[30] Thus, shortly after the colony began, settlers began to clamor for more land to pass to their sons.

While capital may have guided colonialism, the Company also suggested adopting aspects of a tributary form of empire over the indigenous peoples. In 1609, for instance, the Virginia Council instructed Sir Thomas Gates that, if distrust arose with Powhatan, "but if you finde it not best to make him yor prisoner yet you make him yor tributary."[31] But overall, the goal of the Company, funded by shareholders, was to find a way to generate profit. In their letter to Gates, for example, they suggested four ways of doing this; mining, trade, tribute from the land, and "the fourth is labour of yor own men in makinge wines pitche Tarre sope ashes, Steele Iron Pipestaues in sowinge of hempe and flaxe in gatheringe silke of the grasse, and pvidinge the worme and in fishinge for Pearle Codd sturgeon and such like."[32] In other words, the desire of the Company was not to become dependent upon tobacco production, but to create a diversified economy through the construction of profitable social relations. To accomplish this, they sent over men to start ironworks, saltworks, build sawmills, breed silk worms, and so on, although their attempts proved of limited success as tobacco quickly became king.[33] Initially, agricultural production was run collectively.[34] But in 1609 small amounts of land were distributed to individuals, and in 1614 the first group of Company men finished their contracts and were allotted 3 acres per individual, or 12 per family. Independent farmers were expected to feed themselves in addition to providing two and a half barrels of corn a year and working for the Company one month per year.[35] This started the tradition of private individual agricultural social property relations that would continue to grow.

By 1618–19 the Company introduced full private property into the agrarian landowning structure by allowing "fee simple" land. In contrast to "fee tail" land in which an individual's ability to alienate land was dependent on personalized relations with state authorities, under fee simple land individuals were given independent mastery of their land; the difference between "holding by grace" and "owning by right."[36] This was part of political restructuring in 1619 in which martial law was replaced by a limited representative democracy. An elected general assembly was set up, run by the colony elite. The Virginia Company encouraged this with the hope that giving settlers some of the rights and privileges they had back home might encourage more to come and build profitable plantations.[37] Although landholdings would be fee simple, to regulate production and satisfy the basic subsistence needs of the colony, farmers were required to grow corn for the Company, as "every man to sett 2 acres with corn (Except Tradesmen following their trades) penalty forfeit^r of corn & Tob^o & be a Slave a year to ye Colony."[38] The Company also kept land on which its agents hired tenant farmers. These tenants were to pay half of their profits to the Governor, Treasurer, and Company.[39]

Rights to individual capitalistic ownership of land did not go uncontested though. Under Charles I, after the Virginia Company lost control of the colony to the Crown in 1624, Royal Governor Sir John Harvey arrived in 1630. He was given instructions by Charles I to transform Virginia's ownership rights to something closer to a system of subinfeudation as opposed to capitalist private ownership. He declared all preexisting patents invalid and created new ones that would require settlers to pay rents to proprietors and a quit rent to the empire.[40] But these changes proved very short-lived, and several years later the Puritan colonialists expelled Harvey from the colony.

By the 1620s the path that Virginia would follow which set up the basis for the uneven development of the southern colonies was in place: primary commodity production and forced labor. As slavery gradually came to dominate in the next half century of expansion, capital and unfree capitalist labor came together. This was a small part of the broader uneven development of the making of international capitalist relations. Capital accumulation in Virginia developed as part of a spatially expanding world market and as one node on the broader trans-Atlantic world. This was solidified by the formation of a legal structure supporting capitalist private property rights. Virginia lawmakers imported English law and modified it to fit the pressures of capital accumulation in the colony. This included creating a legal structure which would enforce the collection of debts, punish indentured servants' deviance, and support the development of chattel slavery.[41] Territorial expansion continued as the headright system developed. Colonists who could afford their way to Virginia would be given 50 acres, and anyone who paid for another to come over would also be given 50 acres.[42] And most importantly settlers started growing tobacco.[43] The Company itself, though, was very critical of tobacco production, and repeatedly complained, particularly as they saw planters neglecting corn production at the expense of tobacco.[44] Also, given the lack of specie money, tobacco also served as the major currency of the colony as the Company even collected taxes in tobacco.[45] It was also used to pay rangers who policed the frontier.[46]

Just as the Company shipped and sold women to male settlers, so they additionally sent over children. For example, in January 1619 it is recorded, "the Citie of London have by Act of their Common Counsell, appointed one Hundred Children out of their superfluous multitude to be transported to Virginia; there to be bound apprentices for certaine years."[47] During this time they also carried over servants to be exchanged with settlers in return for their passage.[48] By then, the use of indentured unfree labor began to take off in the colony, encouraged by the headright system. For the next few decades, indentured servants, more than slaves, would provide the main source of labor for the colony.

Throughout the seventeenth century, it is estimated that at least half to two-thirds of immigrants to North America were indentured servants and this rate was particularly high in the Chesapeake region.[49] Indentured servitude generally took two forms: either the servant would make a contract before leaving Europe or else servants were sent without contracts, to make them on arrival.[50] Servants themselves were a form of unfree commodity; they could be bought or sold on the market. And, in effect, indentured servitude functioned as a type of indirect wage; to pay for their passage across the ocean they were required to work as servants for a number of years until given their "freedom dues"; usually a piece of land and basic resources to survive. But while servants made up a high proportion of immigrants, their proportion of the total population declined over time. While in 1630 servants may have made up over 40 percent of the population, a decade later they made up perhaps a quarter of the population (depending on the estimate) and between 7 to 10 percent by 1700.[51] In other words, some servants died and some gained their freedom.

Indentured labor combined with tobacco production and family labor set the basis for Virginia's growth. While the colony had perhaps 8,000 people in 1642, thirty-five years later it had 40,000.[52] This immigration was made possible by social conditions within England. Many of those sent were poor and working people who were swept off the streets, convict labor, or wage laborers who chose to go given poor opportunities for employment in English capitalism. Historians have noted, for example, a correlation between immigration, wages, and tobacco: "servants indentured themselves to Chesapeake planters when English wages declined and tobacco prices rose; they refused to go when English wages rose and tobacco prices dropped."[53] Not all indentured servants were necessarily young men and women though. Blurring the line between indentured servant and tenant farm family, Richard Smyth and his wife and children were brought over in 1620 in an indenture and had their expenses paid for and were given a piece of land to work in return for "one third pte of all English corne & of maiz or Indyan wheat and the one halfe of all other pfits fruite cattle seeds & increase whatsoever raysed taken or had from the ground or land of them."[54]

But while in many ways the Virginia colony was organized around capitalism from the start, not all farmers practiced capitalist production. On Virginia's eastern shore, where settlers were connected to the world market through merchants, social life appears to have been organized around non-capitalist forms of production in the early and mid-1600s. Production tended to be organized around family farms, connected through kinship and friendship networks which generally did not stretch between walking distance of farms, as most people did not own horses, and in which most commercial exchange took the form of barter and personal loans and gifts. In some cases, there were tenant farmers. But this was a way for working farmers to attempt to raise themselves up to become independent petty-commodity producers, rather than a continually dependent tenant or laborer class.[55]

Likewise, by the late 1600s one account of the inhabitants of Virginia more generally suggests, "of Grain and Pulse they commonly provide only as much as they expect they themselves shall have occasion for, for the Use of their Families, there being no Towns or Markets where they can have a ready Vent for them, and scarce any Money to serve for a common Exchange in buying and selling."[56] Settlers also often produced their own clothing, as one complained that Lieutenant Governor Francis Nicholson recommended an act to Parliament "*forbidding the Plantations to make their own Cloathing;* which, in other Words, *is desiring a charitable Law, that the Planters shall go naked.*"[57] That being said, traders including William Byrd linked backcountry settlers to broader world market relations as they made sure commodities could pass from the frontier of Virginia eastward, as his commercial networks in the 1680s extended to England and the West Indies.[58]

But gradually slavery took hold. By this time, Virginia was a latecomer to slavery in the Americas, but its adoption would condition the southern developmental path. Slavery in Virginia emerged out of the making of Atlantic world slavery and the first dark-skinned people presumed to be slaves were brought over in 1619. Early language tends to conflate slave and servant though; the distinction itself was vague as indentured servants were sometimes called "slaves" and as black servants were also in some cases not necessarily slaves for life. For example, a record from 1675 discusses the case of Philip Corven, a black servant, who was to serve Mr. Humphrey Stafford for eight years, "then, next ensueing, and then fhould enjoy his freedome & be paid three barrels of corne & a sute of clothes."[59] But Mr. Stafford sold Philip to Mr. Charles Lucas, who forced him to serve three years longer. Due to this, Corven petitioned the court for redress. And racial ideology in this era remained at a formational stage, as the term "race" itself was not used. Rather, native peoples were referred to as infidels or savages, in contrast to Christian settlers. But early racial stereotyping was in full force. As one record puts it in 1622, "they are (saith hee) by nature sloathfull and idle, vitious, melancholy, slouenly, of bad conditions, lyers, of small memory, of no constancy or trust ... lesse capable then children of sixe or seauen yeares old, and lesse apt and ingenious."[60] Native Americans were also enslaved, for example, in 1685 a man named Crawford petitioned against Roger Jones for harboring three Native Americans who he claimed to have purchased as slaves.[61]

By the 1640s Virginia court documents record sales of black slaves and around this time the first records of laws based around race in Virginia were recorded such as a 1643 Virginia tax law for tithable persons that shifted from all working adult men to all adult men and "Negro" women.[62] And by the 1660s the racialized state began to solidify, for instance, a law was passed in 1662 in Virginia doubling fines for those caught fornicating with a "Negro" man or women, and interracial marriage was banned in Maryland two years later.[63] While early on the distinction between slave and servant was somewhat unclear, fear of slave revolt along with the creation of a shared sense of whiteness, even among servants, reinforced divisions between supposedly superior white people and inferior red and black skin especially after Bacon's Rebellion in 1676.[64] While by 1675 there were perhaps 2,500 slaves in Virginia, between 1700 and 1750 an estimated 75,000 slaves entered into the Chesapeake region, most coming directly from Africa.[65] And by the beginning of 1700 the line between slave and servant was set, as one writer of the time put it, "their Servants, they distinguish by the Names of Slaves for Life, and Servants for a time."[66] Through 1740, when the Virginia economy began to diversify beyond tobacco into commodities like wheat and iron, slaves and tobacco provided the basic recipe for the growth of capitalism in the Chesapeake. While the Virginia Company eventually collapsed and the colony was taken over by the British state, which charged quit rents, it was this general process of uneven development, conditioned by the way the American south articulated with the world economy that set the basic path for the expansion of capitalism through the south.[67] Economic development would be further encouraged by the state as, for example, among other incentives, "for Encouragement of Manufactures, Prices were appointed for the Makers of the best Pieces of Linnen and Wollen Cloth, and a Reward of Fifty Pounds of Tobacco was given for each Pound of Silk."[68] Thus, while the colony was controlled by the Crown rather than the Company, it would continue to encourage capitalist development and enforce the power of capitalist law.

The settlement of New England

In their own time, most settlers may have believed they were extending what New England Puritan leader Cotton Mather called "Christ's Empire."[69] As one poem from the era put it, "yet there a mighty future is begun, and men and things a race of empire run."[70] As empire was built by the hands of colonial New Englanders, by the mid-1800s one commentator said of Increase Mather, Cotton's Father, "by these wise exertions, crowned with complete and extraordinary success, he laid the foundation upon which Washington, Franklin, and their compatriots established the vast and extending empire of the United States of America."[71] But even by this time not every American necessarily celebrated empire. The esteemed women's rights activist Lydia Marie Child lamented the destruction of Native Americans, saying, "in the struggle to obtain the sole empire of this country, the settlers showed little scrupulosity in regard to the means used to ensnare or seize by violence the natives."[72] Thus, for her, empire represented the tragic destruction of native peoples. It also led to a distortion of the culture of white Americans themselves.[73]

While in Virginia the pool of laborers dispossessed by the rise of English capitalism provided a basis for the creation of a labor market of indentured servants, in the northern colony religious and political-economic conditions in England pushed Puritans to search for a new space to create their "city on a hill." In 1534 King Henry VIII repudiated the Catholic Church and became the leader of the Church of England. Following this, the Anglican Church became a structure formed around a state-religion nexus, where bishops and archbishops were appointed by the monarch, reinforcing each other's power. Yet the new Church held on to vestiges of the old ways. Rote learning and demonstrations of prayers and rituals and obedience to hierarchical church authority remained the norm. In 1625 Charles I came to power and appointed William Laud as Bishop of London in 1628 and Archbishop of Canterbury in 1635. Charles and Laud encouraged a form of Anglicanism much closer to Catholicism than Puritanism, emphasizing obedience to authority and conformism. Under Laud, the Church also removed dissenting ministers and censured Puritan literature and practice.[74] In this context, Puritans searched for a new land to move to. While some fled to the Dutch Republic others started a new colony across the ocean.

The Puritans were not the first Europeans to visit the New England region. John Cabot explored the area at the tail end of the 1400s and in 1524 Giovanni da Verrazzano sailed to Narragansett Bay.[75] But in the context of increasing religious intolerance, settlers traveled over in 1620 and from 1629 to 1640, the era of the Great Migration, about 80,000 people left England, with perhaps 30 percent of those going to New England.[76] The demographics of New England settlers were very different than those who went further south. Many came from the Greater East Anglia region where economic conditions had deteriorated.[77] Colonists were primarily families of middle class status and perhaps 40 percent were over the age of 25.[78] In other words, the New England colony was comprised of a high proportion of mid-life families, in contrast to the younger adventurers and servants that emigrated to Virginia. This difference gave New England a unique demographic pattern relative to other American colonies, and a distinct and more self-reproducing logic of population expansion, so that by 1700 the population was 100,000.[79]

The question of the motivations of early New England settlers has been up for debate.[80] As the New England Company—which became the Massachusetts Bay Company—emerged out of the ruins of the Dorchester Company, it appears that the interests of religious freedom prevailed over the interests of profit.[81] Investors in the company in many cases did not invest simply to profit, but also brought their families to New England to settle. In the colony, these shareholders became political leaders and landowners as the colony itself was governed from New England.[82] Of course calculations of profits and finances were necessary for the operation, for instance, "the ioynt stock being thus managed, at the end of 7 yeares … the said stock, as the pceede & pfitt thereof, to bee devyded to every man pportionably, according to his adventure."[83] And the company's records demonstrate much time was spent managing finances and tracking down those who were behind on their payments. But overall, as expressed during a general court, "lastly, vpon the mocon of Mr Whyte, to the end that this business might bee pceeded in wth the first intencon, wch was chiefly the glory of God."[84] Managing finances, it appears, was less about generating profit so much as building a successful colony organized around religious discipline and order. And, of course, this also meant that the colony was to "wynn and incite the natives of the country to the knowledg and obedience of the onlie true God and Savior of mankinde."[85] Thus, along with building their own Protestant utopia, the settlers desired to "civilize" those "savages" indigenous to the country.

For Max Weber, the Protestant ethic, and specifically the "calling," provided an ideological basis for the development of New England capitalism.[86] But Weber never dealt with the problem that, in fact, New England went on to develop complex non-capitalist forms of social life. Specifically, the social property relations that predominated in New England were far from purely capitalist. Social regulation and the maintenance of a Puritan hierarchy took precedence over the law of value in regulating land control. Although fee simple landholdings were established and promoted by the Massachusetts Bay Company, rather than being regulated by market forces, they remained socially controlled. New England colonies were organized around town authorities who were generally also in charge of land distribution. Towns did have some variety in their regulations. For instance, Watertown declared in 1638 that land could only be sold to a freeman of the congregation, New Haven required strangers to have permission of the court to obtain land, and in 1659 in Hadley it was decided that no one could purchase land without three years of occupation and with approval of the town.[87]

These are just three examples of many; overall the ownership and control of land was regulated according to what was acceptable to the local Puritan hierarchy rather than abstract capitalist land markets regulated by the law of value.[88] Landholdings were not equal; generally, those who invested more in the community and had more social rank and status and influence were able to secure larger holdings.[89] But land was not a speculative, profitable investment, rather, landholdings were regulated based upon use value rather than exchange value. In order to settle in a particular community, for instance, one needed permission from the government.[90] Some land was also settled in common and regulated within the jurisdiction of particular towns so that freeholder settlers in those towns had access to forests to gather wood from, and so on.[91] This landholding pattern also drove the expansion of what might be called an *empire of townships*. To continue to grow the township, community, and religious-based society, as the population expanded so new towns were incorporated and more territory brought into the colony. For example, in 1635 Marblehead was created, Concord later that same year, Dedham the next, and Watertowne in 1637.[92] Generally, town space was designed to allow fifty or sixty families to settle there and obtain "competent" lifestyles, so that future settlers would be pushed to start their own towns, expanding the empire.

Early on, the colony aimed to stimulate production, but this was as much or more for the purposes of the general good and success of the colony rather than the endless accumulation of capital. In 1628, for instance, the company agreed to bring over Thomas Graues and his family and pay him to locate iron mines, as well as other metals and minerals. In return, the company would also grant him 100 acres of land "to alloue me some competency of necessary victualls for the subsistence of me and my ffameley till the next season of plantinge & reaping after there arryuall."[93] Additionally, the company impressed workers to build public works.[94] Also, wages for artisans were continually set and readjusted as the economic relations were built around a moral economy of "just price" which took precedence over pure profit-seeking behavior.[95] Court cases record that those who charged above these amounts were fined, the most well-known case being that of merchant Robert Keayne who used his last will and testament as a space to defend himself after developing a bad reputation for repeatedly overcharging for goods.[96] Similarly, those who set up mills had to do so with permission of court officials, and the prices they could charge farmers to use their mills were limited by law.[97] The colony was also linked into the world market. John Winthrop's journal, for example, records trade with nearby neighbors, the Dutch, the French, and the Virginians, and extending as far as Bermuda.[98] But just because the colony emerged as part of the expanding Atlantic and world trade system did not necessarily mean the social relations that articulated with this system were necessarily capitalist.

The Puritan ideology itself could be very critical of those who put profits above the common good. One sermon from 1621 criticizes the "vein" and "corrupt" "heart of man" who,

> yea and doth not experience teach, that even amongst processors of religion, almost all love and favor that is shewed unto others is with a secret aim at themselves, they will take pains to do a man good, provided that he will take twice so much for them, they will give a penny so as it may advantage them a pound, labor hard so as all the profit may come to themselves, else they are heartless and feeble.[99]

Rather, "a *man* must *seek the good, the wealth, the profit of others*."[100] In other words, fair and just "profit" was not self-gain and aggrandizement, but contributing to the general good of others. The Puritan work ethic, though, was not simply internalized by the population. Rather, use of force was a regular part of settler life. Those who were idle or slacking, for instance, were punished by the court.[101] Laws made sure each settler worked hard to build the colony. Additionally, gender regulation through, for example, laws regarding acceptable clothing and punishing sexual deviance were regularly enforced. Laws were put in place, for instance, against wearing lace and "other superfluities tending to little vse or benefit but to the nourishing of pride & exhausting of mens estates, & also of evill example to others."[102] Additionally, "And that hearafter no garment shalbee made wth short sleeves, whereby the nakedness of the arme may bee discovered."[103]

Laws regulating sexuality and expressions of gender were deemed necessary as in some cases the Puritans were not so pure. In one case even, "William Hatchet, for beastuality wth a cowe, is condemned to be hanged, & the cowe to bee slayne & burnt or buried."[104] More commonly, though, those that engaged in "fornication" and adultery were regularly punished. And while these cases were often between settlers, including servants, it appears there were also sexual relations between native peoples and settlers, for example, "It is ordered, John Dawe shalbe seuerely whipped for intiseing an Indian woman to lye wth him. Vpon this occacon it is ppounded with^{r} adultery, eith^{r} wth English or Indian, shall not be punished wth death."[105] Later, though, it was decided that the death sentence could be enforced for adultery. Sexual deviance, as with other crimes, could also be punished through slavery as, in one case, "John Kempe, for filthy, vncleane attempts wth 3 yong girls, was censured to bee whipped both heare, at Roxberr, & at Salem, very severly, & was committed for a slave to Leift Davenport."[106] In another case, homosexual activity was also recorded as "Capt. Wiggin, governor at Pascataquack, under the Lords Say and Brook, wrote to our governor, desiring to have two men tried here, who had committed sodomy with each other."[107]

While indentured servants existed, and black slaves were not absent, generally household labor based around the patriarchal family was the most common form of labor organization. And independence meant to be free from dependency on wage labor.[108] As Alan Taylor puts it, "diligent and realistic, most New England families sought an 'independent competency.' 'Independence' meant owning enough property—a farm or a shop—to employ a family, without having to work for someone else as a hired hand or servant. A 'competency' meant a sufficiency, but not an abundance, of worldly goods."[109] That being said, along the coast fishermen organized their relations of production around capitalistic lines, albeit not as simply a wage labor/capital relationship. Generally, fishermen were too poor to own ships themselves, so companies of fishermen made agreements with outfitters to rent boats and purchase supplies. Suppliers would, in turn, take their catch and give them a previously agreed upon rate of return for their labor.[110] Many fisherman, then, were dependent laborers working in a profit-driven industry, but were "clients" rather than wage laborers.

Artisans and farmers were also participants in market relations. Most towns needed a few artisans—blacksmiths, shoemakers, and so on—and artisans were also more concentrated in larger cities such as Boston. Additionally, town artisans also tended to own farms, and engage both in farm and artisanal labor. Farmers themselves were also embedded in market relations, producing both for subsistence and to sell crops on the market to obtain goods they could not produce themselves.[111] But, of course, market relations don't necessarily mean capitalist relations; historically, markets existed long before capital took control of and reorganized social production on a mass scale. And New England was a colony linked into both local markets and the world market. New England merchants sold commodities such as fish and timber to the West Indies in return for molasses, rum, and sugar, and by 1700 Boston became a major center of trade, and had the second largest shipbuilding industry in the British Empire after London itself.[112]

The social structure also began to form around an early racial ideology, although the term "race" itself was yet to be used. Rather, natives were called "savages," and said to have a particular inferior disposition. As to their origins, Cotton Mather stipulated that the devil likely hid them there to avoid Jesus Christ's "absolute empire" over them: "and though we know not *when* or *how* those Indians first became inhabitants of this mighty continent, yet we may guess that probably the devil decoyed those miserable salvages hither."[113] This incipient racial ideology also justified wars and the dispossession of Native Americans. But while the idea developed during the rise of English capitalism (made most famous by John Locke) that if the natives failed to improve the land the colonists had the right to settle and labor on it, in fact the land was well worked by the native peoples, albeit very differently than the settler way. Among other things, the natives cleared fields to plant crops and regularly burned forests to clear the underbrush but keep the taller trees in place, in doing so making it easier to travel through forests and hunt the abundant animal life. When European settlers came, they tended to take over paths, crops, villages, and land previously worked by native peoples, taking credit for their achievements without acknowledging this.

Overall, the early colony of New England had capitalist elements, but was not simply a society in which all aspects of social life were regulated by the law of value. Much of social production was still in the hands of patriarchal families, and the goal of this production was not the accumulation of capital but expansion of the patriarchal household form (as will be discussed). Production and exchange on the market was more about obtaining land for future generations—particularly male children—than it was about profit in itself. This type of social reproduction also gave the colony a logic of spatial expansion driven by patriarchal household reproduction more than the accumulation of capital.

Gender and the origins of American capitalism

As capitalism became the world's dominant social system it inherited and transformed diverse gender forms and inequalities across the globe. In the American context, racialized gender inequalities defined the colonial era and, over time, gender norms and family structures were remade to fit with the logic of capital accumulation.[114] Within Europe, and similarly in North America, the norms of white womanhood and masculinity that solidified capitalist relations in the dominant zones were built through the de-feminization and de-masculinization—or hyper-sexualization—of "the other"; the victims of empire building.[115] Imperialism was not just a political-economic, but a cultural process. As Edward Said explains:

> Neither imperialism nor colonialism is a simple act of accumulation and acquisition. Both are supported and perhaps even impelled by impressive ideological formations that include notions that certain territories and people *require* and beseech domination, as well as forms of knowledge affiliated with domination: the vocabulary of classic nineteenth-century imperial culture is plentiful with words and concepts like "inferior" or "subject races," "subordinate peoples," "dependency," "expansion," and "authority." Out of the imperial experiences, notions about culture were clarified, reinforced, criticized, or rejected.[116]

Through processes of imperial interaction norms of culture, gender, sexuality, race, class, and power were built, and hegemonic conceptions justifying empire building were historically created. Similarly, through engagements with and the destruction of indigenous populations in North America, and through the making of black slavery, among other developments, hegemonic white conceptions and structures of gender, race, and family were constructed. Over time, these ever-shifting formations grew to fit with the social rhythms of capital accumulation as capitalism formed as a deeply racialized and gendered system.[117] And, for that matter, historically the rise of capitalism was not purely a binary, black and white, process. It went along with everything from prostitution to interracial sex to homosexual relationships and more.[118] In this sense, just as there is no "pure" form of capitalism, so there is no primary way gender relations are constructed within capitalism. Rather, the gender-capitalism relation depends upon the particular historical and political circumstance out of which the relations form. After all, black female slaves in the American south were a form of gendered capitalist labor just as much as white middle class housewives were. If the often discussed housewife-breadwinner family relation did emerge with the rise of capitalism in the United States, this was perhaps due less to the rise of capitalism in itself, so much as the political forms which capitalist relations took.

In the colonial area, particularly in the American north, the family and community relations and gender arrangements that formed did not easily fit into a definition of capitalism rooted in social relations of production/reproduction. To address this problem, I suggest the category *patriarchal household mode of social reproduction* as a useful heuristic ideal type to make sense of both the division of labor and organization of gender in non-capitalist relations in the US context. To clarify, the relations were patriarchal in that they were organized around the male-centered household. The husband was the manager of family and labor and the laws and regulations of society passed through the husband to the family. The term "household" is included as the division of labor and mode of production was primarily done on the household level, especially in the American north. Farm families produced for self-sufficiency first with varying degrees of more or less incorporation into market relations, and often through barter and labor-sharing relations within their communities. And I use the term mode of social reproduction to refer to the ways all aspects of social life entailed forms of labor—the social metabolic relationship between humanity and ecology—from women producing children to the production and remaking of gender norms before capitalism and during the transition.

Gender in colonial America

The Puritans living in the colonial northeast would be confounded by many of the gender categories we use today. The concepts of "hetero" and "homo" sexual would not be invented for another two centuries. Rather, gender was a hierarchy in which male and female bodies and capacities were not defined in negation of each other, but in which the man was superior to the woman.[119] As one Puritan put it, "our ribs were not ordained to be our rulers."[120] To be an ideal man was not to be the fierce, independent creature, supposedly tied down to no woman, which would later be encouraged. It was to be the protector of the family, as social life was organized around obtaining "competency" and the reproduction of family life. Inherited from England was the idea that the household was a metaphor for the entire social order: just as the father was the monarch taking care of his domain, so the father-monarch had the responsibility to take care of his family.[121]

Additionally, in colonial and early America, unlike the later era, in which child-raising was increasingly relegated as a woman's supposedly natural role, a father's social role was to take responsibility towards his children and cultivate affection. Writing about his son, who appears to have been sick, for instance, William Fleming wrote,

> but O' my Dear a pang darts through my heart when I think on Lenny, my hopes my expectations dash'd to the ground, not from a want of Abilities but from want of having those abilities properly formed in his tenderer Years. At least this is the light that an affectionate Father views it in. I may be deceived in his capasity, even this would be a comfort to me, as it would be a less implication of negligence in the management.[122]

Through the age of 6 or 7, boys and girls wore the same gowns until boys were "breeched," given male-designated clothing, and put on the path to manhood.[123] From here, fathers would also guide boys, teaching them the values they would need to become husbands, fathers, and eventually heads of households.

The social organization of sex was also much different than it would later become. Married Puritan couples were encouraged to enjoy sexual pleasure as part of a healthy marriage, of course in moderation. And while pre-marital sex, "self-pollution," and other forms of sexual deviance were strictly disallowed, community responses to sexual deviance depended on circumstance. Colonists "often placed personal loyalties and the needs of the local community before the imperative to enforce moral absolutes."[124] This likely included some amount of tolerance for (what we now might call) homosexual behavior. Nicholas Sension, for example, was taken to the General Court in 1677. On trial, a variety of witnesses gave testimony to Sension's advancements towards other men since the 1640s. In other words, while it was known Sension may have had proclivities towards other men, they were tolerated as he was considered, overall, a harmonious member of the community.[125] And in general, gay relationships in colonial American history, in fact, may have been more common than archival records indicate. Men regularly wrote letters to other men in loving, passionate language which might suggest, at times, something more than platonic friendship.[126] And although records are limited, historians have noted that it is difficult to imagine that Virginia colonists, living in a society in which men greatly outnumbered women, did not engage in sexual activity with each other.[127] And on the frontier, for example, even male-male intimacy tended to be much more openly stated than it would in the latter era. After his sister Annie Henry Christian's husband, William Christian, was killed in Kentucky, Patrick Henry wrote to her in 1786 also suggesting in the letter, "Pray tell Mr. Bullitt I wish to hear from him and to cultivate an intimacy with him and that he may command any services from me."[128]

Through the late 1700s husbands were considered "friends" and "protectors." After her husband's death, for example, Annie Henry Christian wrote to her sister-in-law Anne Christian Fleming,

> I must enjoin secrecy from you on this distressing subject, the Man whose connections might have promised protection to my Family, as turned our Enemy & God of heaven only knows for what, only because he found me & my poor children deprived of our Protector & Friend & saw us left destitute & helpless.[129]

Marriage in early American history could also be seen as a relation of friendship. As Richard Taylor Jr. in Kentucky wrote to his recently married nephew,

> I am pleased to hear you are so agreeably married, and wish you and your consort a great deal of happiness, which will depend much on your united efforts to please each other; and live in harmony with your neighbors. I am pretty certain you have industry, which will be necessary in your new situation.[130]

As today, throughout the entire history of the United States, in fact, gender was never organized strictly in a binary. Perhaps the most famous early example of this is the case of Thomas(ine) Hall. What started as an accusation against Hall for laying with Richard Bennett's maid turned into an exploration of Hall's complex gender identity and performances.[131] Hall claimed that he was both a man and a woman, and had practiced different genders throughout his life. In England he claimed his name was Thomasine, and he lived as a girl. Later, to join the military he cut off his hair and performed as a man. Returning from war in France, back in England he again became a woman and worked in needlework, until becoming a man to travel to British North America. After a lengthy trial, involving several physical searches of Hall in which it was seen he had a penis, but he claimed it did not function sexually, the court decided that, from then on, while Hall would wear male clothes it was also necessary he wear women's headwear and an apron, as the court enforced his clothes to represent a punishment in which he would not be considered by the community to be a "pure" male.[132]

Hall's case is one example of gender fluidity in colonial America. Complex gender roles go back, in fact, to early American white-settler colonialism. As Richard Godbeer argues, "Puritans characterized certain roles as masculine and others as feminine, but these were not attached inflexibly to male and female bodies."[133] This was also reflective of the gendered division of labor. While it was the case that women and men had different roles in the household, women doing more domestic tasks as opposed to husbands farming, hunting, and so on, it was not unusual for women to take over men's tasks as so-called "deputy husbands," particularly if the husband was sick or traveling. The complexities of gender in colonial and early US history were also reflected in the complex language used to describe people. As Greta LaFleur puts it,

> it should not be surprising that research on eighteenth-century gender has demonstrated that an incredibly wide vocabulary existed to describe different forms of socially recognizable gender, including terms such as macroclitorides, sapphists, tribades, amazons, female husbands, mollies, bachlors, macaronis, viragos, fops, tommies, effeminate men, *petit-maitres*, "unsex'd females," and masculine women, to name only a few.[134]

Of course, women did live primarily in a world of submission to fatherly power. But compared to, say, the capitalist housewife era, women's work may have been more significantly valued, or seen as *work*. Women also retained control over the birthing sphere.[135] Later, with the rise of medical science, women's control over areas of social life such as birthing would be diminished. But as Mary Beth Norton has argued, "the adult woman occupied a clearly defined place in the seventeenth-century family—so much so that she was seen more as a part of that system and less as an autonomous person. Indeed, her authority derived from her role as mistress of the household."[136] Women were expected to take care of managing the house, and the affairs of the husband. And laws of coverture meant that marriage was also a relation of dispossession. This went back to England where, as Amy Dru Stanley argues,

> like the wage contract, the marriage contract was founded on consent and created a relation of authority and subordination premised on reciprocal exchange: the common law named the wife a dependent and bound her to serve and obey her husband in return for his protection. Like the servant, she owed her husband her labor and its proceeds, though in exchange not for wages but for subsistence.[137]

The marriage contract, then, effectively served as a labor contract between husband and wife in which the dispossessed wife was to serve the husband as a subordinate through her labor. This was reflected in American colonial law. Colonies set laws in which, when married, a woman forfeited whatever right to property she might have: her property became her husband's property.[138] There was some variation in this, though, and widows in some colonies, for instance, had the right to own a portion of their dead husband's land and sell it if they desired. This was uneven between colonies. In Massachusetts, for example, it was common upon a husband's death for all his possessions to pass to male heirs who were legally instructed to take care of the widows while in Maryland, to take another case, it was even possible for a remarried widow to retain ownership of her previous husband's land after remarriage.[139]

These gender norms also meant that men had the right to define and control women's sexuality through the use of force or violence. In the case of rape, for example, its definition had been decided by white men, which continued through the post-Revolutionary era.[140] While it was generally agreed that sexual relations were to be legally consented on, what consent meant was a male-defined category.[141] It was expected that some degree of male to female pressure and violence would occur in sexual relations; women would naturally resist men's urges until, realizing their sexuality, they would consent. And if a woman was raped, it was not unusual for her to be blamed; if a man raped her, it must have been due to the fact that she had somehow seduced him by failing to control her passions. It was also highly racialized; a black man who raped a white woman, for example, would easily be charged while, say, a white man who raped a black woman would rarely.

In Virginia, where environmental conditions were harsher, gender relations also played out somewhat differently. By 1620 the Virginia Company began to send over "Tobacco Brides" to marry men who they hoped had a higher social status than their own.[142] But most women who went to the colony came as indentured servants where they proved to be cheaper to Virginia colonists than men which, in some cases, meant their conditions could be worse than male servants. And while women indentured servants were often tasked with housework—as was a women's role—it was not unusual for them to also be put to work in the tobacco fields by the relatively poor farmers who purchased years of their lives.[143] Thus, in the colony which had the most capitalistic relations, women's role as commodified indentured labor could fuel small-scale capitalist production. Additionally, in the south, pre-marital sexual relations may have also been more difficult to regulate. As settlers scattered throughout Virginia, Maryland, and South Carolina, pastors often proved too far and few between to formalize marriage relations, although missionaries did, at times, go so far as to travel to find cohabitating couples who they could formally marry.[144] So while the colonial elite and religious leaders may have held strict views on proper marriage and sexual relationships, it appears that settlers and farmers themselves had more informal relationship patterns and customs.

Lastly, the social reproduction of the patriarchal family drove empire westward. As J. Hector St. John Crèvecoeur put it,

> I envy no man's prosperity, and with no other portion of happiness that that I may live to teach the same philosophy to my children; and give each of them a farm, shew them how to cultivate it, and be like their father, good substantial independent American farmers—an appellation which will be the most fortunate one, a man of my class can possess, so long as our civil government continues to shed blessings on our husbandry.[145]

In other words, a husband's duty was to provide land to his future male offspring. In this sense, as long as the population expanded, so the patriarchal household mode of production was necessarily spatially expansive.

Reformism, white hegemony, and the remaking of gender

By the beginning of the 1800s, as the increasing dominance of capitalist relations remade the patriarchal household mode of social reproduction, reformist movements began that, over time, pushed against the sexual and gender fluidity of the earlier era towards a more "binary" form of gender relations dominated by white middle and upper class conceptions of femininity and masculinity. White women were the purifiers of the family against the corruption of market forces, and against the troubled behaviors of blacks and other non-white racial categories as gender, class, and race shaped each other. And while these new gender relations were organized around family and households, they also stretched well beyond this into science, medicine, public health, criminality, and broader relations of social normalization and discipline. These new relations would constitute the racialized gender background of American colonization and capitalism.

One of the issues the founding patriarchal elite faced was how to create a white, hegemonic social order. This also entailed the creation of a national identity. The new country was a diverse place and it was not clear how a new national hegemony might be built.[146] Additionally, the uprooting of the political order that the revolution created also led to the opening of a new space of sexual freedom for Americans.[147] For the country's elite, untamed sexual behaviors, racial intermixing, and fluid gender categories were a threat to the new state. Sexuality beyond the limits of what the ruling elite viewed as "civilized" had to be tamed for the stability of the government. In other words, for social stability, it was necessary that patriarchy run through the family to the state and back again.[148]

By the late eighteenth and early nineteenth centuries, to establish hegemony, increasingly middle and upper class men and women asserted their gender norms as the proper civil norms for society as a whole. This was seen most prominently in the rise of reformist movements and benevolent societies.[149] In some cases, these societies simply aimed for tasks such as poor relief, and were even led by blacks and emerged from black communities. In other cases, they aimed to curtail the anomie of society to, for example, limit men's urge to drink alcohol or engage in aggressive behavior. The American peace movement of the 1830s, for example, saw war and violence as in large part due to men's aggressive behaviors. By viewing war and aggression as "manly," men's attempt to live up to their masculine ideals created a culture of violence and militarism.[150] By remaking manhood and limiting these tendencies, a more stable social order could be built, it was believed.

Central to this was marriage. In the early republic, marriage was still relatively flexible, in some respects less set in stone by the state than sanctioned by couples and recognized by local communities. But over time state-sanctioned marriage, along with the idea that the only legitimate sex was sex in a married relationship, solidified as, for example, from 1820 to 1860 states continually remade divorce laws as separation transformed towards a more solidly state-enforced relationship.[151] And by the 1840s, what Stephanie Coontz calls the "triumph of conservative domesticity" was achieved.[152] This was organized around the new middle class. While the idea of separate spheres for men and women existed before this, by the 1840s an American middle class stabilized, internalizing the value of women's space as the "pure" household against the men's corrupt marketplace world, which became, in many respects, the dominant hegemonic ideology and structure of "legitimate" sex and gender relations in the country. As one commentator put it,

> the American shopkeeper's wife and daughters are never seen at the scene of business, for which they are neither intended nor qualified; and, being unable to assist him in trade, are more happily employed in preserving the purity and sanctity of his fire-side. They give him that which he would otherwise be obliged to resign—a home in the bosom of his family.[153]

This was also a racial ideology and structure.[154] White woman's space was defined against what was not white. Black women, who often had to work to survive, and "free" black men, without the privileges of whites, were devalued as less "masculine" or "feminine," or overly sexualized, in that they could not fulfill the ideal of white masculinity and femininity.[155] This was reflected in standards of hygiene and science. Historically, going back to the colonial era, whiteness was seen as pure and clean, in contrast to dirty blackness and brownness. This was further solidified as (somewhat) regular bathing became a norm for white Americans and as soap advertisers began "to depict soap as an imperial agent, capable of civilizing the brown peoples of the world."[156] And while the idea that race was "biological" had been around in the eighteenth century, in the decades before the Civil War race increasingly became an object of science. In this, race was seen along a biological spectrum in which whites were seen as the perfect or superior race, and blacks as the most inferior.[157]

Additionally, the development of separate spheres did not take on the same meaning in southern plantation capitalism. While in the south politics and economic production were led by the white planter class, plantations were essentially capitalist households which produced for profits on the market while generating self-sufficient production to reproduce the plantation society itself, the most capitalistically rational way of obtaining basic goods given the general structure of the south. Plantations themselves were at times considered personal empires—conceptualized in gendered imperial terms. Fox-Genovese notes one case in which southerner Mary Moragne discussed her mother's break from housework as resting from the "weight of empire."[158] And patriarchy ran through each aspect of southern society as, while white mothers occasionally took care of the plantation when their husbands were away, their space was primarily one of domestic management and production. Yet male space was not that of "the market" in contrast to women's space as "the household"; the organization of capitalist patriarchy went through states through gender and household in a broadly organized social hierarchy built on the empire of black slave workers fighting to build their own family lives through the abuse of the slave system.

Capitalism also encouraged the development of the prostitution industry. In New York, for example, brothels flourished in the decades after the revolution, organized according to the class geography of the city. While some women who became prostitutes were simply the victims of the violence of capital, and inability to find other work, some of New York's leading female brothel owners became both rich and famous, such as Julia Brown, who was a regular at the city's high level social events.[159] And many capitalist landlords were happy to lease their real estate to brothels, as it brought high returns. Prostitution was also organized around race and some degree of gender non-conforming behavior was in some cases tolerated. For example, as Timothy Gilfoyle records, in 1836 Peter Sewally, a black man, was convicted of grand larceny. In the case, it turned out, though, that Sewally lived in a brothel and went by the name of Mary Jones. Under this alias, Sewally dressed in female clothes, greeted guests, cooked, and performed domestic work.[160]

More generally, what was "normal" or "abnormal" also increasingly became a science. During the last half of the seventeenth century when prosecutions against witches reached their peak, for instance, it was possession or a deal with the devil, rather than madness or insanity, which was used to explain deviant behavior. Around 80 percent of those accused were women, and around three-quarters of accusers were men, as supposedly women were more susceptible to the devil's influence. But by the first quarter of the eighteenth century, behavior which would have been considered witchcraft was increasingly seen in terms of sanity. Over time, "madness" became less interpreted through spiritual terms, and more in biological terms.[161] And in 1833 the opening of the Worcester State Lunatic Hospital signaled a new era in treating madness. Like race, "normal" (that is, white hegemonic) sex and gender were also seen in scientific terms, perhaps most abrasively in the development of a science of homosexuality as a medical illness. By the early 1800s, European doctors began to view gender deviance through a scientific rather than religious lens, as would American doctors for whom everything from homosexuality to masturbation could be seen as the result of illness, the medicine being techniques including institutional confinement and shock treatment.[162]

In summary, the transition to capitalism in the United States both created, and resulted from, a political history in which the development of white hegemony punished all those that did not fit into its dominant categories of "normal" relations. And the forms of masculinity and femininity built through the rise of capitalism were also *imperial gender forms*, fueling the rise of Manifest Destiny and the fulfillment of the imperial visions of, for instance, Andrew Jackson's violent manhood.[163] The new more capitalist gender form centered around the hegemonic breadwinner-housewife relation as a specific political form which deemed other racialized gender categories as deviant. In this sense, the "totality" of capitalism stretched well beyond the narrow confines that analysis of class struggle and modes of production in themselves produce, to race, complex gender relations, science, social deviance, and beyond. To write the history of capitalism and gender simply within the lens of households and kinship relations misses this history and, in doing so, substitutes a partial, economistic narrative of capitalism's social totality for its broader, more complex history. The rest of the book will examine how these relations played out as the society with capitalism became a capitalist society.

2
The Expansion of Empire

The early United States was a society on the move. Travel writers, for example, were continually fascinated with the pace of expansion as the population pushed west. As the Marquis de Chastellux put it in the early 1780s, "whatever mountains I have climbed, whatever forests I have traversed, whatever bye-paths I have followed, I have never travelled three miles without meeting with a new settlement, either beginning to take form or already in cultivation."[1] The Marquis found that:

> any man who is able to procure a capital of five or six hundred livres of our money, or about twenty-five pounds sterling, and who has strength and inclination to work, may go into the woods and purchase a portion of one hundred and fifty or two hundred acres of land ... at the end of two years, the planter has the wherewithal to subsist, and even to send some articles to market: at the end of four or five years, he completes the payment of his land, and finds himself a comfortable planter.[2]

In this context, this chapter outlines the history of white-settler expansion into Massachusetts, New York, and Pennsylvania. The goal here is not to provide a complete history, so much as to chart the course of capitalism on the expanding early western frontier and show how, gradually, over many decades, social life became subsumed to capitalist relations of production. In particular, the chapter emphasizes the diversity of social life in the processes that drove colonial expansion.

In 1630 less than 5,000 white settlers lived in the North American colony. That number reached almost 112,000 by 1670, half a million by the 1720s, and was over 2 million by the eve of the American Revolution. Among other states, the population of Massachusetts rose during this period to 235,308, New York to 162,920, and Pennsylvania to 240,057.[3] The growth of the white-settler population, also fueled by immigration from England, Scotland, Ireland, the Low Countries, Germany, and elsewhere, pushed westward expansion. In 1850, for instance, while about three-quarters of the surveyed so-called "native" US population lived in the states where they were born, a quarter did not.[4] Every year thousands upon thousands of white colonialists moved further west. But the population laboring to build the racialized and gendered empire did not necessarily move west to spread capitalism. Many frontier settlers may have moved to escape a rising capitalist dependency in the east, only to find themselves competing with speculators who viewed the west as a great space for potential profit.

White-settler colonialism also gradually became a capitalist-driven industry.[5] Cities were built on the western frontier serving as conduits for empire as, for instance, journeying through the old northwest, William Amphlett wrote in 1818, "Pittsburg is the head-quarters of all those who are about to settle in the States of Ohio, Indiana, Kentucky, Illinois, or the countries bordering on the Mississippi."[6] While many settlers initially self-organized their means of transportation, over time the movement of people became increasingly commodified. On their way to the frontier, Amphlett observed, settlers could hire a wagoner to transport their luggage. "Most of these waggoners are the proprietors of their own teams; many of them farmers, who employ their horses in this manner, when their work is not wanted at home; others make it their entire business."[7] In other cases, "many emigrants purchase horses and waggons at Philadelphia, and take at once their families and their luggage, in order to be masters of their time, and travel on as suits their inclination or convenience."[8] In other words, as families decided to move west they produced their own strategies and technologies of expansion yet, by the middle of the century with the transportation revolution, steamboat and railroad companies combined territorial and capitalist expansion.[9] But—on the ground—the frontier population had not yet necessarily internalized the power and habits of capitalist time discipline.[10] To be "free" was not yet necessarily to be a living commodity within capitalism.

The social pressures behind expansion were numerous. While military force and violence against indigenous people played a role, socially, expansion was also pushed by the extensive (spatially/geographically expanding) logic of growth of the patriarchal household mode of social reproduction. This mode of life entailed a particular land-labor ratio necessary for its expanded reproduction in which younger generations could obtain land to reproduce the family farm and obtain competency and independence. In the eighteenth century, average family sizes reached as high as seven or eight, decreasing to around four or five by the middle of the nineteenth century.[11] Much of this decline was in rural areas, given that these populations tended to have more children, and it also appears that there is a direct correlation between declining land availability and a decrease in the fertility rate.[12] Simply put, when frontier households could obtain land with relative ease, and reproduce the patriarchal household mode of social reproduction on expanded scales, the fertility rate stayed high as population increase articulated with the mode of production to push further white-settler colonialism. As capitalist market relations began to subsume these relations of production, one result was declining household sizes and fertility rates as, additionally, family structures began to change as younger generations found themselves increasingly dependent upon commodity relations.

As colonization spread, a mapmaking industry also developed in which the imagery of empire was commodified and sold, bringing together the "imagined community" of the new American nation.[13] Historically, ornamental maps became popular to display in state buildings as well as on the household walls of the nouveau riche and rising middling consumer classes in Western Europe.[14] These habits transferred to the United States as the mapmaking and atlas industry grew after the revolution. Abel Buell's *A New and Correct Map of the United States of North America: Layd down from the Latest Observations and Best Authorities Agreeable to the Peace of 1783* is said to be the first full map of the country produced by an American for the American market.[15] Soon after others followed, as maps, expressing the image of empire, became a popular commodity to display for wealthier classes in the urban United States.[16] Over time, as capitalism deepened, mapmaking itself became increasingly scientific not only glorifying empire, but also outlining the locations of roads and resources in more detail for capital to access and appropriate. Thus, the population grew and the course of empire was charted.

Massachusetts

As the previous chapter argued, the British colonies in North America were born as a product of the larger history of European colonialism. Just as English farmers crossed the ocean to escape "primitive accumulation" on the island, so English investors saw North America as a potential space to generate profits.[17] From the start, English merchants attempted to transport colonialists to the American colony for the purposes of generating profit. This represented an attempted symbiosis or articulation of mixed modes of production. As Bernard Bailyn puts it, "the theory was simple and convincing: costs could be reduced and profits greatly increased by sending settlers to New England, where, as self-sufficient residents, they could catch fish, collect furs, and process other products for shipment to the entrepreneurs in England."[18] The hope of merchants was that, however the settlers organized their means of production, it would at least be subsumed to capital to the extent to which profits would be generated back home.

But the social relations that did form were not so easy to subsume. This was reflected in the early patterns of uneven development in Massachusetts that formed both capitalist and non-capitalist elements.[19] While the Massachusetts/New England town has often been thought of as an example of bottom-up American democracy, paving the way for the legacy of today, as Kenneth Lockridge put it, "the equality of the society was nothing less than the equality of economic interests which lies at the heart, not of modern pluralistic democracy, but of Marxist-Leninist democracy."[20] Dedham, for instance, was founded as a utopian Puritanical dream, a "Christian Utopian Closed Corporate Community."[21] The seventeenth-century town had a population of 500 and was an agrarian community of yeomen and husbandmen who organized their lives around a patriarchal household mode of social reproduction. The average adult man had approximately 150 acres of land, and, while engaged in barter and generally non-monetarized trade with other community members, was also relatively self-sufficient in meeting basic needs. It was not an equal society; social position was determined by community status, and those with higher status also tended to have more land and wealth, and were more commonly chosen to be selectmen. But community decisions tended to be made from the bottom up including the distribution of property and use of a common field system although the latter became increasingly fenced in through the mid to late 1600s.[22]

Similarly, although coastal towns may have tended towards more commercially oriented production for the world market, in some cases the social relations of production were also decisively non-capitalist. Towns including Gloucester, while lacking the potentially conflict reducing religious and cultural coherency of Dedham, developed similar productive relations. With ample land, newcomers to the town were given allotments, and commonly owned and shared land existed through the end of the 1600s.[23] Much of production, including the use of local timber or the licensing of a cornmill and sawmill were oriented more towards sustaining the community of the town rather than production for profit.[24]

In Deerfield by the late 1680s around 235 people had settled. This population was generally young, three-quarters of them under 40, and tended to marry before the age of 25 after obtaining and developing a piece of land to obtain competency and start a family.[25] Many of the settlers immigrated from other relatively nearby towns, while some traveled from further south and east as expansion was a gradual process in which many settlers took small steps west to pave the empire. Relations of capital and profit-seeking behavior were not necessarily absent in new settlements. In Deerfield, for example, John Pynchon owned and rented land for a profit through the 1680s.[26] But the relations of production that formed were similar to other settlements throughout the colony. Farmers generally owned their own land, tools, and livestock. Some land was held in common, albeit with the holdings of the wealthier higher than others.[27] But most production was to reproduce the relatively self-sufficient household and most trade was on a barter basis as a dense network of debts and interdependencies developed.

But while, on the one hand, these non-capitalist relations formed, on the other hand, aspects of capitalism also developed. In 1641, for example, John Winthrop Jr. returned to England with the support of the Massachusetts General Court to locate investors for iron production. He was eventually successful and in 1643 the Company of Undertakers of the Ironworks in New England was formed. After attempts to start ironworks in Braintree in 1644 and 1645, in 1646 the construction of ironworks on the Saugus River began and became the primary site of production, although the Braintree ironworks also remained open.[28] To produce iron, the company needed laborers. Skilled workers were recruited from Britain and Ireland. Less skilled workers were hired from the local Massachusetts labor force. Some workers were paid wages; others were contracted as indentured servants. But a stable labor supply remained difficult to obtain. The English Civil War provided some impetus for the importation of new workers as, for instance, hundreds of Scottish soldiers were captured and sent to New England, the Chesapeake colony, or the West Indies in the early 1650s. In 1650, sixty-two of these prisoners were taken control of by the Company of Undertakers, thirty-six of those making it to Saugus.[29] Many of the workers imported also did not conform to Puritan standards of life, yet the colony made exceptions. Overall, by the middle of the 1600s, some capitalist relations did exist in the colony.

Capitalist relations also formed in coastal towns, linked into broader movements of the world market. English, along with other European fisherman, worked their way to Newfoundland throughout the sixteenth century, hunting for cod and herring. By the time the New England fishing industry began to take shape it was rooted in a long tradition of North American fishing and nautical exploration. By the end of the 1620s, the colony appointed a master to hire seasonal servants to go on fishing expeditions given the low labor supply of the colony.[30] After the outbreak of the English Civil War in 1642, the flow of immigration from England to the Massachusetts colony, and the capital that entailed, dried up. Prices decreased, credit diminished, and the balance of trade turned. At the same time, the price of fish across the Atlantic increased in places such as Seville and Madeira, which regularly imported fish from across the ocean. The price of fish also increased in New England itself. And the number of English ships in Newfoundland dropped from 340 in 1634 to under 200 by 1652.[31] In response, New England merchants channeled their capital into the fishing industry, stimulating decades of growth.

While a substantial portion of fishers owned shares in vessels, perhaps 60 percent did not. Their option was either to contract with a company or rent out a boat with other fishermen. As the industry continued to develop, its capitalist character deepened. While, for example, previously a group of fishermen might rent a boat than share the catch, by the mid-1670s increasingly crews worked for merchant capitalists who owned boats and rented them out in return for three-eighths of the profits.[32] While workers might not directly be paid a monetary wage, they were paid indirect wages in the form of a share of the proceeds from the catch; in effect, they functioned as a dispossessed proletariat class dependent on selling their labor power for a wage, albeit not in the classic Marxist conceptualization. As one observer of the time put it, "the equipment of the ships and crews employed in that trade resemble a privateering expedition; officers and sailors receiving in a measure, the prize-money instead of regular wages. Every man on board has a share in the profits, which is according to his rank and employment."[33] In this way, "they have no wages; each draws a certain established share in partnership with the proprietor of the vessel; by which oeconomy they are all proportionately concerned in the success of the enterprise, and all equally alert and vigilant."[34]

Slavery also existed in the colony from an early age. Pequot's were captured in war in the 1630s, and by 1637 were sold to the West Indies.[35] Black slaves were imported as early as 1638 and played a role in the building of empire.[36] Although the population was not large, it was over 2,674 by 1754. Slaves did much of the manual labor for their owners, clearing and planting fields, constructing buildings, building wells, and so on. Slave labor was used in a wide variety of ways, incorporated into the households of wealthy farmers and artisans to do everything from farming to act as household servants, to in some cases develop artisanal skills such as tailoring. Generally, slaves were purchased by the elite as a symbol of their status.[37] Whether or not slaves were directly put to use by capital, their role as household labor for capitalists may have contributed indirectly to early capitalist development.

Deepening capitalism

Throughout the middle of the 1700s settlers continued to steadily flow into central Massachusetts. While the central-western part of the state had incorporated nine towns before 1740 there were a total of forty-four towns by the mid-1770s.[38] Many communities established new towns in reminiscence of the older New England communal tradition but a population of dispossessed transients, the "wandering poor," also took shape. Some who moved west were the dispossessed, looking to re-start their lives, and they were often greeted by communities which put in place laws and policies to remove them from the towns in which they tried to settle. As land became less available in more established towns with better soil, some took to the hills. The town of Pelham, for example, was settled in the 1740s and by the 1760s most producers worked on an estimated 4–7 acres of cleared land, and had ten or more for pasture and orchards.[39] They continued to reproduce the patriarchal household mode of social reproduction even amongst the pressures of limited land plots and debt.

But these rural communities were gradually pushed and pulled into capitalist relations in a slow and uneven way. Christopher Clark's study, for instance, shows the ways that farming families in the Connecticut Valley were gradually, over decades, brought into capitalist relations. In the late eighteenth century farmers were not self-sufficient. They regularly exchanged goods and services with neighbors and the few merchants around the area. But they spoke in a language of "give and take" rather than "buy and sell" and exchange relations were built into community and kinship relations.[40] Neighbors swapped labor, depending on resources and community obligation. And debts were exchanged in services and labor, although occasionally money, and were built on social trust as they often went for many years without being settled. Overall, farmers worked to develop competent lifestyles—that is, comfortable lifestyles given the social needs of the time—and provide resources, particularly land, for their male heirs.

Over time, this mode of life became increasingly incorporated into capitalist relations. Debt became one avenue of the enforcement of market relations. Between 1811 and 1822 on average about fifty people a year were imprisoned on debt charges as indebted farmers were forced to produce for the market in order to pay their creditors.[41] As the population increased and land became more difficult to come by, the size of farms also shrank. In early settlements it was not unusual for farmers to claim 200–400 acres, but by the early nineteenth century a middling farmer might have 50 acres.[42] This meant that patriarchal inheritance relations became more difficult to reproduce as less land was available to pass on to heirs. Given this, more and more of the population began to look for new routes of social reproduction. In some cases, for instance, young farmers unable to secure land found work in paper and textile mills. Women's labor also changed. The rise of industry coincided with the development of outwork, especially after the 1820s.[43] As manufactured textiles became more common, households could purchase clothing and focus on other work. Women, for example, produced buttons and hats, working within their own homes, supplied by merchants through the putting-out system. And most famously, the Lowell girls helped fuel the US industrial revolution.[44]

Similarly, in Franklin County farmers lived to "earn competency."[45] In other words, their goal was not capital accumulation, but social and familial stability and comfort. But, as capitalism gradually took hold, farmers searched for new ways of finding competency through its power while still attempting to reproduce the patriarchal household mode of social reproduction. One of the main strategies of lowland farmers was to raise cattle and then hire drovers to sell it in cities such as Boston or New York. By the 1820s profits in the cattle industry diminished, after which farmers shifted their capital to broom corn production, while upland farmers began to specialize in the production of broom handles.[46] And in the 1850s farmers also began to experiment by producing tobacco for the market.

In Essex County, although, as discussed, a capitalist fishing industry took off, rural society was structured around patriarchal household relations. Relations of exchange were personalized, based upon kinship and community, rather than profit.[47] Yet, like in the western countryside, as the population increased and land became more difficult to come by, young people searched for new sources of employment. One option was military service; the Seven Years' War, for example, provided soldiers with payment in wage form, acclimating them to be wage laborers. Those who were close to the coast could participate in the fishing industry. And others became craft producers and artisans.[48] All of these functioned to erode the independent patriarchal household lifestyle.

Rural capitalist transformation was also accelerated as capitalist social relations were expressed through industrialization. Increasing proportions of rural society began to acquire competency through manufacture rather than agriculture. For instance, in Greenfield in 1771, 87 percent of male household heads owned some improved land, and most that did not were younger people waiting for inheritance. By 1820, 56 percent of adults were employed in agriculture, 38 percent in manufacturing, and 7 percent in commercial occupations.[49] In Dudley and Oxford, patriarchal household relations remained dominant through the start of the nineteenth century. Here, capitalist development and industrialization developed together. Between 1810 and 1830 about twenty textile mills were constructed in the two towns. Samuel Slater, who helped start the first factories built on the British industrial model in the 1790s, moved to the region in the 1810s and began constructing textile manufactures. By 1824, he owned three clusters of factories in Dudley and Oxford.[50] Between 1810 and 1830, the amount of land auctioned off due to debts after the death of farmers who owned the land rose from 19.9 percent to 46.2 percent.[51] In an increasingly economically precarious environment, young people were forced to search for new methods of social reproduction. Attempting to sustain family competency, they entered into the market, in doing so gradually dismantling the previously dominant mode of life. In some cases, this meant engaging in outwork. In other cases, they became wage laborers. By 1832, 816 workers were recorded working in the textile factories in the two towns. Around 40 percent were women, 35 percent men, and the last quarter children between 8 and 16. All of them were "free" wage laborers.[52]

By the 1720s, towns were being developed on what is, today, the western edge of the state. One observer noted, "the country people generally manufacture their own clothing, and make considerable quantities of tow cloth for exportation. The other manufactures are ashes, maple-sugar, bricks, pottery, and iron ware. All this 'surplus' goes to Boston."[53] And another traveler through western Massachusetts stated, coming across a settler,

> he was settled in the midst of the forest, surrounded with rocks and woods, and his habitation had the most dreary appearance. He however made a subsistence, raised plenty of grain, and made his own sugar from maple trees. This practice I found very common; the forests in this part of the country abound with the maple and sugar is extracted with great ease.[54]

What became Great Barrington, for example, was settled initially during that decade. While some settlers of Dutch heritage came from New York, and some from further south in Sheffield, many came from towns further east including Westfield and Springfield.[55] By 1800, the town produced a variety of goods from potash to pottery to hats and shoes, to wool and flax, and so on. Some households appear to have been incorporated into a putting-out system as they were provided with looms to weave wool and flax after which the product was completed at a fulling mill.[56] But the majority wore homespun clothing, and producers, from blacksmiths to hatmakers, tended to own their own means of production. Similarly, Pittsfield, a new town of log cabins in the 1750s, was a community of freeholders. Land was divided into plots, not entirely equal based upon the status of those who received them, and some land was held in common.[57] Not everyone in Pittsville was necessarily a landowner. As early as the 1760s, perhaps three or four dozen laborers were temporarily hired.[58] But in general settlements on the far western edge of the state followed a similar trajectory of those further east.

By the last decades before the Civil War the state was well on its way towards capitalism. Industrial production itself, according to the state's own survey's, rose from $86,282,616 in 1837 to $295,820,681 in 1855, although the actual number was higher than this due both to the fact that the survey did not look at every industry and for tax purposes some people likely underestimated their production.[59] While industrial development was uneven, as even far western towns developed various mills to process raw materials, generally the west tended to serve as a space producing agricultural goods for the more industrialized eastern parts of the state. Through decreasing land availability, incorporation into monetarized debt networks, an increasing emphasis on commodity production, and gradual development of a larger and larger dispossessed proletariat, life choices were increasingly constrained by the power of capital, forcing younger generations to incorporate into capitalist relations or head further west to the frontier.

New Netherland

New York was born into the battleground of empires. From New Netherland and New Sweden to New York, French and British battles during the Seven Years' War, to the eradication of native populations, and, finally, the making of a nationally American imperial formation, New York—the empire state—emerged as a key component of the rising American Empire. And unlike New England, which experimented with communal forms of landownership and developed a strong moral economy, or Virginia, which developed a slave-based political economy, New Netherland, from the start, developed along a capitalist trajectory, although New York State would later unevenly develop not-so-capitalist elements.

The colony was started for profit and politics. Through the seventeenth century the Dutch emerged as the leaders of European and Atlantic world capitalism, and the colony of New Netherland demonstrated this relationship. European explorers first arrived in the New York region in 1524 when Italian Giovanni da Verrazzano, sponsored by France, anchored near Staten Island. But motivation to colonize the region did not develop until Henry Hudson, under employment from the Dutch East India Company, explored the region in his search for the fabled Northwest Passage in 1609.[60] Following Hudson's initial exploration, other Dutch ships began to enter into the region, which by 1614 took on the name New Netherland. In 1614, following these explorations, four companies merged to start the Compagnie van Nieuwnederland. The Dutch States General granted the company a patent to monopolize trade in discovered areas initially for three years. Several years later the West India Company was formed. By this point, Dutch ships had begun sailing across the Atlantic from Brazil to Africa in search of merchant profits. They imported sugar from Brazil and spices, ivory, and gold from

West Africa as the Dutch emerged as a colonial power in competition with the other European powers.[61]

On June 3, 1621, the West India Company received its charter. The company acquired monopoly rights for trade and navigation within West Africa and the Americas, along with rights to act as a military and naval power and function as a governmental structure.[62] It formed as both a political and economic organization: its goal was to interrupt the Spanish Empire and create profits through trade for its investors. The company was also given the responsibility to "advance the peopling" of unsettled land, and effectively granted the right to colonize foreign land, incorporating it into the Dutch Empire. In 1622, following a dispute between the Dutch and English ambassador, Sir Dudley Carlton, who suggested the English had previous claims to North American territory, the West India Company began to organize plans for a small settlement in New Netherland. Through 1624 and 1625, the Dutch began to send settlers to the colony. In March 1624, for example, thirty Walloon families sailed to the colony. The company also brought over cows and horses in an attempt to make a self-sustaining colony.[63] But the main goals of the settlers were set as, first, to act as a defense force against possible English colonization—the Walloons were required to serve as a military force if called upon—and to engage in the fur trade.

Throughout 1625 and 1626, more settlers, along with plants, trees, seeds, and so on, sailed to the colony. Of course, the land was far from unsettled, and relations with natives would condition the patterns of Dutch colonization. The two main settlements that formed were Fort Orange (present day Albany) and New Amsterdam (present day New York City). In 1626 an Indian war broke out around Fort Orange. Local commander Daniel Van Crieckenbeeck decided to disobey company orders of neutrality and join the Mohicans warring against the Mohawks. Several Dutch soldiers were killed and, with the threat that the Mohawks might wipe out Fort Orange, colony commander Pieter Minuit traveled to Fort Orange in spring 1626. Minuit made a deal with the Mohawks in which settler families would be moved to Manhattan, and from that moment onwards New Amsterdam became the center of Dutch activity in the colony.[64]

By the late 1620s two fractions developed within the West India Company. On the one hand, some argued for the continuation of the colony primarily as a commercial venture. On the other, some argued that continued resources needed to be put into colonization itself, and

New Netherland could be transformed into a self-sustaining agricultural exporter. As a compromise, they put in place the patroon system under the charter for Freedoms and Exemptions in 1629. Patroons were manorial fiefdoms granted to the colonial elite. Patroons were given limited rights to govern their patroons and sailing rights. They were also given the right to trade in beaver pelts, with the cost of one guilder for each pelt obtained. But the patroonship system was, in most cases, ultimately not successful, with only one patroonship, Rensselaerswyck, succeeding in the long run.[65]

While the colony was driven by a profit-seeking fur industry, to succeed it also needed to develop other components such as artisanal production and farming. This entailed the formation of a labor force and class structure. By 1664, before the English conquered the colony, the population was reaching 9,000. Most immigrants came from the United Provinces, and between 1657 and 1664 close to 70 percent of these were married couples.[66] Additionally, perhaps a quarter of immigrants were not Dutch but from other parts of Europe. Besides Europeans, black Africans arrived as early as 1626. Many of these were captured from Portuguese and Spanish colonies, already "seasoned" from working on sugar plantations. Initially, black slaves were employed by the West India Company and were common by the 1630s. By 1664, perhaps as many as 700 slaves were in the colony.[67] The colony also had an example of what has been called "half freedom." In 1644, eleven slaves who had worked for the company for close to two decades petitioned for freedom and were granted a status somewhere between bourgeois freedom and slavery.[68] This meant that a slave, after many years of service, could be freed but would have to pay a rent to the company in the form of agricultural goods and livestock for the rest of their lives. Secondly, if called on by the company they would be forced to work for the company for a wage. Finally, their children (born and un-born) would be required to serve the company as slaves.[69]

This status of half freedom demonstrates the continuum of free-unfree labor forms in the colony. Half-freed slaves were not slaves, nor were they free workers, but something in between. In addition, slaves, half freed, and white and free black labor were interchangeable from colonial capital's perspective. Slaves and free laborers, for example, worked together as longshoremen. Slaves could also be hired out as wage laborers. Patroon owner Stuyvesant, for instance, regularly hired out his forty slaves.[70] Soldiers also worked as a form of indentured wage laborer. They were recruited by *zielverkopers* (meaning "sellers of souls"). Recruits were lodged and boarded by *zielverkopers* until hired out. When hired they would be given wages two months in advance, which they usually immediately gave to their boarders in return for debts for food and lodging.[71] Cadets, then, served as another form of wage laborer, partly "free" and partly indebted servants.

Expansion in New York

By the middle of the seventeenth century, the Dutch were the most powerful capitalist center of power in Europe. But Dutch capitalism emerged in an era of rival empires, and the Dutch were soon targeted by the English and French for control of the emerging Atlantic world market. In 1651 England initiated the Navigation Acts. These stipulated all trade into England had to be conducted in English ships, or ships from the country of origin, and were targeted to diminish the Dutch entrepôt trade.[72] This triggered three Anglo-Dutch Wars through the next three decades, and in the first of these England captured New Amsterdam in 1664, changing its name to New York. While the Dutch briefly recaptured it in the third Anglo-Dutch War in 1773, from hereon, New York was a part of the British Empire. After restoration, Charles II gave New York to his brother James. The latter was given dictatorial powers over the colony to govern, provided his laws did not go against English law.[73] Under James, the Duke's Laws were passed in 1665. These laws, in contrast to the local politics of town meetings in New England, did not make provisions for localized elections.

By 1756 the population of New York was around 97,000 people as opposed to 220,000 in Pennsylvania.[74] One reason for this was due to a strong presence of Native Americans in the state who continually pushed back early settlers. In 1690, for example, a French and Iroquois attack on Schenectady, the most significant colonial settlement outside of New York City besides Albany, killed sixty people.[75] And the French and Indian War further deterred movement west into the territory. But in 1768 the Treaty of Fort Stanwix further solidified white claims to western land, and paved the way for New York to be divided between speculator patent holders whose interests were primarily in using the land as a space to produce profits for themselves.[76] The Revolutionary War also created an obstacle for westward expansion into New York. Settlers were attacked in the Cherry Valley region; they were killed and their settlements burned, including German Flatts, the westernmost settlement in the region.[77]

In addition to native resistance to settler colonialism, the other major obstacle to the colonization of New York was the manorial system. Unlike the other British colonies in North America which practiced fee simple landownership, in New York land was granted to the elite in the form of manors. Tenants then moved to the land in return for regularly producing agricultural products for the lord of the manor. Although manor lords invested in improvements—mills and so on—potential tenant settlers tended to seek out other land that they could own. This has led to suggestions that New York manors were something closer to feudalism than capitalism. Staughton Lynd, for example, argues the Livingston Manor had a "quasi-feudal" character.[78] The reasons for this have to do with the system of surplus extraction: landowners attempted to directly coerce tenants into giving up a portion of their surplus product to the landlord in return for use of the land. Tenants were required, in general, to give one-tenth of their wheat to the manor, ride with the horse team once a year, and buy wood from the manor's sawmill. Additionally, manors often had manor stores that sold spices, rice, molasses, and so on, which tenants rarely had choice but to purchase from.[79]

But manors such as Livingston may have been less of a quasi-feudal mode of production than a kind of capitalist institution that utilized tenants rather than wage workers, given the paucity of labor available at the time. As David Hamilton Grace has argued, "from the very beginning, New York's great landholders were fully market oriented with no open field or commons traditions standing in their way."[80] While their cultural habits may have had an aristocratic flair, lords of the manors aimed to use their land to make a profit through tenants, quit rents, and investments. Livingston, for instance, aimed to generate a profit from his tenants, and also, similarly to other landowners, invested in gristmills, sawmills, a bakery, and a brewhouse as a way to encourage tenants to work under the manor.[81] For Livingston, landownership was a way to engage in for-profit tenant farming. While the tenants themselves may have organized their relations through a patriarchal household mode of social reproduction, this became formally subordinated to capital as they produced commodities Livingston and his heirs could use to make profit.[82] In this sense, also, the anti-rent strikes beginning on manors such as Rensselaerswyck in 1839 and after were not exactly "feudal" per se.[83] Rather, they were a kind of reaction to an exploitative form of market-dependent tenant capitalism in which the Rensselaer family, for instance, profited from the direct exploitation of tenant farmers by acquiring the results of their labor either in commodities such as wheat which could be sold on the market, or else in direct monetary rents and fees on, for example, the alienation of land.

By 1776, settlers had generally not ventured beyond the Hudson Valley and Mohawk Valley.[84] While the British Proclamation of 1763, following the French, British, and Indian War of 1754–63, restricted settlement west of the Appalachian Mountains, the frontier of New York had not yet reached this point.[85] In most central and western New York counties, although some settlers did come between 1763 and 1776, it was not until after the revolution that many parts of the state were fully settled with white colonialists and most western counties were not started until at least the 1780s.[86] In 1788, a group of investors led by Oliver Phelps and Nathanial Gorham purchased about 2.5 million acres of New York.[87] By 1790, though, the investors struggled to make a profit and sold off two-thirds of it, or about 2 million acres, to Robert Morris who sold off much of this to the Holland Land Company several years later. Unlike the manorial system, these speculators purchased the land with the intent of selling it.[88] Several million new acres of privatized capitalist space were opened in central and western New York for settlers to purchase.

This land ended up in the hands of the Holland Land Company. Dutch capitalists viewed the space across the ocean as a potential investment outlet for their capital, and purchased 3.3 million acres of land in the 1790s. They hired Joseph Ellicott, an experienced land surveyor, to turn this investment into profit.[89] After surveying the land, and beating out competing development proposals, Ellicott was hired to manage the territory's development. In contrast to speculators who simply purchased the land in order to sell it for a profit, Ellicott pushed an agenda of company-led capitalist development. This meant gradually opening up more of the territory for sale, and encouraging small and middling farmers to settle and, slowly, build up the local economy. This entailed, firstly, low or non-existent down payments for settlers.[90] Settlers were given provisional sale of the land, which meant that they would not officially own the land until the settler who purchased it cleared and improved an agreed upon portion of the land and made payments to the company for the land fronted.[91] The company also invested in roads—so that producers could gain access to markets—and encouraged millers, taverners, blacksmiths, and other necessary settlers to come by offering them discounted land and loans. And, in some cases, the company itself financed the construction of mills. It also meant building roads and developing water routes so settlers' goods could arrive at distant markets.[92]

The social relations which formed on the western and northern frontiers of New York resulted in a tense symbiosis between Dutch capital and the patriarchal household mode of social reproduction. Settlers arrived from other parts of greater New England, pushed out by declining land availability further east.[93] The goal of many settlers on the New York frontier was not to put the land to profitable use, but to provide for their families and obtain competency. Settlers such as Stephen Durfee, a pioneer of Palmyra, noted that early settlements had a culture of friendliness due to mutual dependence. But he also notes the struggles of that time, particularly alcoholism as whiskey distilleries were built and trouble with taxes as money was scarce, and many farmers lost property due to inability to pay.[94] Joseph Sibley who settled around Monroe County says, "in the early years, there was none but a home market, and that was mostly barter:—It was so many bushels of wheat for a cow; so many bushels for a yoke of oxen, &c. There was hardly money enough in the country to pay taxes."[95] Sibley also notes that early settlers practically lived "from hand to mouth," and were self-reliant for most of their production, although dependent on a local store for black salts. And in 1819, Frances Wright notes on a trip to Rochester, then a town of perhaps 200 houses, "every man is a farmer and a proprietor; few therefore can be procured to work for hire, and these must generally be brought from a distance."[96]

Similarly, in Chautaqua County, Judge L. Bugbee, describing his childhood memories in an 1885 speech, points out that most early settlers first moved to bark-covered cabins, building log cabins as soon as they could. Neighbors all attended cabin raisings as part of their obligation to the community.[97] As these communities developed, it was rare to find wage laborers, and when farmers needed an extra hand they might exchange labor with a neighbor, or else plan a day in which other community members worked together, for instance, to haul and burn logs, followed by a night with a meal and festivities. In these communities, much of basic production of goods such as textiles was done in the home. This changed with the onset of industrialization, for example, in 1823 a textile weaving factory went up in Jamestown and by 1846 the town was exporting $30,000 of textiles.[98]

Similarly, gender relations reflected the practical conditions of frontier settlements. As one female settler in Chautauqua County put it:

> It was not fashionable then to be weakly. We could take our spinning-wheels and walk two miles to a spinning frolic, do our day's work, and after a first-rate supper, join in some innocent amusement for the evening. We did not take particular pains to keep our hands white; we knew they were made to use for our advantage; therefore, we never thought of having hands just to look at. Each settler had to go and assist his neighbors ten or fifteen days, in order to get help in return in log-rolling time; this was the only way to get assistance.[99]

In other words, frontier women in western New York were less concerned with protecting the racial purity of their white skin or the bourgeois household than the practical tasks of settlement life and labor.

Ellicott, acting as capital personified, though, had to work to make sure returns went to the company. In this regard he quickly encouraged settlers towards market incorporation. Settlers had plenty of ecological resources to remake, and a potash industry formed early on as trees were cut and burned, and lye was extracted from the ashes and burned into black salts which merchants purchased from settlers and sold as far as Montreal.[100] Markets for livestock, wheat, maple syrup, and timber also formed as settlers were formally incorporated into market relations. And Ellicott also pushed for capital-led state formation as he successfully lobbied Albany to create a new county, Genesee County (which itself would later be further subdivided), in 1802–03.[101]

Similarly, William Cooper actively pursued capitalist development in Otsego from the 1780s. He believed that by selling plots of land to poor freeholding families on long-term credit, rather than renting the land, the farmers would be more productive and enthusiastic about improving the land they themselves owned. But in order to pay back their debts, farmers would need access to markets and encouragement to produce for the market. He acquired maple sugar and potash kettles to help settlers turn their raw materials into commodities and organized cattle drives for settlers to sell their livestock on the market. He also built a store and warehouse which linked frontier settlement to the Atlantic world market as goods came from as far as the West Indies and Britain and frontier potash made its way to New York City.[102]

Towns such as Rochester and Syracuse were also planned, in many respects, along capitalist lines. As Diane Shaw puts it, "[Rochester] was to be a commercial city, built for profit and attractive to business interests."[103] The city was planned along a grid pattern and divided into districts to serve milling, commercial, and civic zones. Public buildings were not to be the center of the town, but placed on the edge of the commercial zones, symbolizing the fact that the most central land was to be used for commercial, rather than political, purposes. These cities, along with Buffalo, exploded in the decades following the construction of the Erie Canal; a state-led project to further capitalist development. Carol Sheriff notes that "most inhabitants of the Erie Canal region embraced market opportunities with a mixture of impulses; they were neither wholly pre-capitalist nor wholly capitalist in outlook."[104] That being said, the canal was primarily built by Irish wage laborers as immigrant labor played a central historical role in the making of a wage labor-based American working class.[105]

Overall the making of white-settler empire on the frontier of New York was an uneven process in which emerging capitalist interests attempted to will and subjugate the patriarchal household mode of social reproduction to the logic of capitalism. While capitalist interests opened and developed new land, much of the labor organization itself—the social relations of production—were organized in a non-capitalist mode of production. Early empire building in New York was thus not entirely driven by capital.

Pennsylvania

As the capitalist-state elite were working towards New York's development, Pennsylvania was, by that time, on its way towards the predominance of capitalist relations. The colony's white-settler roots go back to Henry Hudson who noted the existence of the Delaware Bay as early as 1609, and while the English and Dutch sent a few explorations to the region following this, the first serious settlement appears to have begun with the Dutch in 1623. New Sweden was started in 1638 until conquered by the Dutch in 1655.[106] Of course, New Netherland was soon taken over by the English, and the development of Pennsylvania would begin to take off under the leadership of William Penn. Penn found himself in the curious situation of being a Quaker during a time of religious intolerance in England, and an elite member of English society;

a friend to the courts of Charles II and James II. The state owed debts to Penn's father, Sir William Penn (whom the younger Penn claims he named the colony after), and Penn petitioned Charles II for land in what became Pennsylvania in lieu of paying the debts in cash. In return, he received the right to settle the territory.[107]

Penn famously constructed a "holy experiment." Quakers, as their critics called them, or the Religious Society of Friends as they called themselves, led by George Fox, believed that following their inner light was the path towards salvation. Viewed as a challenge to state ideology, an estimated 15,000 at least were imprisoned between 1661 and 1685, with estimates ranging as high as 60,000 imprisoned and 5,000 killed.[108] Quakers also proselytized throughout the colonial world, from North America to the West Indies, and sought out new spaces to practice their religion. By the time Pennsylvania was created Quakers had already established a presence in the colonies. And persecuted within England, Quakers sought out a new land to create their utopian world.

Penn's connections granted him this space, and while Penn's ultimate goal was to create a society of religious freedom in which Quakers and other denominations could practice freely, he also lived in a world going through a transition to capitalism, with lineages of a feudal past still holding on. This shaped Penn's approach to land distribution and settlement. While Penn saved some manorial lands for his future heirs, and distributed some to manor lords who promised to develop the land, much of the land was distributed to settlers who would, in turn, pay quitrents to Penn.[109] Quitrents were a form of tenancy inherited from pre-capitalist England, and continued on as a historical structure into this period.[110] But they overlapped with emerging capitalist relations of commodified land markets. In this sense, Penn's social actions represented something closer to capitalism than feudalism. Selling land and collecting quitrents was a method of profit generation for the Penn family. But the social relations that formed on the Pennsylvania frontier were not necessarily capitalist. As Gottfried Achenwall reported to a German audience after interviewing Benjamin Franklin:

> In Pennsylvania, where the Penn family own all the land, anyone who wants to improve the land, chooses a piece, pays the landlord for 100 acres 10 Pound Sterling local money, and binds himself to pay an annual rent of half a penny for each acre—he then becomes absolute owner, and the little ground rent can never be increased. Sometimes

> the hunter builds a wooden hut, and the nearest neighbors in the wilderness help cut the timber, build the log hut, fill the crevices with mud, put on the roof and put in windows and doors, and in return the owner pays them with a gallon of brandy.[111]

While Penn's deed gave him "possession" rather than ownership of the land, it was quickly subdivided into commodified shapes that could be sold for a profit.[112] Perhaps the greatest example of this is Philadelphia. Penn saw that a successful colony would need a central commercial city, just as England had London. He commissioned Thomas Holme, surveyor general of the providence, to lay out a plan for the city. Penn's idea was to develop a commercial center with small lots of land given out, surrounded by larger lots as suburbs. Purchasers would buy lots by lottery, and the space itself would be designed in a grid pattern, facilitating rational flows of capital and people.[113]

The population of the Philadelphia region rose from 2,200 in 1700 to 19,000 by 1760 as the population of Pennsylvania rose from 18,000 to over 200,000 during this period. A class structure formed around the city's international mercantile connections. Merchants comprised an important segment of the population and were linked into circuits of capital extending to Africa, the West Indies, and Europe. But the majority of merchants in the latter part of the eighteenth century were not wealthy gentlemen, but of middle and lower classes, while perhaps 15 percent were part of the Philadelphia elite. Next to merchants formed a group of shopkeepers along with artisans, apprentices, laborers, sailors, slaves, and other social groups. Perhaps 10 percent of the working population consisted of mariners and dock laborers, including black workers and occasionally Native American workers.[114] And, of course, there were also the poor and destitute, served by the cities almshouses.

While Philadelphia was planned as a kind of capitalist city from the start, its development used a variety of labor forms. In some cases, slaves were imported, first primarily from the West Indies, and by the middle of the century merchants were trading directly between the city and the African coast.[115] More common than slaves were indentured servants. In the middle of the eighteenth century, approximately half of all laborers in Philadelphia were some form of unfree labor (servants or slaves) and two-thirds of servants were purchased by artisans. But during the Revolutionary War, the pace of servants transported across the ocean slowed. It picked up again later, and was followed by a 1788 British ban on the emigration of skilled workers from Britain and Ireland, and the Passenger Act of 1803 that reduced the number of immigrants a merchant could carry. These policies, along with the confusion of the Napoleonic Wars, limited the number of new servants, encouraging producers to rely more heavily on wage laborers. At the same time, economic problems hurt the artisan class, forcing them to sell their labor power for wages. A depression hit in 1765 following the Seven Years' War, and between 1765 and 1769 prices decreased, putting artisans out of work. From the end of the 1760s through the 1790s, wages for cordwainers, tailors, journeymen printers, and others tended to decline. In this context, master mechanics found it more profitable to invest in the growing wage labor force, rather than hire servants.[116] And prison labor was also used.[117]

While Philadelphia was a city destined towards capitalist development from its origins, it became a central node on broader relations of uneven development throughout the rest of the territory. Further west what developed was not simply a New England style society of English immigrants, but complex creole cultures mixed together.[118] In particular, besides the English, Scotch-Irish and German settlers poured into Pennsylvania. For instance, between the settlement of the colony and the American Revolution, perhaps 111,000 German colonialists made their way to Delaware Bay, and while early on more Germans than Irish migrated, by the end of the eighteenth century as many Irish appear to have been arriving as Germans, as German immigration during this era hit its peak in the 1750s, and Irish immigration in the 1780s. While in some cases families immigrated, perhaps half of all German immigrants came over as indentured laborers. Commonly, young single men came over, and to pay for the cost of their travel, upon arrival the merchant who filled his extra space (besides goods) with potential servants sold them to a buyer. Their contracts, in this case, were not negotiated in advance, but upon arrival. These "redemptioners" might be sold to a variety of people. Artisans might need an extra hand, or households an extra laborer. Or speculators hired servants to clear and improve their land, using servants as an investment to generate profits.[119]

Capitalist relations also formed in the iron industry. In the early 1700s, large plantation manor owners were hiring workers to produce iron.[120] And soon after this, investors pooled their capital in companies such as the Durham Iron Works, built in 1727, to produce iron for profit. A variety of labor forms were used in this industry, scattered throughout early southeast Pennsylvania, including wage laborers, indentured servants, apprentices, and slaves and free blacks. Due to labor shortages, for example, in 1727 a petition was created to eliminate duties on black slaves brought into the colony to work in the iron industry, and although it failed, duties were reduced two years later.[121]

In the west, instead, the social relations that formed took on a variety of not-so-capitalist characteristics. The Moravians provide an example in contrast to the capitalistically forming Philadelphia landscape. Under Count Nicholas Ludwig von Zinzendorf, they purchased 500 acres in Pennsylvania in 1741 and started the town of Bethlehem. Moravians organized their age, gender, and labor relations around "choirs"; little girls and boys choirs, older boys and girls choirs, single brothers and sisters choirs, married couples choirs, and so on. They ate and slept in choirs, worked in choirs, and often worshiped in choirs. They also raised children communally, rather than living in nuclear families.[122] Within the choir system, women tended to have positions of power alien to other parts of the colony. They could participate in governing bodies, give sermons, and so on although the top leadership was all male. In sum, the Moravians organized a communal society antithetical to capitalism. As one traveler noted:

> all manner of trades and manufactures are carried on in this place distinctly, and one of each branch; at these various occupations the young men are employed. Every one contributes his labor, and the profits arising from each goes to the general stock. These young men receive no wages, but are supplied with all necessities from the various branches of trade. They have no cares about the usual concerns of life, and their whole time is spent in prayer and labor; their only relaxation being concerts, which they perform every evening.[123]

But over time Moravians became integrated into the expanding hegemony of capital. Most significantly, the colony had acquired debts that they were not able to pay off. This was coupled with an ideological shift in which Moravian leaders became increasingly dissatisfied with elements of communalism, such as the collective raising of children. In the 1760s, the colony began to make changes to cope with these pressures, and by the early 1770s families were reorganized to live together and some industries began to operate privately. While some parts of the colony were kept communal at first, such as stores, inns, farms, blacksmithing, and pottery production, some farms were leased to tenant farmers as privatization was introduced. In 1771 the colony also started its first constitution that, among other things, set prices and wages and prevented land leased by the colony to be purchased or sold to landholders without the colony's permission.[124]

By the beginning of the nineteenth century, the original Moravian dream began to collapse. The Revolutionary War disrupted the colony as many men left to fight in the war, and pressures from within and without the colony forced a series of changes in the structure of governance. For example, in 1818 a General Synod was held for the first time in seventeen years that would, among other things, reduce the degree of commercial regulation. As time passed, the community could not resist the changing world around them as, for example, coal was discovered around the area and developed into an industry by the Lehigh Coal and Navigation Company, and as Bethlehem increasingly found itself linked into new networks of transportation and circuits of capital. So in 1844 the Board of Supervision finally decided to dismantle the lease ownership system, open the city up to non-Moravians, and adopt a secular government, enacted the next year.[125]

Westward expansion early on was driven by similar forces as elsewhere: population increases, decreasing land availability, and rising land prices placed limits on the ability of patriarchal, independent households to reproduce their means of production, forcing younger generations to commodify their labor or move further south or west. Lancaster, for example, was initially developed by Andrew Hamilton, an associate of the Penn family, who acquired the land through a complex set of maneuvers. Aware that the land was the designated seat of the newly created Lancaster County, he gave money to a friend, James Steel, who purchased the rights to the land from an Englishman who still held them, and sold it to his son, who obtained a patent from the Penn family in 1735.[126] Like many developers on the "urban frontier," Hamilton desired to turn the land into profit.[127] Soon after the developing town was settled by a primarily German population. Settlers were granted titles upon an agreement of building a substantial house within one year and paying regular ground rents to Hamilton. Additionally, some settlers appear to have attempted to profit from Hamilton's own speculation by purchasing several lots, building houses, then selling the lots for profit.[128]

While profit-seeking activity through the commodification and distribution of land played a role in settlement itself, the social relations from below were not necessarily organized along capitalist lines.

Prospective husbands for the most part did not come of age until 21, although occasionally married earlier. Generally, at 21, if working as an apprentice, their time would be over, and often fathers supplied sons with some combination of land, tools, livestock, or money to start their own independent family lives. Women often married younger than men, sometimes in their late teens, although marriage ages tended to rise gradually between the 1740s and 1800s, and, upon marriage, were also given inheritances.[129] Before a man married—and as marriage was viewed as a way to quell the potentially violent tendencies of masculinity—it was expected that he would be well on his way towards obtaining the means necessary to build an independent patriarchal family. But over time the patriarchal household mode of social life remained difficult to maintain. Land warrants were given out at decreasing rates, and the size of the holdings also decreased. For example, in Lancaster County between 1771 and1780, 665 warrants were given out, with 45 percent of those being under 100 acres. In contrast, from 1791 to 1800, 119 warrants were given out and 70 percent of those were under 100 acres.[130] This land also increased in price, raising the costs to begin a new family, and forcing younger generations to move elsewhere in search of cheaper land.

Further west, the reflection of non-capitalist relations in the region around Pittsburgh, for example, can be seen in the wills left by those who died. These wills dictated the distribution of property after death, and, given the coverture laws of the era, this meant that a husband, as in one case, would even specify to leave a wife's clothes to her own use.[131] Generally, though, fathers would distribute land to their sons, often giving a larger portion to the first born who would also be designated the role of providing for the widow and potentially other sons and daughters, while daughters were given other more liquid assets such as livestock, clothing, and other valuables, although there were also exceptions in which land was left to daughters.[132]

Squatters, settlers, and class conflict

As settlers moved west, tensions arose from a variety of angles in western Pennsylvania. While Penn may have attempted to develop a "peaceable kingdom" in which land would only be acquired from native populations through their cooperation, settlers on the frontier did not have the same attitude. Tensions between French and British imperial aspirations also deepened as the French pushed their claims to frontier land, culminating in the French and Indian War and, following this, Pontiac's Rebellion.[133] In the countryside, frontier squatters resisted competing claims of landowners and restrictions against western expansion which might create conflicts with native peoples. By 1730 Scotch-Irish immigrants from Ulster, Ireland, were squatting in Conestoga Manor. James Logan, who was secretary of the providence, gained the support of Reverend James Anderson of Donegal Church to remove the squatters. Anderson recruited a volunteer force and, with the help of the magistrates of Lancaster County and the sheriff, burned down about thirty cabins and evicted the settlers.[134] Over the next decades, tensions between frontier settlers and state and speculative capitalist forces would set the contours of class conflict and capitalist development in the region.

White-settler colonialism also entailed the removal of native peoples. This land was acquired through the typical American colonial pattern of using violence against the natives, deceiving them, and forcing them to sign treaties with the colonialists. In Pennsylvania, perhaps the most famous case of this was the Walking Purchase of 1737. Although objective evidence was never fully demonstrated, Quaker folklore suggested that at some point William Penn and the Delaware Indians had made an agreement in which Penn, along with Delaware representatives, were to walk for three days west of the Delaware River, at the end agreeing upon a boundary, after which Penn would buy it in exchange for a particular amount of goods.[135] And while the Delawares also had some socially collected, somewhat vague memories of a land agreement with Penn, it was nothing close to the final decision that was forced upon them.

Penn's heirs, under pressures of debt, decided to expand their holdings of Pennsylvania territory, which meant widening their control into this area. Thomas Penn produced a 1686 document that he argued was evidence for the Delaware-Penn agreement west of the river. The native peoples were hesitant to settle to an agreement based upon the document. Following this, Andrew Hamilton drew a map that was both inaccurately scaled to misrepresent the amount of territory the settlers claimed, and documented only the Delaware and Lehigh Rivers. Between these, though, lay the Tohickon Creek, purposely left out of the picture so that the natives would mistake the Lehigh for the Tohickon. Thomas Penn used this map to get the Delawares to agree to a purchase, based on an agreement in which the Delawares would get to stay on any land they previously occupied within the purchase. Following this, Penn hired three groups of walker surveyors to head west and northwest to map out the territory determined by the length they could walk in three days, in doing so acquiring 710,000 acres of land.[136] As settlers moved to the area, over time, the Delawares were pushed out of the territory as their pleas against the injustice of the land acquisition were ignored by white settlers.

While whites in pursuit of land and speculative profit pushed the natives west, some settlers became "white Indians," mingling with native populations in something closer to Richard White's "middle ground" than strict, clearly delineated racial and cultural borders.[137] In some cases, squatters asked permission from natives to settle the land. They also engaged in small-scale trading of products such as corn, tobacco, and alcohol. And settlers even rented land from Indians as tenant farmers.[138] But settlers also commonly warred with native peoples. Perhaps the most famous case of this is the Conestoga massacre by the Paxton Boys in 1763.

The Conestogas lived in territory granted to them by William Penn, but by the middle of the eighteenth century Penn's more benevolent type of colonialism (if such a thing can exist) was supplanted by a more brutal form. On December 14, about fifty settlers burned down Conestoga Town and killed six natives. The Conestogas regrouped in Lancaster, but thirteen days later the Paxton Boys rode into town and slaughtered the remaining fourteen. The boys then began to march to Philadelphia to inform the government of their grievances, but were stopped in Germantown by a contingent of Philadelphia's leading political figures, to whom they left two spokesmen to present their case. This was a crucial turning point in the history of Pennsylvania as "for the first time in the providence's history, a group of colonialists engaged in an extralegal, large-scale, and organized act of racial violence."[139]

This violence came after the conclusion of the Seven Years' War (or the French-Indian War). The war severely disrupted native-settler relations as throughout the region Delawares attacked settler farms, killing hundreds. This challenged the patriarchal authority of settler colonialists. It threatened their status as "men" striving for economic "competency" based upon control and improvement of land, and the labor of their children, wives, and indentured servants (and rarely, slaves). It also encouraged settlers to increasingly group the ethnically diverse native peoples into one overarching racial category.[140]

In addition to facing indigenous peoples, settlers and squatters also had to contest with an emerging capitalist American social formation.

For example, in 1804 a surveyor under the employment of Pennsylvania land speculators was shot dead by a group of an estimated eighteen white people wearing native garb.[141] He was one of many killed by white settlers fighting off emerging capitalist forces as settlers fought against large-scale speculators taking control of land they believed they had the right to. Throughout the eighteenth century, squatters were continually purged by the government. For example, in 1748 local justices of the peace, along with several Shamokin Indians, expelled squatters from Sherman's Creek, the Juniata Valley, and Great Cove. They found sixty-one illegal dwellings, and agreed to burn down the settlements. For the authorities, the land had to be legitimately purchased before it could be settled.[142]

In 1768, the Fort Stanwix treaty was signed, giving Thomas Penn the right to claim land in the Wyoming Valley and Shamokin region. The Penn family hoped to profit from the land and hired speculators to settle and develop it in return for land grants. But those hoping to profit from the territory soon clashed with white squatters who claimed the land for themselves. While the settlers sent letters pleading their case, claiming to have purchased the land from the natives, the Penn family viewed their claims as illegitimate. These claims were also located in a broader struggle between Pennsylvania and Connecticut to control the region. Connecticut settlers feared that the new treaty would deprive them of their settlements and sent a letter signed by sixty-three of them, including Lazarus Stewart, previous leader of the Paxton Boys, pleading to sustain control of the land they settled.[143] Conflict between Pennsylvania and Connecticut claims would continue until the Trenton decree of 1782, fully enforced in the next four years, which stated that the land belonged to Pennsylvania, although Connecticut settlers already there could stay.

By 1790 nearly 13,000 white settlers lived in the western counties of Allegheny, Washington, Fayette, Westmoreland, and Bedford. Perhaps 37 percent were English, 7 percent Welsh, 17 percent Scotch, 19 percent Irish, and 12 percent German, among other nationalities and ethnicities.[144] However, compared to other parts of the western frontier, Pennsylvania tended to have a relatively high percentage of landless peoples. For example, during the Revolutionary War many soldiers were paid in land grants, yet many of these grants were sold to speculators.[145] By 1780 around one-third of Pennsylvania's population did not own land.[146] And many of those who did own land were still producing little beyond subsistence. In the 1780s perhaps 75 acres were needed to produce surplus product, depending on the quality of land. The median taxable person held about 100 acres of land. Additionally, much of the land that was held was still not cleared, thus agriculture could not be produced on it.[147] Overall, this suggests that while market relations of course existed, for many settlers they remained marginal to the social reproduction of the family. Traveling at the foot of the Alleghenies, finding a tavern or house to stay each night, one traveler said "of these articles, the coffee was only not the produce of their own land! What people, therefore, can be more independent?"[148] And another stated,

> the Pensylvanians are an industrious and hardy people, they are most of them substantial, but cannot be considered rich, it being rarely the case with landed people. However, they are well lodged, fed, and clad, and the latter at an easy rate, as the inferior people manufacture most of their own apparel, both linnens and woolens, and are more industrious of themselves, having but few blacks among them.[149]

Through the 1790s the patterns of landholding continued to consolidate in fewer hands. In Fayette and Washington counties, for instance, around 59 percent of the taxable population owned land. In addition, the size of landholdings for poor and middling farmers tended to diminish, in part due to the fact that as fathers passed land on to their male heirs, the size of the lots decreased. At the same time, large-scale landowners tended to increase the size of their lots. In Washington and Fayette, for example, from the mid-1780s to mid-1790s the top 10 percent of landowners raised their control of land.[150] Increasingly, the population had to find other means of social reproduction. Tenants as a percentage of the population may have been as high as 12 percent in the 1780s and 20 percent in the 1790s.[151] Others found work as artisans or, in some cases, wage laborers, although these class categories were not always clearly delineated as, for example, artisans were also sometimes landowners.

These shifting conditions in western Pennsylvania set the basis for the Whiskey Rebellion of 1791–94. Through the 1780s and 1790s, settlers were increasingly economically squeezed as landlessness rose, plot sizes decreased, and living standards worsened.[152] Meanwhile, political power was increasingly centered in the hands of the eastern elite. This was confirmed by the Constitutional Convention of 1787. The convention was a response to several factors. First, many of the so-called founding fathers themselves were bondholders and part of the ruling class elite. Yet those in debt called on individual states to print money to lower their debts. One goal of the convention was to disallow states from producing bills to lower the value of these debts. The constitution also solidified a balance between northern states increasingly dissatisfied with slavery and southern slaveholders who viewed it as a part of their liberty.[153]

But, perhaps most importantly, Shays' Rebellion in western Massachusetts brought George Washington out of retirement and sent a message to the American elite that something had to be done to quell what they commonly called an "excess of democracy."[154] With the doors locked and guarded, the so-called founding fathers constructed a constitution that centralized governmental power and would insulate policy making from popular pressures. The new constitution itself was unconstitutional, according to the previous Articles of Confederation. It was accepted as soon as it was approved by nine states, although the articles stated that all states had to accept these changes. Overall, "the convention decided to make the new national government considerably less responsive to the popular will than any of its state level counterparts."[155] Among other things, the remade government would have the direct ability to levy taxes from citizens and construct a large standing army that could be used to quell outbreaks of violence, such as Shays' Rebellion.[156]

For western settlers, struggling with wars against the natives and economic poverty, whiskey was the one commodity they could count on for market exchange. They could convert their surplus grains into whiskey production, a sustainable and in-demand commodity. Short of specie, whiskey also served as a form of currency. Thus, a tax on whiskey was, in essence, a challenge to the basic livelihood of settler yeomen. But for a newly formed, struggling federal government, a tax on whiskey appeared to be a reasonable way to increase state finances. Between 1790 and 1796, for example, five-sixths of the federal operating budget went towards war; especially Indian wars, as the United States tried to clear the frontier of natives through a series of wars in the early 1790s culminating in the Battle of Fallen Timbers in 1794. For Secretary of the Treasury Alexander Hamilton, then, whiskey excise taxes seemed to fit into part of a practical strategy to fund the new state.[157]

By 1791, western frontiersmen were sending letters to the government to reject Hamilton's proposed excise tax, under pressures of wars with natives, lack of profitable outlets to sell their surplus production to, and lack of specie. In particular, the state wanted to drain what specie was available in the region to pay for the wars. These pressures culminated in resistance to the tax. The first major meeting protesting the tax occurred at Redstone Old Fort on July 17, 1791. Leaders gathered and resolved to appoint delegates to investigate their respective counties to get a sense of public sentiment and meet again in Pittsburgh in September, although it was not until eleven months later that the meeting was held.[158] Early on, then, much of the protest was in legal, civil forms, and only later would violence break out on a large scale.

By the summer of 1792, a year and a half after the tax had been passed, no attempt to collect it had been made. But in August, inspector John Neville hired newcomer William Faulkner to host a place to process taxes at his residence. Neville placed an advertisement in the *Pittsburgh Gazette* saying they were prepared to process whiskey stills at Faulkner's place. Several days later approximately twenty men in war paint traveled to Faulkner's place and shot holes through a sign on the front of his house, and shot the ceiling in every room in the house. They also considered burning down his house, but decided against it for fear it might start a fire that would catch other houses, and instead drew a knife and threatened to tar and feather Faulkner if he kept the inspection office open. Neville continued to have trouble renting a place to register and process taxes. In June 1794, for instance, John Lynn agree to lease Neville a part of his house. Following this, twelve men in blackface visited Lynn and took him to a remote forest where they cut his hair off, removed his clothes, and tarred and feathered him. These are just two of many cases of gangs visiting those who complied with the tax, or rented space to enforce it, that were met with racialized and gendered forms of violence as whites disguised themselves as natives, blacks, or women to hide their identity.

By the middle of 1794, the international situation had changed. The French Revolution had triggered a shifting of circumstances, leading American politicians to fear the possibility of war with Spain and Britain. And General Anthony Wayne's victory at the Battle of Fallen Timbers opened up a new space in the west for speculators to profit from. In this context, fed up with years of resistance to the whiskey tax, Alexander Hamilton and other leading American politicians began to consider more extreme techniques to subdue the rebels. District Attorney William Rawle ordered the appearance of more than sixty distillers, and on June 22 Marshal David Lenox journeyed west to serve the notices. After an exchange at the home of William Miller in which Lenox and Neville attempted to give Miller a copy of the summons, and three or four dozen settlers chased the two off, Lenox fled to Pittsburgh and Neville to Bower Hill. Two days later, in search of Lenox, rebels surrounded Neville's place, believing Lenox to be there. Neville ordered them to stand back, and fired, killing Oliver Miller. More shots rang out on both sides, and several of the protestors were injured. Miller's death set a new precedent in the conflict whereby settlers moved beyond the law to fight for their cause. Another assault on Neville's home led to the death of James McFarlane, a hero of the American Revolution, further adding fire to the rebels' cause. The violence continued to grow, spreading to Maryland, and at its peak 7,000 rebels gathered for a meeting at Braddock's Field on August 1. As violence and protest spread, the federal government used 12,500 troops to quell the rebellion.[159]

The rebellion is often thought of as a conflict between farmers and the eastern elite, but in many respects it represents social and class conflict arising from patterns of uneven development. While settlers wanted to be involved in market relations, and whiskey was a method of doing this, many of them were more generally protesting the overall social conditions in which they found themselves. While George Washington (a major western land speculator himself) and Alexander Hamilton were fighting for a rational, organized, increasingly capitalistic society, the rebels fought for control of their land and livelihood, fighting for something closer to a patriarchal household mode of social reproduction rather than full on capitalism.

The convention of 1787 and subsequent crushing of the Whiskey Rebellion (and Fries Rebellion in 1799) set the basis for the destruction of less market-dependent household relations in the west.[160] As taxes were enforced, specie increasingly necessary, and the monopoly of force controlled by the federal government, producers became engaged in "petty-commodity production"; that is, increasingly integrated into and dependent upon market relations even if the restructuring of the organization of production itself was a slow process to develop. In other words, capital inserted itself into these preexisting patriarchal household relations and gradually transformed them.

By 1800 the frontier era of Pennsylvania's history was coming to a close. By then, what land was left unsettled was primarily that of unproductive soil and rugged terrain.[161] But settlers would continue to move west to produce new spaces of empire. By the early 1800s Pittsburgh, for example, was on a path to capitalist development on the urban frontier. In what might be considered an early form of military-industrial complex, deputy quartermaster and military storekeeper Issac Craig, who also helped start the first glass manufactory in the region and owned land on which he worked tenant farmers, encouraged local production for military uses, in doing so stimulating the economic growth of Pittsburgh. Craig might be considered as a nascent capitalist subjugating the frontier to capitalism. Brought to the frontier through his military service, he remained, channeling capital to profitable uses. In 1803, for example, he wrote to Samuel Hodgdon discussing the establishment of the manufactory, the costs of which exceeded expectations as he organized skilled workers (who were apparently not as skilled as he would have hoped) and built lodgings for their families.[162] Besides investing in manufacturing, Craig also owned land which he rented to tenant farmers.[163] But while tenant farming was a for-profit mode of production, given the paucity of money and rough frontier conditions, Craig also accepted other mediums of exchange. This is due to the fact that his letters reflect collecting rents from frontier farmers was a continual struggle for wannabe capitalists. In one case, for example, he mentions he "would take A good Horse if brought here and a few well grown hog."[164] Thus, even frontier capitalists resorted to non-monetary means of compensation, as the money supply was not large enough and market relations too undeveloped to guarantee paper money as a measure of value and means of circulation.

Overall, capitalism in the early northwest developed gradually and incrementally, with some zones, particularly cities such as Boston, Philadelphia, and New York, forming as urban centers of capitalism as eastern capital expanded west and gradually pressed against small farmers. The formal subsumption of settlers by capital meant that the power of profit-seeking behavior slowly and gradually took a larger and larger role in the dictation of social life. As the next chapter will show, however, by the early 1800s in both the American north, south, and grey area between, expansion was not yet necessarily overdetermined by the power of capitalism.

3
Kentucky and Ohio

For minister Lyman Beecher:

> The West is a young empire of mind, and power, and wealth, and free institutions, rushing up to a giant manhood, with a rapidity and a power never before witnessed below the sun. And if she carries with her the elements of her preservation, the experiment will be glorious—the joy of the nation—the joy of the whole earth, as she rises in the majesty of her intelligence and benevolence, and enterprise, for the emancipation of the world.[1]

Through expansion the United States would realize and extend its powerful masculinity over "she"; the west. And for Frederick Jackson Turner, famously, the vast western space was where American democracy was realized and reproduced: "American social development has been continually beginning over again on the frontier."[2] The primitive conditions frontier settlers found themselves in renewed the individualist American culture characteristic of American democracy.[3] In other words, the culture of American "democratic" Empire was continually renewed through westward expansion.

This chapter will continue the story of capitalism and colonization into Kentucky and Ohio. The reproduction of manhood through empire drove settlers into these territories for a variety of reasons, from patriarchs establishing personal domain over their families to building an empire of slavery. Between formed a complex borderland of interchangeable labor forms, including free workers and slaves, as slavery was not simply "one" form of social life in itself, but took on unique characteristics in different parts of the United States.

Geographically, "the west" was continually redefined. By the early 1800s it was, for instance, "that part of the United States, which has received the term Western, relatively to the part east of the Aleghany mountains, lies entirely in the valley of the Mississippi, and the Basin of the Canadian Lakes."[4] But the west was also more than geography and ecology. Over a hundred years ago Turner viewed the west socially rather than geographically. For the writer, "the west, at bottom, is a form of society, rather than as area."[5] And for westerners writing in their own times, they were the west; the edge of the frontier.[6] But rather than using "west" as a social category, it has more often than not been used as a geographical category. To put it in other terms, the geographical concept of "the west" which was reconstructed after the frontier had closed stopped referring to the west as it was, and transposed a historical-geographical category "the west" on to a history in which the real "west" was lost.[7] In this context, this chapter also examines the ways that Kentucky and Ohio were the wests of their own time, and suggests both entered into the American union somewhere between capitalism and non-capitalism.[8]

The origins of American movement into the Ohio Valley emerged out of a long history of competition for power between the French, British, and Native Americans. By the time the French arrived, down from the Great Lakes, in the last half of the seventeenth century, they encountered native groups devastated by the spread of European disease, and the Iroquois offensive of the 1650s and 1660s that pushed other native populations away from the Great Lakes region.[9] From then on, the native peoples, and most significantly, the Iroquois confederacy, found themselves caught between Anglo-French interimperial rivalry. But by the 1740s the balance between these forces began to falter, and over the next four decades, shifted. The Ohio Valley transformed from a space of competing and cooperating interactions, to one of Anglo dominance as the American Revolution set the stage for the ethnic cleansing of the native peoples and establishment of white-settler dominance over the region.[10]

In 1742, the Iroquois agreed to the Treaty of Easton, granting land previously held by the Delawares to the Penn family. Two years later, in 1744, they agreed to the Treaty of Lancaster. In return for 800 pounds of currency, 300 pounds of gold, recognition of Iroquois leadership over native tribes, and the right of Iroquois to pass through the land to battle Cherokees and Catawbas, they gave up their rights to remaining claims on land in Virginia and Maryland. These treaties were pushed by the desire for western Anglo speculators to profit from western lands; by 1745, Virginia granted close to a third of a million acres around the Ohio River to a syndicate of speculators.[11] As the British became increasingly active, pressuring the balance of power in the Ohio Valley and beyond, the War of Austrian Secession spilled over into King George's War from

1744 to 1748. During the war, the British blocked goods shipped for New France, making it increasingly difficult for French traders to compete with British traders. As a result, some native groups shifted their allegiance away from the French towards the British. For example, the Miami leader La Demoiselle shifted alliance from France to Britain, and established Pickawilly to trade with the British. As a response to British pressure, from both Virginia speculators and Pennsylvania traders, and shifting native allegiances, following King George's War the French intensified their efforts to exert control over the Ohio Valley. This was in large part due to the fact that the French wanted to maintain a geographical link between their empires in Canadian and Louisianan territory. So in 1752, the Marquis de Duquesne arrived in Quebec with orders to drive the British from French claimed territory by mobilizing the Canadian militia to build a series of forts in Ohio country, two of which were under construction by the next spring.

In reaction to increased French militancy—as a result of increased British presence into territory the French saw as theirs—and the gradual hollowing out of the Euro-Native American middle ground, British politicians back home grew more worried about French dominance on the frontier of their North American Empire. This was also caused by increased British fear after the War of Austrian Secession returned to the status quo with the Treaty of Aix-La-Chapelle, but weakened the British-Austrian alliance. As a result, the British, led by the Duke of Newcastle and Lord Halifax, pushed further to assert their control over the empire across the ocean. Influenced by reports coming over from the colony, the king agreed to support the colonists in constructing forts in the contested area and, if the French attempted to interfere, use force, provided that the British colonists were defending themselves from the supposed French aggressors. Tensions increased after French Ensign Coulon de Villiers de Jumonville and thirty-five men traveled to warn the British against their incursions into French territory in late May of 1754. Famously, led by George Washington in alliance with the Mingos, and the Half King Tanaghrisson, the British attacked the French, killing Jumonville and triggering the beginnings of the war which evolved, more broadly, into the Seven Years' War (or the French-Indian War).[12]

The war ended in 1763 with British victory. And it was through the attempt to consolidate the British Empire in North America that policies were put in place, such as the Proclamation of 1763 and Stamp Act of

1765, that led to the gradual transition from "resistance to revolution" which culminated in the American Revolution.[13]

Settling Kentucky

Following 1763, for the next decade, the main populations entering into what became the state of Kentucky were Native Americans and Long Hunters. The latter often traveled in groups to the territory with the goal of making profits from hunting furs and skins. Following the treaties of Hard Labor and Fort Stanwix, white settlement across the Appalachians led to the first permanent settlements in Kentucky. The atmosphere also changed after the appointment of Lord Dunmore as governor of Virginia. At the end of 1772, Dunmore granted Thomas Bullitt the right to survey Kentucky. Bullitt organized a group of over thirty men to survey the land. After a conflict, in which William Preston, surveyor of Fincastle County (in which Kentucky was located) refused to accept Bullitt's expedition surveys, Dunmore overrode part of Preston's complaint by issuing patents around the Falls of Ohio based upon surveys by Bullitt's team.[14]

As white settlers ventured into the Ohio Valley tensions also rose between natives and settlers. This culminated in a series of violent conflicts in March and April of 1774. Additionally, the Shawnees did not recognize the treaties of Hard Labor or Fort Stanwix, which had been negotiated with the Cherokees and Iroquois. They still considered Kentucky their rightful hunting ground. These tensions culminated in Lord Dunmore's War. The war consisted of one major battle: The Battle of Point Pleasant on October 10, 1774, in which white colonialists, headed by Andrew Lewis, led an expedition of around 1,300 troops, fought the Shawnee, headed by Cornstock. After the loss of much life on both sides, Cornstock retreated and in the subsequent Treaty of Camp Charlotte, agreed to allow the colonists to remain south of the Ohio.[15] But conflict and violence between settler and native would continue for some years to come.

The first full-fledged white settlement in Kentucky was Harrodsburg, started by James Harrod (who had participated in Bullitt's expedition) in 1774. The settlement was short-lived though. In July of that year, following Shawnee attacks, the settlers fled the colony.[16] The next year, Harrod returned to his town, finding another group of settlers, the McAfee brothers, nearby. But the most famous of early settlements was Boonesborough, started by Daniel Boone. Although Virginia and North

Carolina made it illegal for private individuals to purchase land from natives, the Transylvania Company, led by Richard Henderson, made an agreement with Cherokee chiefs for the land. Under the company's sponsorship, Boone was to create a road into Kentucky and start an initial settlement, in return for a personal allotment of land.[17] Here the logics of capital and settlement came together: while the company was interested in developing the land as a commodity, settlers, more interested in obtaining their own land and living "competently," pushed westward. Boone and his expedition set out on March 10, and as quickly as March 25 were attacked by natives. Two of the expedition were killed, and some went back. But those who stayed located a place to build a fort—Boonesborough—and began to plant crops and survive by hunting local buffalo herds.[18] Thousands of settlers would follow Boone's Wilderness Trail through the Cumberland Gap as Kentucky became a part of what was, after the conclusion of the American Revolution, an expanding American state.

Early expansion into Kentucky was driven by two main forces. On one side, settlers flooded in to create a patriarchal world of competency and independence. On the other, speculators viewed the vast space as a potential commodity to make profits. These dual forces, and the class struggle that evolved between them, shaped the early history of the state. The Virginia land act of 1779 attempted to reconcile this difference. It granted preemptive rights to settlers who could purchase 400 acres below non-resident prices. If improvements were made, they could preempt an additional 1,000 acres at a higher rate. All other lands not settled or designated for soldiers were put up for sale through Treasury warrants for the price of 100 acres for 40 shillings.[19]

The selling of warrants, particularly as the value of Virginia's currency depreciated, encouraged speculation. Within a year, Treasury warrants for almost 2 million acres were sold. And "land jobbers" established these claims by stacking logs in a square and calling it a cabin, or clearing a small portion of land, so that speculators could claim to improve it, justifying their purchases to the state. Additionally, a wide range of conflicting and overlapping claims formed. As a result, a commission was set up that, in the winter of 1779, heard over 1,400 claims and dispensed 1,334,050 acres of land. But many of these claims remained vague, with borders not clearly defined or surveyed, and for decades to come, disputes over Kentucky land claims would continue. Conflict over land also led to a somewhat different landownership pattern compared to other parts of the frontier. Most significantly, by 1792, the year Kentucky became independent from Virginia, two-thirds of white male adults did not legally own land.[20] And these landownership patterns would shape the contours of capitalist and non-capitalist relations in this part of the United States.

The origins of capitalism in Kentucky

Some scholars have argued capitalism came with white settlers from the start. For one author, "Kentucky farmers, whether or not they had slaves, were profit-minded. Like most enterprising American farmers, they were not satisfied with the idyllic little self-sufficient homesteads of agrarian myth."[21] And another writer suggests, "the eager multitudes journeying to western Kentucky raised families, governed themselves, and created a society in America's mythic wilderness: the west, the frontier. Rich or poor, these pioneers came to western Kentucky committed to private property and capitalism."[22] Other scholars are not so convinced that capitalism dominated the early white-settler Kentucky landscape. Stephen Aron, for example, sees expansion into Kentucky as driven, on the one hand, by profit-seeking speculators, and on the other, by homesteaders and patriarchs in search of land to obtain independence and competency, and reproduce their masculine independence.[23] And Craig Thomas Friend criticizes the binary between capitalist (or market, as in much of the debate the two are conflated) and non-capitalist relations, instead arguing that early Kentucky was characterized by a mix of relations in which, while profit-seeking activity occurred, farmers also participated in market relations to reproduce their community obligations and relations that were not-so-capitalist.[24] This section suggests that the latter are correct. While the power of capital did penetrate Kentucky early on, at the same time, many settlers came with other less-capitalist motivations. But, as elsewhere in the country, over many decades, capitalist relations eventually won out.

By 1790, Kentucky had a total population of 73,077 out of which 11,830 were slaves and 114 free blacks. By 1800, the population was 220,955 with 40,343 slaves and 741 free blacks. The population continued to skyrocket, and by 1860, the state had 1,155,684 people; 225,483 were slaves and 10,684 were free blacks.[25] But Kentucky's early population defied anything clearly resembling a "pure" capitalist or non-capitalist order. Most significantly, Kentucky landownership patterns—and social property rights—took on a character unique to the state due to its legacy as a part of Virginia. While between 1792 and 1802 the rate of landlessness decreased from two-thirds to one-half, at the start of the century, many farmers found themselves to be dependent tenant farmers rather than fee simple landowners.[26] The prominence of tenant farming created a situation in which, although many farmers traveled to Kentucky in hopes of obtaining competency through safety-first farming, they could only do so through tenant farming and market production. As Friend puts it:

> familial and communal obligations required older residents to pass property on to the next generation. Land, therefore, held a premarket value, a communal significance integral to the stability of society. Yet, because land early became a commodity exchanged by profiteering speculators, property also took on a monetary association that could not be ignored. In a society where less than one half of the householders owned land, the need for capital to purchase land and create a farm compromised aspirations to live in self-sufficiency.[27]

For speculator landowners, tenant farming was the most reasonable way to make profit from the land they owned. In this sense, it represented a formal subsumption of labor to capital, in which capital—through tenant farming—subordinated patriarchal households, and forced these households towards market production, but did not control the organization of labor itself. In other words, capital leached on to, but did not transform, the means of production. Tenants were also often required to make payments in currency, rather than in kind, forcing them to develop a mixture of subsistence and commercial production.[28] Overall, for tenant farmers, it was not that farmers came with capitalist motivations: rather, they were subsumed under a kind of capitalist dominance through the lack of means to live outside of dependence.

From the start, speculators viewed the western land as a space potentially subsumable to capital; a space of great potential profit. For example, Samuel Beall and John May teamed up to speculate in Kentucky. May writing to Beall, as early as 1799, stated,

> I wrote to you yesterday proposing a Scheme for purchasing the Land which is British Property in Kentucky County as I have Reason to believe, from the Scarcity of Money in that County, that it will sell

> lower than the State Price; it is Choice Land, at any Rate would be a profitable Purchase.[29]

By the next year May wrote,

> I have met with Col Logan from Kentucky who brings me a Letter from my Brother George who writes me a very great Profit may now be made by the Purchase of Settlement & Preemption claims, as many of the Claimants have not yet money to clear out their lands.[30]

Early on, capitalists like May looked for frontier settlements held by settlers who perhaps would not have the money to purchase the land they worked. May, for example, regularly complained of those who obtained land without warrant. The speculators bought up Treasury warrants produced by the state as well as military warrants given to those who fought in the Revolutionary War but sold their land claims (which they were given in lieu of wages). For instance, "My Brother George has been very industrious in procuring Locations & has enabled me to enter all our military Warrants, I believe very well; and I hope I shall procure Locations enough for the others as well as for the Treasury Warrants."[31]

May also brought a slave with him to the frontier, as slaves provided labor for empire building. At one point his slave even escaped, although soon found the harsh frontier conditions perhaps no better than his other life, as May wrote:

> he is a most valuable Slave and one that I thought I could have trusted with any Thing and any where, but when I left … Falls last October I left him too much in the Way of Temptation and he fell in ith some worthless Negroes who pursuaded him to run away & attempt to get with the Indians; however after ten Days Absence he thought it prudent to return. I fear this will be a bad place to bring Slaves to, being so near … Indians that they will frequently find their way to them.[32]

For settlers looking to profit from the land in particular, access to markets was a central concern. General William Henry's correspondence from the early decades of the 1800s, for example, repeatedly discusses the market opportunities provided by settling in different locations with family members. In 1817, for instance, he wrote to his brother regarding the latter's apparent migration to Missouri in which he says that the distance from the market there is so far that "the farmer will be a drudge one half of the year to make a subsistence for his family … the other half on dealing it out to them."[33] He goes on to say that while the distance to the market is also far in Kentucky, in Missouri commerce is especially difficult as it faces an uphill current and a disadvantaged geography, thus "You never can be eminently commercial."[34]

This logic of capitalist rationalism seems to have guided many of Henry's calculations. For example, in another letter he writes, "the widest door stands open for profitable speculation than can be found in many other sections of the U.S."[35] After purchasing land in Kentucky he rented it out to a farmer in return for improvements. Believing that the land in the region would greatly increase in value as the population increased, for Henry land was a commodity to generate profit from. Yet the worker, in this case, was not a wage laborer but a tenant farmer who did not pay anything, but improved the land with his labor in order to increase its value. Surplus value was generated from this labor—realized in the improved value of land containing the labor of this worker—but was in the form of non-waged labor. A logic of capitalist "self-interest" was also discussed by other frontier settlers. As one letters states,

> He wishes for your Orders as to the price & manner of disposing of it. Not being improbable, but that in a little time we Shall have some Salt of our own for Sale, I have concluded on consideration that it would not do so well with us, as we must in point of duty to Mr. B, as well as Self Interest give the preference of Sale to his.[36]

Additionally, for Henry, "patriarchal longevity" and "independence" were not separate from capitalism; far from it. Writing a reflection on his thirtieth birthday, he wrote, "the cares and wants of my family are increasing apace, but they shall only incite me to … efforts for the attainment of that solid independence, 'without which,' … 'no man can be happy, nor even honest.'"[37] While he used the language of "independence," he attempted to realize this primarily through speculation in commodified land.

The complexities of early capitalism in Kentucky might also be seen through the life of Annie Christian.[38] After her husband died in 1786, she wrote to her brother Patrick Henry: "we are enjoying blessings of peace here and a great plenty of every necessity and I hope I shall always be independent, as my dear deceased friend has left us all possessed of an ample support."[39] But for Christian being independent did not mean living self-sufficiently or outside the market; quite to the contrary. Her husband left her with a variety of capital, including a saltworks and slaves, which she worked to produce a profit to pay off her family's debts and sustain her children. This meant hiring workers to produce salt and regularly renting out slaves. In a representative passage, for example, she writes to her mom,

> Yesterday our Negroes, were hired out, Mr. Wallace got Hannibal at 14, & he is to have a thousand weight of Pork at 6.0.0 which pays a debt for him to Capt. Taylors Estate I sent Woodfolk after the Negroes were hired, to collect what money he cou'd for Mr. Wallace, & as soon as the weather permits I shall have some salt brought here for sale.[40]

While Christian aimed to make a profit to obtain independence, she also complained of a scarcity of money, writing, for instance,

> I had not seen Mr. Bullitt for more than a year till now, he has directed me to have Salt sold for Cash at what ever it may bring, Money being so scare in our Country , as occasiond (!) me to sell hetherto (!) upon Credit Salt to the amount of 640 pounds due next fall.[41]

But while money was a necessary part of capital accumulation, often times given the paucity of paper money, other means of exchange were used to realize surplus value.

Christian's example also went against what historians have often assumed are characteristic of gender roles on the frontier; specifically, women's subordination to husbands. After her husband died, Christian herself took control of their means of production and management of resources, although she continued to engage in some traditional women's roles. For example, she wrote to her sister, "I rec'd yours per John Duglass with the books which I am highly obliged (!) to you for, Altho' I have been so busie making our Negroes Cloaths (!) I have not had time to give them a reading yet."[42] Thus, she did take on the typical role of producing clothes for the slaves in the household, even as she defied what is the often assumed position of frontier white-settler women. More generally, gender roles on the frontier tended to be perhaps less clearly defined than sometimes suggested. For instance, Will Trigg writes of a Mr. Wallace who remarried, saying:

> She is about 4 feet 2 inches high, well set, weighing near or quite 220, aged 50, has traveled as much as Cook whose voyages you have read, remarkable shrude and cunning, has consequently learned all the manners, ingenuities Generalships & tricks common in any and all the Countries, is well Versed in Sea phrases, understands all the tacks & turns of the Wind and its perfectly acquainted with the management of all the rigging from the Bough Spirt to the rudder (don't you think this is information enough for the Old man) She is remarkable neat & I believe kind to the children.[43]

Descriptions such as this suggest that variations of socially acceptable femininity may be broader than otherwise conceived. But empire itself was often driven by masculine dreams of control. William Fleming wrote, for example, "I can not be see the advantages of moving as soon as it can be done with saftey to this Country and would be willing to know the Country tho roughly before I fix on a plan to move my Famely to."[44] As in this instance, often husbands first went west, in some cases with slaves, to search for land and security for their families before bringing their families to the western edge of empire.

Tensions between speculative profits and patriarchal independence also shaped the formation of the state.[45] If the capitalist state is a "condensation of class" and social forces, then, in this case, the state in a society becoming capitalist represented the working out of a variety of class and social forces that, in the long run, enabled and supported capitalist development.[46] Throughout the 1780s Kentucky politics differentiated into three loosely defined "parties." The partisans, representing "the rabble," at their peak made up perhaps as much as half of the state's (in becoming) population.[47] By 1783–84, partisans were in support of separation from Virginia, with the hopes that Virginia's large, speculative land claims might be annulled. During these years they even settled on land claimed under Virginia land grants, with the hope that they could claim this land through headright after independence. The Court Party, called so because it contained many lawyers and those engaged in legal and political professions, in contrast, was an elite party of Kentucky capitalists, and often more urban based. They had a strong economic interest in separation with the hopes of developing state policies to promote what might retrospectively be called import substitution industrialization strategies. They also, for example, started the Kentucky Society for Promoting Manufactures in 1789, and imported machinery from Philadelphia and cotton from Tennessee to manufacture cloth. This same year, members of the society went so far as to agree not to purchase luxuries from other states, with the goal of promoting the production of liquor, clothes, and so on within Kentucky. Finally, the county party was a more rural-based elite party, including plantation owners, who were interested in protecting their Virginia land grants. And many of the members were land surveyors themselves.[48]

The Kentucky constitution of 1792 (and its update in 1799) enshrined the rights of the Kentucky elite to private property. It also legally protected their rights to own slaves, and for immigrants to bring new slaves into the state, although it was not legal to bring in slaves as merchandise. But it did not resolve the land disputes, which continued well into the nineteenth century. Throughout the 1790s settlers and squatters continued to hold land in Kentucky they did not own. In 1795, for example, the legislature passed a bill making it possible for settlers to purchase preemption ownership of land of 200 acres at the cost of $30 for each 100 acres. This was done based on the idea that settlers would not be able to obtain the same rights to the land, but settlers ignored this and expanded their unowned holdings. The state continued to legislate based upon these developments as they arose. For example, two years later, in February 1797, a law was passed allowing settlers in the Green River area, who moved there before July 1798, to preempt either 100 or 200 acres at either $40 or $60 per 100 acres, depending on the quality of land. Settlers were given a year to pay, and by 1799 a mess of claims and debts was amassed, so that one auditor estimated $352,612 was owed by settlers to the state.[49]

Often times, through a state-capital network, those who controlled the emergent government also profited from these positions using familial and personal connections.[50] People in positions of political power and in control of land distribution directly worked with, and profited from, the commodification and sale of land as state formation and capitalist development were deeply intertwined in personal networks. Kentucky capitalists also created a Society for the Encouragement of Domestic Manufactures in 1817.[51] The primary stated agenda of the society was to promote the domestic consumption of manufactures and become less dependent upon foreign importations, so building up the national political economy of the emerging empire. Institution building such as this suggests a concerted effort on the part of the elite classes to promote economic growth through capitalist development. Circuit court judge

Adam Beatty, for example, produced a variety of agricultural goods and his letters reflect that he was continually concerned with the status of the world market. He also wrote a variety of essays commenting on the application of science to agriculture and how to produce more efficiently beginning in the 1830s, reflecting the capitalist obsession/necessity with productivity increases.[52]

Overall, the formation of the state protected the private property rights of Kentucky capitalists while also providing some space for settlers and yeomen with limited degrees of integration into Kentucky capitalism to continue to find patriarchal independence through the ownership of land plots and limited market dependence. In this sense, the space of state was a space of class conflict and cooperation wherein a variety of class forces could find a balance, albeit one in which the capitalist elite ruled the state and assumed they would continue to do so in the developing capitalist state.

Economic development, gender, and slavery

Following its state independence, capitalist development, linked into broader world market relations, continued unevenly in Kentucky. On the one hand, white men grew rich through agriculture and livestock production, from selling hemp bags to Louisiana to shipping cotton to Britain to importing and producing cattle, hogs, mules, and even racehorses. On the other, the labor that built Kentucky within the United States was constructed from the efforts of chattel slaves and women who worked to reproduce and expand the white, masculine controlled empire.

By the fall of 1784, the first Kentucky crops were transported on flatboats down the Mississippi River.[53] From the 1780s and 1790s onward, after a short era of close to self-sufficiency, agricultural production in the state increasingly took on higher degrees of market participation.[54] And parts of the state, such as north-central Kentucky, became more and more commercialized from the 1790s onward. Kentucky yeomen found themselves in an area between the moral and the market economy.[55] While, on the one hand, they tended to engage in safety-first agriculture, placing patriarchal household and community obligations and relations over production for the market, over time small farmers became increasingly integrated into, and dependent on, merchants and the commercial economy. As Friend again puts it:

> customers traded homespun, butter, and wood for books, refined clothes, and European goods. In many ways, a network of dependency tied the merchant to those customers who provided him with foodstuffs as well as profit. Indeed, an argument may be made that even as the use of barter and account-book credit satisfied commercial relations between merchants and customers, they also symbolized the communal obligations between friends and neighbors. Although they consistently advertised for cash in order to meet the demands of eastern suppliers, local merchants never abandoned barter—the exchange of one commodity for another—as a transaction. Although the cash supply in Kentucky fluctuated, the continued use of barter suggests that citizens still operated with some premarket notions of economic exchange.[56]

This went hand-in-hand with increased demand for imported goods. From early white colonial settlement, Kentucky was not separated from world market relations. By 1775, Richard Henderson, for instance, opened a store at Fort Boonesborough selling commodities on credit. Pioneer women tended to bring with them goods, including china, that reminded them of their more "civilized" lives back home.[57] And by 1802, one estimate by François Michaux suggested that seven-tenths of Kentucky goods were imported from England, and goods came from as far as India and the Caribbean.[58] It was not unusual for relatively self-sufficient yeomen to trade with merchants for goods including higher end English garments or ceramics that they could not produce domestically. Overall, "consumption of manufactured goods and metropolitan styles thus transformed the Kentucky backwoods into a consumer frontier: an economic border region situated between subsistence and capitalist modes of production, containing elements of both economic systems."[59]

But outside of this limited market integration, other social classes in Kentucky developed relations that might somewhat more "purely" be considered capitalist. By 1810, manufacturing had taken off in the state. That year listed were 15 cotton factories, 13 hemp mills, 38 ropewalks, 33 fulling mills, 4 furnaces, 3 forges, 11 naileries, 267 tanneries, 9 flaxseed oil mills, 2,000 distilleries, 6 paper mills, 63 gunpowder mills, and 36 saltworks.[60] By 1840, $5,945,000 was invested in manufacturing, and by 1860 that number was $20,256,000. Additionally, by this time, the state had 3,450 manufacturing establishments that paid out a total of over $6 million in wages. While the majority of workers in Kentucky manufacturing were white men, white women and black slaves also labored for Kentucky's capitalist class and slaves were even used in textile mills and hemp factories.[61] Besides manufacturing, farm production became a major component of early Kentucky capitalism. While early on farmers operating for profit focused on producing crops such as corn, tobacco, and hemp, by the mid-1830s, livestock production dominated.[62] By 1835, Bourbon County alone exported 40,000 hogs, 10,000 cattle, and 3,000 horses and mules.[63] Kentucky capitalists such as Henry Clay, in search of higher profits through increased technological development, also started a scientific farming movement. The second Kentucky Agricultural Society, between 1838 and 1842, for instance, lobbied the government to start an agricultural school, conduct a geological survey, and collect agricultural statistics.[64] Or, to take another example, Kentucky cattle producers invested in new scales in the 1850s to increase productivity.[65]

Capitalist development was also facilitated by the state. As early as 1797, Kentucky's General Assembly passed legislation forcing all males over 16 years of age to labor a certain number of days each year on road construction and repair, and over the next half century many roads were built and maintained using this system.[66] Of course, while the state wanted to build roads (often times with the goal of linking farmers more deeply with the market), many of the resources for this were in private hands. One solution to this was to construct toll roads, which was done in 1797 on the Wilderness Road. Additionally, in 1817 the Kentucky legislature authorized two turnpikes, one from Lexington to Louisville, and one from Lexington to Maysville to be underwritten by selling stock at $100 each, to get the $350,000 necessary for the construction, although the plan failed after the economic crisis two years later.[67] This set a precedent, though, as selling stock to private holders to finance toll roads became an important strategy in future projects. And it was out of the battle for federal funding (as leaders like Henry Clay pushed for internal improvements) that Andrew Jackson vetoed federal funding for the Maysville Road, putting in motion a legal precedent against federal funding for roads as unconstitutional. The state, though, continued to locate ways to channel capital into roads, creating a Board of Internal Improvements in 1835 and hiring engineers to supervise projects and improve engineering practices.[68] And both the state and private capital invested in hard-surfaced, stone roads, so by 1837 the state had invested $2.5 million, and private investors $2 million in these roads.[69]

Kentucky also contained a vast network of rivers, and the deepening of Kentucky capitalism (and Kentucky's deepening integration with a developing capitalist United States and world market and interstate system) was further facilitated by the rise of steamboats. The first upriver trip to Kentucky from New Orleans to Louisville appears to have been in 1815, and after this a group of Lexington capitalists financed a commercial steamboat which left for New Orleans, although it did not return.[70] Through the 1820s steamboats began to compete with, and eventual win out over, keelboats and flatboats, and soon an entire economy developed around them as warehouses and watering holes lined the rivers where steamboats commonly traveled. Steamboats regularly took Kentucky hemp, among other commodities, down to New Orleans so that southern cotton could be put in hemp bags and shipped to England. Over time, boats that could traverse more shallow water were constructed, and the state also facilitated the steamboat industry. In 1836 Kentucky began work on a series of locks which opened in 1842.[71] Here, as with roads, public investment stimulated the further advancement of Kentucky capitalism.

By 1830, Lexington, not near a major river, found itself left out of the steamboat boom. As a response, investors began to channel their capital into a new technological frontier: railroads. By October of that year, the first tracks were laid, and by the summer of 1832 a half mile of track was ready for operation.[72] From here on, private capital flowed into railroads and by 1860 the state had close to 600 miles of operative tracks. Much of the initiative for this construction came from private hands, although occasionally local governments did support the process.[73]

As with other states in the south, Kentucky was a slave state. Much of the labor that built the United States came from their muscles and minds. By 1790, Kentucky had 11,830 slaves, and that number was 225,483 by 1860. The relative peak of Kentucky slavery was around 1830, when 24 percent of the population were black slaves. The average slaveowner held about 5.4 slaves.[74] And overall, as of 1850, a little over a quarter of white families owned slaves.[75] Kentucky was less a land of large plantations and more a land of smaller slaveowners. For example, in 1850, 9,244 people owned one slave, 13,284 families owned one to five slaves, 1,198 families held twenty to fifty slaves, 53 families had fifty to a hundred slaves, and five families owned over a hundred slaves.[76] Slaves were brought to Kentucky with the first white settlements. The census of Harrod's Fort, for instance, found twelve slaves over 10 years old, and seven below 10 years old.[77] And it was not unusual for slaves to be the vanguard of expansion. For example, masters would, in some cases, send an overseer to manage slaves to land purchased a year or two before the master moved there, to clear the ground, plant crops, construct houses, and so on.[78]

While some large plantations did exist in Kentucky, particularly in the Bluegrass region, it tended to be a land of small-scale slaveowners, with some exceptions such as Robert Wickliffe, the largest slaveowner in the state, who had 200 slaves. These plantation kings tended to focus on producing livestock, and often hemp, perhaps the crop that was most suited to plantations in Kentucky.[79] But large-scale monoculture never took off in Kentucky as it did further south, although cereals (corn especially), tobacco, and hemp were the main crops cultivated. Cereal producers, though, found that it could often be more profitable to substitute temporary white seasonal labor, rather than fully owned slaves, to harvest their product. And, as noted, many producers shifted their capital into livestock and industry that did not depend on large-scale slaveowning.[80] Overall, slaves were an important part of the Kentucky economy but many slaves were also incorporated into smaller scale family production, rather than large-scale capitalist plantations.

And, as throughout the United States, expansion was built on a foundation of women's oppression. As elsewhere, marriage remained a relationship of dispossession. Richard Sears, for example, tells the story of Sarah Burnam. In 1859 Burnam sued for divorce from her husband. As the author puts it,

> Sarah K. Burnam testified that her husband had taken control of all her property, including her slaves and dower land, from which he was receiving all the proceeds. She claimed Harrison Burnam had defrauded her of all lawful rent for use of her land, which had belonged to her previous husband.[81]

And while Harrison Burnam admitted he rented out slaves she brought into the marriage and kept the proceeds, the court ruled in his favor: after all, when a woman was married all her property became legally his and he had the right to profit from it. These laws stayed in place until 1894, when married women gained the right to own their own property, and 1900, when they were granted titles to their own earnings.[82]

The deepening of capitalism in the state also changed women's role in the household. On the frontier women often engaged in more muscle-intensive manual labor.[83] They also participated in market production. It was not unusual for women to produce goods, such as textiles, to sell on the market to obtain small luxuries. But over time, as capitalist relations deepened, so did the separation between "home" and "workplace," and "public" and "private." Women were increasingly pushed into the private realm: to be a good woman meant to be a good mother and housekeeper. Women in Kentucky, as in other parts of the south, were now supposed to be submissive appendages to their proud and honorable husbands. Thus, "the image of the self-sufficient frontier woman receded in antebellum Kentucky with the emergence of the dependent southern belle and her matronly counterpart, the southern lady."[84] The deepening of capitalism made women into invisible workers in the private sphere, subordinated to their masters: white men.

Ohio

By the middle of the eighteenth century, Ohio territory emerged as a key pivot in the international battle for empire waged between the British and French. Additionally, many of the native populations within Ohio had only recently settled there, as migration of Delawares, Shawnees, and Senecas increased after the 1720s, pushed by white colonialism and conflict between native groups.[85] From the seventeenth century onward, there was a series of Anglo-French wars for control over North America including King William's War, Queen Anne's War, and King George's War.[86] These, as mentioned, ended with the French-Indian (Seven Years') War and British victory, which then set the basis for the American Revolution as the British attempted to augment their control over a colony that increasingly saw British taxes and control as unnecessary.

After the French-Indian War and Pontiac's Rebellion, which resulted in the British Proclamation line of 1763, against British authority settlers, "lawless banditti", continued to move into Trans-Appalachia. In 1774, an estimated 50,000 whites lived on this frontier. On the native side, while the Treaty of Fort Stanwix was signed in 1768 with the Iroquois, it was not agreed upon by the Shawnees, who attempted to create an alliance with other native groups against colonial incursion. Tensions continued to rise between settler and native, and on May 3, 1774 a group of Virginians murdered several innocent Mingos after offering them liquor, then murdered eight more who came in search of them including, most likely, war chief Logan's mother. Under Logan's call (and against others such as Cornstock who warned against such aggressive behavior) the Shawnees aligned with the Mingos and began to attack settlers below the Ohio River on the Pennsylvania frontier. Settlers responded as Captain John Connolly, with the support of Lord Dunmore, and interested in land speculation, fought back culminating in the battle of Point Pleasant on October 10, 1774. The result was settler victory as the Shawnees were forced to accept the Treaty of Fort Stanwix.[87]

The Revolutionary War also brought violence to Ohio territory. For many native communities, the British appeared a stronger potential ally than the expanding Americans. Then in 1777, Shawnee chief Cornstock, his son, and two others were murdered by a white militia. This led to six years of war in Ohio country between Americans and native peoples.[88] Following the end of the Revolutionary War, as the emerging United States played off European powers to acquire as much North American territory as possible, the 1783 Treaty of Paris gave the United States about 900,000 square miles of territory, about 70 percent of which was west of the British 1763 line.[89] With the American Revolution over, the stage was set for the white settlement of Trans-Appalachia and the ethnic cleansing of indigenous peoples. And after decades of violence, the last natives left Ohio after the Wyandot Treaty of 1842, in which the Wyandots traded all of their Ohio lands for 148,000 acres west of the Mississippi, $10,000, and an annual sum of $17,500, payments for improvements, and their debt of $23,860 was taken over.[90]

By 1783, Ohio was part of the frontier borderland.[91] Incorporating the territory more deeply into the American state first meant dispossessing and removing the native peoples. But Native Americans were not the only population that needed to be eliminated in order for the United States to gain control of Ohio territory. There were also the "white Indians"; squatters and frontier families who settled the land without care for the capitalist privatization of the land pushed by speculators such as George Washington. These "white Indians" were white by ethnicity, but living in a cultural way too similar to Indians to be considered "white" enough to become members of the emerging racialized, white dominated United States.[92]

During and after the American Revolution, squatters continued to head west in search of open land. One traveler noted in Ohio,

> the first clearers, or *squatters*, as they are called, look out to a situation where they can find it, and clear and cultivate a piece of land. A second class come after them, who have got a little money, and they buy up the improvements of the first settlers, and add to them, but without buying the land. A third and last class generally come for permanent settlement, and buy both the land and improvements.[93]

And later he encountered

> an emigrant family, consisting of a man, his wife, and two children. They had travelled far in a quest of settlement, and their means being exhausted, they were obliged to stop short at this place, where they meant to sit down and clear and cultivate a piece of land. In the language of the country, they were *squatters*.[94]

These settlers were not so much concerned with the state and its private property laws, and their view on land itself seems to be more oriented towards the use value of land rather than state sanctioned law.[95] Land was livelihood, their source of freedom and independence.[96] In other words, the aim of these squatters on the frontier was to live in patriarchal household relations of social reproduction, and while they may have supported absolute property ownership, these were not property relations controlled under the power of capital and the capitalist state and legal system.

Both squatters and natives practiced a different "mode of foreign relations" than the developing American state pushed.[97] While natives, for example, had concepts of personal property, they did not view land as private property.[98] Native life was organized around kinship, reciprocity, and use values, rather than capital and exchange values. Squatters also tended to use land as a use value, and exchange with the purpose of obtaining the necessities—and perhaps occasional luxuries—of life, as whether or not the state laid down the law, squatters' ownership came from settlement and use of the land, not state jurisdiction and monopoly on violence. Out of differing relations of production, they developed different structures and ideas of inter-community relations, inconsistent with the law of the American state. In the case of Ohio, these modes of foreign relations proved to be unable to deflect the foreign relations of the expanding country, in which state law, rather than use value, was the absolute authority.

The settlement of Ohio

After signing the Treaty of Fort McIntosh in January of 1785, under orders from the federal government, Colonial Josiah Harmer began to drive squatters off illegally occupied land. Throughout the next two years, the army located settlers' homes and forced them to leave, burning down their houses and destroying their crops. But squatters continued to move into Ohio territory, although, as one author notes, "if the squatters could not be driven off the land, their society would be restructured in ways that would insure that they would behave as the citizens of a model republic."[99] This was part of the function of the Northwest Ordinance of 1787. The Ordinance was the most important in a series (others were in 1784, 1785, and 1790) which set the structure of American colonial policy. Most importantly, it enshrined the rights of private property holders in the Northwest Territory, and created a system in which the United States could spread and incorporate new territories. Among other things, the Ordinance disallowed slavery in the territory, although it did institute a fugitive slave law.[100] It also set a three-stage process for a territory to become a state. First, the state would be administered by a governor, secretary, and three judges until the population reached 5,000. At that point, an assembly with an elected House of Representatives and congressionally selected legislative council would be set up, and a congressional delegate without voting power selected. Finally, with a population of over 60,000 a territory (or space within a broader administered territory) could become a state, on equal terms with other states.[101] The Ordinance also further institutionalized the 1785 survey system, which placed land into townships of 36 square miles, each parcel subdivided into 6 mile by 6 mile squares.[102] This gave the American territory a grid-like pattern that remains to this day, facilitating flows of capital and preventing the sort of claims problems that existed in states such as Kentucky.

The spatial expansion of American power was organized in order that the state could sell land to serve as a source of federal finance. Additionally, it created a legal structure which speculators could take advantage of and provided a way for small farmers to purchase, legally, fee simple land titles. And in Ohio, both the federal state and power of capital over the territory and population were strengthened by the methods used to incorporate the territory into the young state. The most significant way this came out was through war. Often the American military-industrial complex seems to have its origins in the aftermath of the Second World War, symbolized by Eisenhower's famous warning. But the link between military spending and private profit goes back to an early era of US history in regions such as Ohio.

In the first half of the 1790s, the federal government, under Secretary of War Henry Knox, waged a series of wars against Ohio natives that resulted in, first, humiliation, and secondly, victory. Throughout the 1770s and 1780s, violence between native and settlers continued throughout the entire Ohio country region. Natives, for example, often targeted settlers' possessions, such as stealing horses, while settlers also attacked natives, creating an insecure environment on the frontier. To address this problem, Knox increased the American military presence in Ohio country. In 1790, with federal funds and 320 trained soldiers out of an army of 1,500, otherwise comprised of mostly untrained militia, Josiah Harmer led an expedition against the Ohio Indians.[103] Harmer and his troops burned Indian crops and settlements, but he lost control of much of his army, who were prone to looting or fleeing at the sound of battle. Harmer's army was relatively unsuccessful. In one battle alone, for example, it lost 75 regulars and 108 militia troops against perhaps 100 natives. Harmer's expedition was followed by Arthur St. Clair's the next year. St. Clair's army, little larger than Harmer's, also failed to subdue the Indians. St. Clair lost hundreds of troops, many killed in a single battle, led by Little Turtle and Blue Jacket, on November 4, 1791, considered by some the worst (or best) defeat of American troops by indigenous peoples. Two years later, led by Anthony Wayne, the United States launched another expedition into Ohio country. Wayne commanded an army of over 5,000, and made one final push to move Ohio from a borderland to a key component of the United States. They were finally victorious with the Battle of Fallen Timbers and subsequent Treaty of Greenville signed on August 3, 1795. In exchange for $20,000 in presents, an annual annuity of $9,500, and an exchange of prisoners, the United States gained control of much of the greater Ohio territory, including present day Detroit and Chicago, among other places.[104]

The American victory was not just a win for settlers, speculators, and the state, but merchants who made profits from the military presence in an early form of military-industrial complex. Merchants supplied the military's needs, such as food and clothes, and links were formed between the military and merchants wherein "the military received supplies, while settlers and businessmen benefited from enhanced security."[105] Military forces contracted out supply purchases, and contractors also contracted out to sub-contractors as military spending stimulated economic growth. This also led to increased state investment in infrastructure. For instance, in the 1790s Kentucky invested in roads, connecting Frankfort and Cincinnati, and Virginia built a road from Clarksburg to Marietta for cattle driving.[106] In these ways, war, commerce, and states worked together to create the infrastructure for imperial and economic expansion.

The conquest and remaking of space was always central to American expansion. In 1785 US geographer Thomas Hutchins led a team to survey the Seven Ranges in eastern Ohio.[107] The township line surveys for four of the ranges were completed by February of 1787, and the state began to sell the lands, although the sales went slower than anticipated, with none of the townships being sold in whole, and 108,431 acres sold between September and October of that year for $117,108, much of which came as government securities that had depreciated in value to begin with.[108] More generally, though, this started the trend of the federal government surveying western lands and selling them (often to private speculators) to generate state finances: in this sense, the early American state and capital aligned over territorial expansion.

Ohio country was a land of many claims. Initially, four eastern states had claims to the land. New York, Virginia, and Massachusetts gave up their claims beginning in 1780, while Connecticut held on to its "western reserve." On the reserve,

> the agriculturalists are mostly occupied in raising supplies for internal consumption of the inhabitants, who manufacture nearly all their own clothing, in their respective families, so that there is little commerce: the chief trade is in salt, and a few ornamental imported goods. The principle exports are cattle and cheese.[109]

Additionally, Virginia held on to some land to allot to soldiers as payment for serving in the military in what was called the Virginia Military District. Besides this, the federal government controlled land, some of which was reserved for military veterans. Land was also sold to private speculative companies. The Ohio Company of Associates gained 1,781,760 acres purchased from the federal government, partly through devalued securities, for instance.[110] The Scioto Company, led by New York capitalist William Duer, gained an option on part of the

Ohio Company's grant, and began to sell claims to the land in France, although the over 500 French who arrived in Ohio territory later learned that they had not, in fact, legally purchased land from the company as the town Gallipolis turned out to be outside the Scioto Company's grant. Eventually though, they were given grant to the land in 1795.[111] Besides the Ohio Company, Judge John Cleaves Symmes also developed a plan to sell lands from the Miami Purchase. While initially attempting to secure a patent of 2 million, then 1 million acres, eventually he was issued a patent in 1794 for 311,682 acres. But, among other things, Symmes sold land that he did not have a claim to and, after much legal trouble, died in poverty in 1814.[112]

For St. Clair, governor of the territory in its second stage, Ohio settlers were "indignant" and "ignorant" people who did not understand the importance of the federal government. St. Clair filled government positions with Federalists like himself who viewed a strong state as necessary to bring Ohio into the United States. But for settlers, and Ohio capitalists, St. Clair's regime was seen as aristocratic and paternal. Leaders for Ohio statehood such as Thomas Worthington, Nathaniel Massie, and Edward Triffin (who became the state of Ohio's first governor) themselves were all invested in capitalist speculation in land, as were many of their allies.[113] With their lobbying, and following Thomas Jefferson's victory and defeat of Federalism, in 1802 the Enabling Act was signed granting Ohio statehood.

The forces which pushed Ohio statehood, and development, then, were several fold. Speculators were interested in profit. The state was interested in using western space as a way to finance the government, and also secure its territory against internal and external threats. And settlers were interested in cheap land and patriarchal independence. How this played out led to, in the long run, the development of capitalism in Ohio, articulated through both the national and world market.

If the related, but not equivalent, factors of market integration and capitalist development might be seen as a spectrum, rather than definitive lines, then Ohio's development presented an uneven development of different relations. William Cooper Howells' story is an example of these degrees of capitalism and not-so-capitalism. Howells' father, a Quaker, took the family to eastern Ohio in 1813. After moving to Mount Pleasant, he joined a textile spinning partnership that soon dissolved. Following this, he went out on his own, with credit from a local English merchant, and obtained machinery for carding and spinning wool to sell on the local market. As a boy, Howells also helped tend the machines, as the family was the reproductive economic unit. Howells' father, in addition to family labor, also hired hands. Through these twists and turns, eventually Howells' father, on credit, bought 40 acres of land for $600 about 5 miles from Steubenville. While the land had been improved by the previous owner, more work was needed, so Howells' father continued to do factory work during the transitional period. On the farm (while Howells' father continued also to work in the city mill) the family practiced composite farming. For example, they grew peaches, many of which they sold in Steubenville. At the same time, they planted wheat (with the help of hired hands) which they used to produce bread for themselves. They also had livestock, such as pigs and cows, as part of their household production. After three years, though, Howells' father sold the farm and the family moved to another farm closer to the city, where Howells' father could more easily maintain his urban work along with their dream of owning a family farm.[114]

While the Howells family moved to one of the more economically advanced parts of the state, the story of Worthington, Ohio, a Scioto Company settlement, tells a similar story. Here, labor was performed in a variety of more or less capitalist forms. As two authors put it,

> household labor was evident in women's weaving and in seasonal activities by farmers such as broommaking and carving wooden handles for tools; itinerant workers were available for common labor and skills such as shoemaking and dressmaking; work was exchanged for needs such as carpentry or the use of a cider press; craftsmen working in their homes produced items as diverse as chairs and hats.[115]

Most families, then, did not live outside the market, like squatters of the earlier generation, nor did they live in a way fully subsumed and dispossessed by the law of value; their social form was somewhere in between.

As throughout the United States, patriarchy was also a deeply embedded historical structure. In 1826 Anna Briggs Bentley and her husband moved from Maryland to Columbiana County, Ohio, a relatively rural area. Bentley's story is one in which the majority of production was organized in the household for family use. On their farm they grew wheat and corn, along with watermelons, cantaloupes, squash, pumpkins, beans, and cucumbers, and also had a variety of fruit trees.

Besides this, the family had livestock such as chickens, and a cow for dairy products (Bentley, for example, made her own butter).[116] For labor which could not be done in the household alone, the community banded together, as in the case of logrolling, which consisted of "rolling in large heaps with the levers the largest saw logs and then piling on the brush and firing it."[117] In return, all that was expected was that supper would be provided for everyone involved. The Bentley family, though, was not completely divorced from the market. But money in this community was scarce, and only used to get the most basic of items, and occasional luxury, such as textiles that could not be easily produced at home. The majority of production, in general, was organized by household gender roles as Bentley produced the majority of household necessities, cooked the family's meals, and so on.

But the development of higher degrees of capitalist relations transformed gender roles, as represented by the story of Celestia Rice Colby. Her parents moved to Ashtabula County and by 1830 settled in Andover with perhaps around 25 families in the area.[118] Her father worked in a variety of roles, such as a merchant, farmer, and speculator, and their family occasionally hired hands to help with production. Colby was raised in a society becoming increasingly capitalist, and her attitude towards gender reflected this as she viewed women's space as private, as she put it in 1854,

> we doubt not that her presence and influence in the councils of our nation would have a purifying effect, yet her influence at home is the lever with which she may sway the destinies of the world. If the great mass of our sex fully understood their duty, and were prepared to fulfill it, how soon, how very soon would the moral aspects of the world be changed for the better.[119]

Colby, during this time, appeared to accept the hegemony of capitalist patriarchy, where the woman's place was to purify the home and save the man, against the pressures of work and politics outside the home. Interestingly, five years later her writings reflected the opposite opinion, and Colby's writings pushed for equal rights for men and women, against the idea of women being confined to the home, as she broke with patriarchal hegemony to a degree and embraced what might be considered a liberal feminism, for her time.[120]

Race and capitalist hegemony in Ohio

In the 1820s, the degree of capitalism in Ohio grew as the population became subordinated to the law of value. In agriculture, increasingly "market-minded agrarianism" prevailed. For example, when Aaron Miller and his brother Daniel traveled to Ohio in 1832, their goal was to locate land that could profitably produce wheat, so that their extended families could move to the region and engage in for-profit production, even if much of the production was still done by the family, rather than a dispossessed working class.[121] More generally, when the first US census of manufactures was conducted in 1822 it showed that several areas, such as Muskingum County, where Zanesville was located, Hamilton County, with Cincinnati, and Ross County, where Chillicothe was located, for example, all had significant manufacturing, with Muskingum having approximately half a million dollars of capital invested.[122] After the middle of the 1820s, in particular, Ohio's connections with the national—and world—market increased as social relations within the state, articulated unevenly with a variety of spatial economic scales, deepened capitalism further in Ohio, connected to wider market relations.[123]

Central to this were new transportation technologies and networks. Following the model of New York's Erie Canal, by 1833 two major canals in Ohio were completed: one from Cleveland to Portsmouth and another from Cincinnati to Dayton. In addition to canals, the national road extended to Columbus by 1833, and to Indiana by 1840. New routes of transportation compressed time and space, and additionally themselves provided a source of jobs for wage workers, which gradually became a more predominant form of labor.[124] But canal building also represented the poverty of capitalism, as

> the laborers who constructed them endured long hours of back-breaking work, for they literally dug the canals with picks and shovels. Disease, including cholera and typhus, raged periodically. Food and shelter were usually deplorable ... immigrants and local farm boys nonetheless showed up eager, at least initially, to make enough money to buy some land.[125]

These canals were also in part dug by Irish immigrants, and convict labor was used in at least one instance. Additionally, steamboat production and use took off, from 1811 to 1825, when twenty-six steamboats were launched from Cincinnati. And these developments were later followed by railroad construction. Railroad construction in Ohio was primarily privately funded, but state chartered, and while construction began in the 1830s, between 1841 and 1850 seventy-six companies were chartered (although many of these did not succeed, or even build). By 1860, the state had 2,974 miles of railroad.[126]

Cincinnati also grew as a center of capitalism in the old northwest. The city's initial growth was due to its location by Fort Washington at the end of the eighteenth century, when city merchants profited from military spending. Soon traders were traveling between Cincinnati and other cities such as Philadelphia, Pittsburgh, and New Orleans as Cincinnati became integrated into circuits of capital and commodity chains stretching across the country.[127] The city itself also became a center of manufacturing, as even before the panic of 1819, a variety of industries developed including textile spinning factories, potteries, foundries, breweries, and distilleries. By 1819 the city produced more than a million dollars of goods a year.[128] And the development of steamboat and capital goods production also became an important part of the economy; one estimate from 1829 suggests that the city exported over $225,000 of steam engines, textile machinery, and sugar mills, the city becoming a producer of not just consumer, but capital goods.[129]

Cincinnati's growth also resulted in class inequality. For instance, the majority of the city's population were either lower-middle or lower class. While on the top, the merchant and capitalist elite ruled, below were clerks, skilled workers, small store owners, and, below them, poor immigrant workers, transients, and manual labors.[130] As a response to the increased pressures of class society, laborers also began to organize. In 1836, for example, workers from a variety of professions including coopers, cordwainers, hatters, tin plate workers, and tailors, among others, began the General Trades' Union of Cincinnati, and in this year a newspaper titled *Working Man's Friend* was in circulation.[131]

By 1838, the city had 2,559 people who owned a total of $4,935,500 worth of real estate. This represented about 6 percent of the population or one out of every five white male adults. And over half, 55.4 percent, of this property was held in 256 hands.[132] By the census of 1840 the city was said to have a working population of 14,544. Within this, 80 people worked in agriculture, 2,044 in commerce, 10,287 in manufacturing and trades, 1,756 in navigation, and 377 in "professions" (physicians, teachers, attorneys, clergyman, and so on).[133] But by this time the city may still have been going through a transition from "artisans to workers."[134] Within manufacturing and industrial production, for example, out of 1,614 establishments, over half had under five workers and only a quarter of the total population of 10,287 workers in the manufacturing and trades category worked in institutions with over fifteen.[135] By 1840, Cincinnati was increasingly becoming a city organized under the law of value, in which larger proportions of the population were dispossessed, although the age of the artisan was not yet over. As a dispossessed proletariat developed, prison labor was also used. As recorded by Joseph John Gurney in the early 1840s, reporting from Columbus, Ohio, at the state prison:

> during the day they are employed in their respective working rooms, in large companies, all in silence—as busy a scene as I ever witnessed—carriage-lace weaving, tailoring, shoemaking, manufacturing saddle trees, carpentering, working in iron, and stone cutting … the several divisions of men were employed in executing the orders of certain joint-stock companies engaged in their respective trades; and I was assured that the payments for the work defrayed the whole expense of the prison.[136]

Prisoners who broke the silence were whipped as unpaid labor generated profits for companies and revenue for the prison.

Beyond the city, by 1819 Ohio had twenty-eight state chartered banks and by 1820 it was third, behind New York and Pennsylvania, in terms of the overall value of manufactured commodities. The War of 1812 also stimulated increased production. For instance, in Dayton from 1814 to 1821, fifteen new manufacturing operations began. And in Steubenville by 1815, 1,200 yards of cloth were produced each month, a steam powered flour mill was in operation, and a brewery was being constructed as capitalists in the city were discussing building a steamboat to more easily sell to the world market.[137] The state's vast ecological environment also provided resources for economic growth. Timber, for example, was readily available, as were salt licks, coal, clay, and shale. The meatpacking industry also grew quickly, and by the 1820s Cincinnati was processing as many as 30,000 hogs a year. And as early as 1804 an iron furnace was set up near Youngstown, followed by their spread throughout the eastern and southern parts of the state.[138]

Whereas Ohio's path to capitalist development enriched a white elite, black workers suffered under the "freedom" of Ohio's entrance into the Union as a non-slave state under the Northwest Ordinance. To call blacks in Ohio "free labor" would be an exaggeration. As a continuum of racialized and gendered labor forms have always been central to the history of capitalism, it was also the case in Ohio. Some former slaves were brought across the Ohio River and forced to sign contracts of indentured servitude. If they refused to sign, their masters would likely have sold them before moving.[139] And the borderland between chattel slavery in Kentucky and free labor in Ohio was also a region in which capital exploited a variety of labor forms as "while some of these men and women earned wages as free laborers, others paid their wages back to their owners, and still others earned no wages at all, toiling as enslaved workers."[140] Kentucky slaves were also hired out; for example, one author notes as many as 2,000 slaves were hired out to Ohio from 1800 to 1810.[141] And on the river itself it was not unusual for a variety of laborers to be used, from northern "free" blacks to slaves, interchangeably; after all, the goal of steamboat owners was profit, whatever labor forms surplus value was generated from.

Ohio also adopted a series of "black codes." The first of these was in 1804, and it stipulated that counties in Ohio had to keep a registry of free blacks who each had to register.[142] Additionally, more were passed in 1807, 1829, and 1830 and the black laws forbade blacks to enter the state without providing a $500 bond with signatures from two white men guaranteeing their appropriate and good behavior.[143] But the black population continued to increase, and by 1829 they made up 9.4 percent of the total population of 24,148. Racialized violence towards Ohio's blacks culminated in the race riots of 1829 in which, from August 15 to 22, white mobs of 200 to 300 people attacked the black section of Cincinnati's Fourth Ward, and, as police provided no protection against the white riots, between 1,100 to 1,500 African Americans fled the city.[144]

Gradually, Kentucky and Ohio, along with the rest of the country, became more and more capitalist. Frontier towns evolved into thriving market-driven cities, work became organized by capital, and, in Kentucky, slavery provided the economic basis for the state's power elite. While many may have entered into these territories without entirely capitalist motivations, over the decades their social relations became increasingly shaped by capital. Meanwhile, even further south, slavery would push the expansion of empire.

4
Slavery and Capitalism

For W.E.B. Du Bois capitalism, race, empire, and American slavery were part of the same historical process. Slaves themselves were part of the mass proletariat, divided by race, which capital exploited. As he argued, "out of the exploitation of the dark proletariat comes the Surplus Value filched from human beasts which, in cultured lands, the Machine and harnessed Power veil and conceal."[1] For Du Bois, the black slave proletariat was the laboring foundation of the modern, capitalist social order.[2]

> Black labor became the foundation stone not only of the Southern social structure, but of Northern manufacture and commerce, of the English factory system, of European commerce, of buying and selling on a world-scale; new cities were built on the results of black labor, and a new labor problem, involving all white labor, arose both in Europe and America.[3]

They were the foundation of an Atlantic world-system which entailed "new dreams of power and visions of empire."[4] And it was this link between capitalist slavery and empire which was at the root of the Civil War. For Du Bois, "it was a war to determine how far industry in the United States should be carried on under a system where the capitalist owns not only the nation's raw material, not only the land, but also the laborer himself."[5]

This chapter picks up on Du Bois' insights to unpack the dynamics of the history of imperialism and capitalism in the old south. Specifically, it aims to reevaluate the extent to which the south was capitalist or not by examining southern development in light of the dynamics of the uneven class structure of the south, emphasizing in particular the fact that "the south" was not one thing, but a complex uneven variety of relations.[6] Specifically, the question I contend with is: to what extent did capitalist relations exist in parts of the south—particularly in plantation slavery—and how did they drive expansion? How did these social relations co-exist and interact with poor farmers and "plain folk"; whites who organized themselves around perhaps something closer to the northern frontier household rather than the plantation?[7] In other words, was the old south a society with capitalism or a capitalist society?

Slavery as capitalist?

The debate over the question of slavery and capitalism has been long running and wide ranging. For some scholars, most influentially Eugene Genovese, southern slavery was not capitalist. Slaves were not "free to choose" to sell their labor power for a wage, and were not guided by the indirect coercion of the invisible hand, but by the direct violence of the whip. Masters were not owners of large corporations and banks, but kings of self-sustaining agrarian complexes based upon forced labor. They aimed to live like aristocrats using the labor of others, guided by an ethos of southern gentility. Overall, "the planters, in truth, grew into the closest thing to feudal lords imaginable in a nineteenth century bourgeois republic."[8] Another position suggests, "perhaps the solution is to regard the South as a society transitional with respects to capitalism, but one in which the transition has never been able to progress beyond a certain point."[9] Thus, while plantation slavery moved towards a type of capitalism, it became stuck or frozen at a point where the transition was not complete. A related point of view argues that "it was a hybrid type of enterprise, with modern features (looking forward to the industrial 'plant') but a basis in extra-economic compulsion."[10] Slavery was not fully capitalist, but partially capitalist and partly something else.

Yet other scholars have argued plantations were in fact capitalist institutions. Most influentially and contentiously Fogel and Engerman, professional economists, argued that slavery was capitalist because slaveowners were rational profit calculators aiming to maximize their profits from slave labor.[11] And many recent works of the "new" history of capitalism also emphasize the capitalist nature of the plantation south.[12] That being said, these recent works have somehow managed to make a case about capitalism while avoiding clear definitions of it, or, perhaps more importantly, engaging with the long history of debate over, methodologically, how to understand capitalism historically.[13] This approach raises a conundrum which both Marx and Weber, among others, spent their lives trying to understand. Concepts do not just build themselves; we collectively construct them to make sense of the world. While, as noted in the introduction, constructing a definition creates a risk in that it may be the case that "capitalist" exceptions may be found in almost any definition of capitalism, it is necessary to have some definition, however precise or loose. Much of this recent work has either fallen back on loose definitions that focus on markets and finance, or, more often, neglected clear definitions and, perhaps more importantly, explanations of methodological processes through which concepts are created in the first place. In other words, to write a supposed history of capitalism without clearly engaging with the conceptual and methodological processes of clarifying what capitalism is in the first place is not to write a history of capitalism at all, but a description of something that could potentially be called capitalism while avoiding naming the system in a clear way.

Having presented a definition in the introduction of this book, the rest of this chapter will make a case for why plantations were, essentially, capitalist institutions. That being said, there has been a tendency to equate all of "the south" with plantation slavery. But this was not the case. Just as in the states so far discussed, in the history of the American Empire there tended to be less clear-cut divides between capitalism and non-capitalism, so much as complex articulations of different types of relations, and the same can be said for the south. So while plantation slavery was capitalist, not all of the south was capitalist. As much as the shadow of slavery hung over all aspects of the south, it was the presence of interactions between capitalism and non-capitalism that characterized southern empire building. Like capitalism further north, the south was a complex amalgam of different types of social labor. And this social order was held together through gendered and racialized social relations.

Slavery and labor

Slaves like Charles Ball were well aware of their economic value to planters. As he put it in his post-escape narrative, "regarding the negroes merely as objects of property like prudent calculators, they study how to render this property of greatest value, and to obtain the greatest yearly income, from the capital invested in the slaves, and the lands they cultivate."[14] For most slaveowners, slaves were capital; an investment. This has also raised a conceptual question: what *type* of capital were slaves? For example, some have argued that slaves were fixed capital.[15] This would mean slaves were not circulating capital that, through labor, created value, but investments more similar to industrial machines, the product of human labor power, which transfer value to the finished good and contain the results of labor, but don't create value directly.[16] But if slaves were fixed capital they could not have been value producers by their own collective labor which, in fact, would suggest value, or surplus value, was not being produced in the south at all. This, in a way, would also have made it impossible for masters to profit from slave labor. Rather, it makes more sense to argue that slaves were a form of variable and circulating capital who collectively produced surplus value and transferred it to the commodities they produced, from the cotton they picked and processed, to the railroads they built, to the factories they worked in. In this sense, as Du Bois noted, slaves were productive of surplus value. And slave labor itself was more flexible than is sometimes discussed. For one, slaves could be, and often were, bought and sold and slaves were sometimes traded to different masters throughout their lives for a variety of reasons from debts to death. Slaves were regularly hired out, a way for planters to profit from slaves during slack times. Some slave capital went into industry, where slaves worked alongside, or instead of, wage laborers. And slaves themselves were also a speculative investment that had a tendency to increase in value over time, and they provided the capital basis for the southern credit system, stretching across the Atlantic Ocean.

First, there was the interstate slave trade itself.[17] Overall, estimates suggest about 835,000 slaves were moved during this period, with some estimations suggesting over a million. While we many never precisely know, following Jonathan Pritchett and taking one estimate of half of all slaves moved as a benchmark, it may be likely that over 400,000 slaves were sold in the interstate slave trade.[18] A vast institutional complex formed in order to profit from the movement of black bodies across long distances. These pathways centralized in the Louisiana slave market where slaves were stored in pens to be sold, either through auctions or else individual sales. And southern newspapers such as New Orleans' *The Daily Crescent* regularly posted advertisements for the buying and selling of slaves. To take one of countless examples, an advertisement for J. Buddy's Slave Depot says,

> house servants and field hands for sale at all times. Slaves will be received on board or sold on favorable terms. The building is a large, three-story brick house, and very commodious as a Slave Depot.

> Particular attention will be paid to the health and cleanliness of all the slaves placed in the Yard.[19]

For merchant capitalists, slaves were a form of liquid capital to buy cheap and sell dear, and this movement of slaves fueled the making of capitalist slavery in the south.

Slave hiring was also a regular practice throughout the south. Estimates as to the percentage of slaves hired out for the south as a whole range from 5 to 15 percent, with particular counties hiring out one-third of all slaves.[20] Hiring out slaves gave slaveowners a certain degree of flexibility with their slave capital. For slaveowning capitalists, hiring out labor was a central way to add flexibility to the slave system, and transform supposedly "fixed" slave labor into a more liquid, circulating form of variable capital. Hired slaves experienced slavery in a variety of ways. And while, on the one hand, it might seem hired out slaves were closer to wage labor than slavery, on the other hand, it could be the opposite case at times: rather than hired slaves having an easier life than non-hired slaves, hired slaves could be subject to just as much brutality.[21] For the slaveowner, the goal was to generate profit by hiring a slave out, with hopes that the slave would not be so damaged that they would continually be usable for profits. For a slave hirer, most often using one year contracts, the goal was to get as much value out of the slave as possible within that time period; that is, work the slave as hard as possible. In these conditions, slaves would be treated just as cruelly as if not hired out; perhaps even more so. For instance, the economy of Washington, DC in the antebellum period used a variety of labor forms. While many of the workers in the city itself were free blacks, along with Irish and German workers, slaveowners who lived directly outside the city regularly hired their slaves to work in the city.[22]

Slave hiring had a variety of dimensions. For example, poor white farmers who could not afford to purchase slaves themselves could hire them temporarily. Slaveowners could rent them to other slaveowners if they thought they might have trouble profiting from the labor on their own plantation. Even industrial companies hired slaves and used hired slave labor interchangeably with white, especially Irish, wage laborers. In Frederick Law Olmstead's travels across the south, for example, he came across a slaveowner, Mr. C., who hired Irish workers to dig ditches, although he preferred black slave labor for most tasks, given that the Irish were supposedly more dishonest and needed closer supervision.[23]

And industries in Virginia, for instance, used a variety of types of labor. For example, Olmstead notes:

> yesterday I visited a coal-pit: the majority of the mining laborers are slaves, and uncommonly athletic and fine-looking negroes; but a considerable number of white hands are also employed, and they occupy all reasonable posts. The slaves are, some of them, owned by the Mining Company; but the most are hired of their owners, at from $120 to $200 a year, the company boarding and clothing them (I have the impression that I heard it was customary to give them a certain allowance of money and let them find their own board).[24]

Slaves in some cases were also able to hire themselves out on their day off to poor whites to earn money.[25] Olmstead even mentions at one point that it was so profitable to hire slaves out to tobacco factories and to build railroads that slaveowners hired out too many, and, in turn, had to temporarily hire white workers to replace them.[26] One reason why planters may have at times hired white Irish workers over their slaves was because they did not want to risk the value of their slave capital on dangerous jobs. He mentions one case of an Irish gang being hired to drain land in which the reply was, "it's too dangerous work (unhealthy?), and a negro's life is too valuable to be risked at it. If a negro dies, it's a considerable loss, you know."[27] Or as a mate on a cotton shipping boat put it, "the niggers are worth too much to be risked here; if the Paddies are knocked overboard, or get their backs broke, nobody loses anything!"[28]

The story continues as both company owned and hired slaves worked interchangeably with Irish and German immigrant labor in many industries. For instance, Olmstead encountered a glue manufacture who "said that, in his factory, they had formally employed slaves; had since used Irishmen, and now employed Germans altogether."[29] Perhaps the slaves that got the closest to living in "quasi" slavery, or "half" freedom were self-hired slaves. While most states had laws against self-hire, it was not unusual for these laws to be ignored. Self-hire was most common in larger cities such as Charleston and Richmond, where a demand for flexible, semi-skilled labor was higher than in the country. Self-hired slaves effectively paid a "body rent"; in other words, they were allowed to hire themselves out as wage laborers provided they paid their masters a continual fee. For masters, these slaves became an easy way to profit simply by ownership. For slaves, this meant, at times, a greater degree of independence. Some, for example, even rented their own homes and saved money to purchase their freedom. But whatever degree of "quasi" freedom some may have had, a slave was still a slave, and more often than not treated as such. Self-hired slaves, for instance, made up a large portion of revolts led by Gabriel Prosser in 1800 and that led by Denmark Vesey in 1822, not content with their supposedly half-free situation.[30] And the term half freedom may have been used in some cases as, for example, Linda Jacob's narrative records being scolded for knowing how to read with "who writes to you? Half free niggers?"[31] Although it is not entirely clear in this context whether half free refers to free blacks or perhaps self-hired slaves, it appears, perhaps, the distinction between slavery and freedom was not always entirely clear-cut. For example, Simon Gray, a slave, was hired out to Andrew Brown and Company where he worked first in the sawmilling industry and eventually as the company's chief boatman.[32] As one scholar puts it:

> as a captain, Simon Gray exercised a degree of authority that is surprising to the modern student of slavery. His crews, usually numbering between ten and twenty men, were made up of both Negro slaves and white rivermen. Some of the slaves were the property of the company, while others, like Gray himself, were hired from their owners by the firm. The white crewmen, on the other hand, were employed by the Negro, who kept their records, paid their expenses, lent them money, and sometimes paid their wages.[33]

Eventually, while a slave his renter even allowed him to engage in his own private business ventures in his free time. Thus, while technically a slave, Gray was perhaps as free as many supposedly "free" white workers.

Most slaves lived and worked in agriculture but not all slave capital was tied up in the countryside. Slaves were used in a variety of industrial enterprises. While industrialization itself started in the south almost as early as the north, its rate of growth was substantially slower. The number of industrial workers increased in the south about 72 percent from 1820 to 1860, and nearly 400 percent during that period in the north.[34] In total, in the 1840s and 1850s, it has been estimated that perhaps 5 percent of the south's 4 million slaves worked in industry, and on the eve of the Civil War the south controlled about 15 percent of the country's industrial capacity.[35] While lagging far behind the north, then, a significant amount of industry did develop in the south, some of it worked by slaves.

In fact, from its origins, American industry used a variety of labor forms including slave labor. For example, Alexander Spotswood, lieutenant governor of Virginia, purchased African slaves to work on the Tuball Iron Works as early as 1720. The Principo Iron Works, outside of present day Baltimore, also used slaves among a variety of types of labor. In 1723, the company employed thirteen slaves, ten white servants, and twenty-six other white workers.[36] Throughout the antebellum period slaves continued to labor in a wide variety of industrial projects. Southern textile producers, for example, used combinations of "free" and "unfree" labor, and in 1860 cotton and woolen industries employed over 5,000 slaves.[37] In general, slaves worked in mining, ironworks, textile, hemp, and tobacco factories, built canals and railroads, and were employed in basically every form of southern industry. Joseph John Gurney, in his journey from Ohio to Virginia, for example, found slaves working in saltworks around the Kenahwa.[38] And Loughton Smith found "a company has associated for purposes of navigation by cutting a canal along the river. Ninety negroes are constantly employed, with four overseers and a head manager."[39] In addition, while industry and agriculture are often considered two different realms, in practice there tended to be a blurry line between them. For example, the production of sugar is often considered a rural activity, but in the Louisiana sugar industry the number of acres cultivated per hand rose from 2 in 1802 to over 5, in some cases as high as 6.6 in the years before the Civil War.[40] Much of this productivity stemmed from a rising organic composition of capital in the sugar industry. This involved, for example, using moving conveyer belts in sugar processing industries in an assembly line fashion with labor organized around clock time.[41] It also involved using steam power, as by the 1860s, 80 percent of sugar plantations were using this new technology.[42] Louisiana planters also invested in railroads, in some cases creating integrated production facilities in which small railroads shipped sugar cane, as it went through its processing stages, to different facilities on the plantation.

Slaves comprised the largest section of unskilled labor throughout southern cities, but also engaged in skilled labor. This was demonstrated in the overwork system. With overwork, slaves were required to produce a certain amount: beyond that they were paid a bonus for their production. Wages from overwork could be used for slaves to purchase a life beyond the subsistence level the majority of slaves lived at. For example, Sam Williams of Buffalo Forge received $5 per extra ton of iron he finished. He, along with other slaves, also held a plot of land on the company's territory that he could work and sell produce for a profit. Using proceeds from these, Williams regularly purchased coffee and sugar, opened a savings account at Lexington bank, and lived a life that might be considered "quasi" free; albeit still a slave.[43] Other slaves saved money to visit families living elsewhere, or even to try and purchase freedom. In all these cases, capital had an interest in investing in slaves, and treating them as not purely "unfree" labor but along a labor form continuum.

Slavery, race, gender, and empire

Slavery, of course, was held together by racism. By viewing slaves and Native Americans as the racialized other, the master class were able to defend expansion and the "peculiar institution" as well as build white supremacist solidarity amongst different classes of whites.[44] As traveler Francis Grund put it:

> the progress of the white race is the soul of universal history; for it is the white race which produced all the changes, and acted as the animating principle on the rest of mankind. The other nations remained stationary, bound by the limits which nature had set to their progress; the white race alone was possessed of the courage to overleap them and to traverse the ocean in a quest for new land.[45]

The white race was supposedly the motivating race behind all significant achievements in human history. Thomas Jefferson thought, while black-skinned people may have a fine ability to remember ideas and actions, they lacked the creative intellectual capacity to create new human innovations, as he says, "it appears to me that in memory they are equal to the whites; in reason much inferior."[46] The spread of the white race across the expanding American Empire, then, was practically inevitable. As Grund again put it, "every race has feared the contact of the whites, in the same manner as a weaker animal dreads to meet one which is more powerful."[47] While it may have been (somewhat) sad or regrettable for the imperial mind that the indigenous peoples were killed and conquered, it was simply the result of the movement of civilization across the North American continent.

When Thomas R. Gray wrote Nat Turner's "confessions" after interviewing him, he included in the introduction of his book, "Nat Turner, the leader of this ferocious band, whose name has resounded throughout our widely extended empire, was captured."[48] For Gray, Turner's rebellion was a challenge to empire. And in the south, empire could be seen as stretching from the household to the polity. As the Marquis de Chastellux put it, more critically, "I mean to speak of slavery; not that it is any mark of distinction, or peculiar privilege to possess negroes, but because the empire men exercise over them cherishes vanity and sloth."[49] Thus, for some, the "empire" of slavery was not something to celebrate, but to criticize. Compared to the more prosperous and economical north, southern slavery tarnished human potential, encouraging arrogant behavior and idleness through the exercise of personal slave empires.

Slavery was, of course, not only racialized, but gendered. American slavery was unique in that it developed into a self-reproducing system, so that, even with the formal abolition of the slave trade, slavery could continue to expand south and west. Often slave women worked in the fields, the same as men, although in some cases their gender was preferred for household tasks. And, as recorded in the story of Harriet Jacobs, female slaves were also regularly raped.[50] The result of this, along with the fact that free blacks and whites did occasionally copulate on consensual terms, led to years of debate over who, exactly, was "black." Milton Clarke's narrative, for example, reveals he was called a "white nigger."[51] And one record of racial categories in New Orleans shows a complexity of racial categories:

Sacatra	griffe and negress.
Griffe	negro and mulatto.
Marabon	mulatto and griffe.
Mulatto	white and negro.
Quartcron	white and mulatto.
Metif	white and quarteron.
Meamelouc	white and motif.
Quarteron	white and meamelouc.
Sang-mele	white and quarteron.[52]

The racial categories of the south were white, black, and red, but they also contained a variety of complexity, albeit one in which if someone was partially black they were considered ripe slave material. In fact, in some cases, young light-skinned female slaves were even sold directly for sexual exploitation, given their lighter skin made them supposedly more desirable for the white master race. And the value of female slaves, "breeding wenches," as they were called, was also dependent upon their potential fertility.[53] A female slave could give a master a high return on his investment if it produced more slaves who, by the fact that their mother was a slave, were legally made slaves themselves.

From Virginia to Texas, slavery spread across the land as the illusion of northerners that "diffusion" would gradually lead to the end of slavery was exposed. White masculine dreams of the profits of empire pushed expansion further along the western frontier, driven most significantly by the cotton boom which supported British industrialization across the Atlantic.[54] Travelers recorded zones of overused, desolate land and abandoned farms in the east while massive slave plantation complexes flourished in the west. As Gurney wrote with disgust,

> The plain fact is, that the lands of North Carolina and Virginia, have been for so many years under a process of exhaustion by slave-labor, that this labor is no longer a source of profit. The negroes themselves are now the only profitable article on the estate, and to breed them for sale insensibly becomes the regular business of the country.[55]

And passing through Virginia, Charles Ball observed of tobacco,

> this destructive crop ruins the best land in a short time; and in all the lower parts of Maryland and Virginia the traveller will see large old family mansions, of weather-beaten and neglected appearance, standing in the middle of vast fields of many hundred acres, the fences of which have rotted away.[56]

But slavery was also an adaptive system. In Virginia, for instance, some producers switched to crops such as wheat or, as noted, employed their slaves in industry. But hundreds of thousands were sent further south and west through the interstate slave trade. Here, white-slave-settler colonialism in the west provided capital with a "spatial fix" against declining profits due to over-exploitation of the land in the east.[57] For plantation owners to move west to search out new profits they would either have to bring over their own slaves, or else purchase new ones after arrival. Moving could also mean a capitalist's slaves were held from circulating for a portion of time. To soften this, and keep slaves as circulating capital, slaveowners would, in some cases, send their slaves ahead. For example, slaveowner John Breckinridge moved from Virginia to Kentucky but sent his slaves to the new state nearly a year before he left. He then put them under control of Samuel Meredith and William Russell to hire out in the time before he arrived.[58] In other cases, capitalists moved west and left their slaves behind in trusted hands, to be hired out until the capitalist was settled and ready to use them profitably. Additionally, it was not unusual for new settlers to hire slaves upon arrival to work towards setting up their new homes. In all these cases, slaves as circulating capital contributed to the expansion of the westward and southward frontier. The slave south was far from a static system: it was a dynamic and shifting modern social order. Capital continually moved from region to region, and from crop to crop, in order to generate surplus value. It has been suggested that as much as 30 percent of the south's economic growth from 1840 to 1860 was due to the movement of population from the old south to the new.[59] In other words, *imperialism was profitable.* The movement of capital southwest opened up new avenues for profits, particularly in the cotton kingdom. This was also driven by the ability of slaveowners to shift to new crops when profit rates declined in the old south: from tobacco to indigo, rice, and sugar, to cotton. In all these cases, slave capital changed forms, either geographically or in terms of what product was produced.

Expansion was a key method for increasing profits from slavery. Specifically, the movement from less fertile, overworked soils in the east to nutrient-rich soil in the west likely contributed to increased productivity. As Olmstead and Rhode note, the center of the cotton world shifted from west central Alabama in 1839 to west of the Mississippi-Alabama border by 1859. In this new territory picking rates increased more than in the east, between 1811 to 1862 rising by approximately 1.52 percent a year in the old south, and 2.13 percent a year in the new south.[60] The movement west opened up new lands, further increasing the productivity of slave society. Finally, it is useful to note that it was not until nearly a century after the end of slavery that the mechanical cotton picker replaced the field hand in the south.[61] This suggests the problem was not one of a lack of desire on the part of slaveowners to invest in more efficient means of production, but that the technological capacities to do so simply did not exist, and would not until well into the age of the generalization of supposedly "capitalist" relations.

Recent research has also highlighted the extent to which plantation slavery was perhaps more economically rational and efficient than some previous perspectives suggested. Olmstead and Rhode's calculations suggest that in the six decades before the Civil War productivity on cotton plantations may have increased fourfold.[62] Increases in the efficiency of production under slavery were both continual and gradual: the product of countless capitalists experimenting with new biological varieties of crops and production organizational techniques. In Maryland between the 1640s and the 1690s, for example, the mean per hand production of tobacco rose from £900 to close to £1,900. Farmers invented new techniques, combining European with African and Native American techniques. Additionally, slaves were gradually introduced, replacing indentured servants, and the skills they brought from Africa may have contributed to this, along with the introduction of labor gangs. This also likely contributed to the declining price of tobacco as the costs of production decreased.[63]

Beyond the cotton gin, productivity increases in the cotton industry were the result of countless farmers experimenting with new breeds of cotton. Initially, there were two main breeds, Sea Island, which grew around the coastal regions and islands of South Carolina and Georgia, and Upland cotton that proved to be more resilient further inland. Farmers continued to experiment, in time creating many new breeds through cross breeding and importing new forms of cotton seed, such as Black Seed cotton, imported from Siam in the 1730s. One successful example was Mexican cotton, brought to the Mississippi Valley as early as 1806. It had a relatively short time to ripen, could be easily picked, and was resistant to disease. Petit Gulf, perhaps the most famous cotton breed, emerged out of this in the late 1820s, developed by Dr. Rush Nutt, and soon spread widely as a regional market for cotton seeds grew.[64] Innovation continued up through the 1850s, contributing to increased productivity.[65]

Capitalist slavery pushed racialized and gendered imperial relations across the southern half of the United States until the Civil War. Yet the social structure of the south itself—and the social forces driving empire—were more complex than this picture alone shows. On the verge of the Civil War, in fact, only about a quarter of southern white families owned slaves, down from as high as around 35 percent three decades previously.[66] And many families that did own slaves owned very few. In many parts of the south, in the sandy regions, poorly or un-drained marshes, and the pine barrens and upcountry where the land was cheaper and less fertile—and less conducive to plantation slavery—"poor white trash" and "plain folk" lived in relations in many ways closer to the northern frontier patriarchal household mode of social reproduction than the capitalist plantation system.[67]

Social class in the south

The white component of the southern social structure was divided along class lines.[68] There were poor whites, barley producing above subsistence, middling whites, petty-commodity producers engaging in "safety-first" farming, and small-scale planters with lesser numbers of slaves than large-scale plantation complexes. There were also white wage laborers, white artisans, and so on. Demographically, before the Civil War, the total population of the United States was 31.4 million. There were around 4 million slaves, perhaps 6 percent of them living in cities, while the total white population was around 27 million. And overall, there were about 8 million whites in the south. The planter class, defined as owners of twenty or more slaves, was around 225,000 people, and around 10,000 planters owned fifty or more slaves, while perhaps 40 percent of slaveowners owned five to nineteen slaves. Around 3–4.5 million whites were small landholders, owning either no slaves, or below five slaves, while perhaps 2.4–4 million whites did not own land at all. And there were almost half a million free blacks.[69]

So "the south" was an uneven place, much more complex than plantation slavery alone. And it was out of these complex social relations that the southern half of the American Empire was built. In other words, southern white-settler colonialism was driven both by capitalist plantation slavery as well as non-capitalist farmer households, which intersected through a relation in which small farmers were regularly pushed west as plantation owners moved to more fertile grounds in the west, taking control of the land, with the whole social order linked together through a system of white supremacy.[70]

Those who lived in the south were well aware of the large class of poor whites they regularly encountered. For slaves, poor whites at times provided an opportunity for trade. For planters, among other things, they could serve as patrollers—"paddyrollers"—out to capture slaves who might escape in the dead of night. As one traveler observed,

> humanity has still more to suffer from the state of poverty, in which a great number of white people live in Virginia. It is this country that I saw poor persons, for the first time, after I passed the sea; for, in the midst of those rich plantations, where the negro alone is wretched, miserable huts are often to be met with, inhabited by whites, whose wane looks, and ragged garments, bespeak poverty.[71]

Another observed in North Carolina, "the inhabitants are mostly farmers, and produce on their farms every necessity of life."[72] And as escaped slave Charles Ball wrote, in the south there was a "third order" of white men,

> in my opinion, there is no order of men in any part of the United States, with which I have any acquaintance, who are in a more debased and humiliated state of moral servitude, than are those white people who inhabit that part of the southern country, where the landed property is all, or nearly all, held by the great planters. Many of these people live in wretched cabins, not half so good as the houses which judicious planters provide for their slaves.[73]

Lastly, as Olmstead wrote,

> I have been once or twice told that the poor white people, meaning those, I suppose, who bring nothing to market to exchange for money but their labor, although they may own a cabin and a little furniture, and cultivate land enough to supply themselves with (maize) bread, are worse in almost all respects than the slaves.[74]

For poorer and low-middling whites, the "farm economy meant a diversified, self-sufficient type of agriculture, where the money crops were subordinated to food crops, and where the labor was performed by the family or the family aided by a few slaves."[75] In some cases, they even squatted on the land, often living in no more than a poorly constructed log cabin.[76] The south might be characterized, then, as Stephen Hahn suggests, as a "dual society" where "alongside the commercialized Plantation Belt arose areas characterized by small farms, relatively few slaves, and diversified agriculture."[77] Regions such as "Western North Carolina, eastern Tennessee, the hilly sections of Georgia, Alabama, and Louisiana, as well as southern Mississippi and Georgia, among others, remained isolated enclaves or on the periphery of the staple economy."[78] While in some cases, poor whites lived near plantation regions, producing small amounts of cotton to sell on the market, in other regions the geography of the south organized along class and ecological lines. And in parts of South Carolina, yeomen tended to congregate in the piney land where they were, as Stephanie McCurry puts it, "masters of small worlds"; small farmers who occasionally owned slaves and engaged in market production, but tended to put the sufficiency of the household first.[79]

But it would be a stretch to argue that yeomen did not want to become capitalists, or were fully insulated from capitalist pressures. A variety of works have come out showing that, in fact, yeomen may have been more market oriented than otherwise argued. In some cases, small and medium slaveowners appear to operate in a similar way to plantation owners. Benton H. Miller of Georgia, William Harris argues, moved from Mississippi to Georgia in 1858 after collecting slaves and debts from the former region. By 1860 he owned fourteen slaves and 900 acres of land.[80] Similar to larger plantations, Miller produced sizeable amounts of cotton for the market, and also planted other crops, especially corn, to make his farm relatively self-sufficient. In some ways, his activities reflected yeoman behavior: participating in reciprocal farm work with the local community, for example, and working alongside slaves in the fields. But he almost produced as much cotton as corn, devoting 32.5 acres to the former and 44 acres to the latter.[81] Corn and cotton were also useful crops because they had different growing seasons, and provided a way to keep slaves busy throughout the year. Overall, much of Miller's orientation seems to be towards capitalist production.

In Maryland the situation may have been similar, and it may have even been the case that some slaveholding yeomen were more dependent on the market than larger planters.[82] In the Mississippi piney woods a similar story also appears to be the case. In Covington, Jones, and Perry counties small farmers did not practice "safety-first" production. First, between one-half and three-quarters of farmers did not produce all the manufactured goods they needed to subsist and relied on the market for those. Secondly, many farmers specialized in raising cattle and hogs for the market. In other words, they used land and labor resources that could have been devoted to sufficiency, deciding instead to produce for the market, often to the extent to which they did not produce enough grain to subsist without purchasing food. There was a risk in that if the grain crop they produced was not enough, it would not feed their families, or the livestock they raised. But many took this risk in order to gain a surplus they could use to purchase more land. Some farmers were successful, and between 1850 and 1860 it appears that farmers, in some cases, were able to increase the size of their landholdings and shift away from livestock towards cotton production.[83] And in Missouri, as will be discussed in next chapter, mixed farming (partly for subsistence, partly for the market) developed from the earliest American immigrants. By the 1820s, particularly along zones close to rivers, much market activity occurred and would continue to grow. Small farmers led this as they practiced "composite farming."[84] This meant farmers diversified between domestic and market production, from producing for the family, bartering with neighbors, and buying and selling from traveling merchants.[85]

Overall, variations on composite farming, with some tending towards more self-sufficiency and some towards a higher degree of market dependence, seemed to be the norm for yeomen plain folk. Of course, it was not just middling yeomen and planters that moved west. Poor whites also migrated with the hope of obtaining a cheap piece of land. Often they squatted, hoping preemption laws would eventually allow them to buy cheap land, although, perhaps more often than not, they were not able to gather the money to fight off land speculators. Landless whites often became tenants or, in some cases, transient wage workers whose lives are not well documented. In 1850, for example, in northeast Mississippi as much as 40 percent of the population were landless farmers, living as squatters or working for absentee landlords.[86]

In summary, the social forces that drove and built the southern American Empire were diverse and uneven. While many small farmers practiced composite farming, depending on the location of the farm family, different techniques seem to have been practiced, with a wide variety of degrees of market dependence or independence. And, as importantly, simply because these farmers were integrated into the market does not mean that they were automatically pursuing capitalist production. For one, the extent to which an exploited, dispossessed class existed that yeomen could use to produce surplus value was limited. While some yeomen owned less than five slaves, this labor was used as often to supplement household labor as it was to produce for profits. Slaves, in other words, could be integrated into the patriarchal household mode of social reproduction. Additionally, the extent to which these social forms were dominated by the law of value was also limited. In fact, most yeomen families could shift towards taking care of their needs as opposed to producing for the market, an action that, often times, remained supplemental to household production, albeit in some regions less than others. And, as the next chapter will show, up until the Civil War, while capitalist plantation slavery would overshadow the contours of the southern political-economic system, "the south" was not necessarily entirely capitalist.

5
The Progress of Empire

The western course of empire continued to expand and by the early 1800s frontier settlers penetrated halfway through the continent into many territories on their way to becoming states. For Henry Schoolcraft, who wrote one of the first thoroughly documented accounts of the region, Missouri and the old west were driven by what he called the "progress of empire."[1] And by 1870 L.U. Reavis commented on the "sublime march of the American people in the course of the star of empire in its majestic career across the continent."[2] St. Louis was to be celebrated as the center of growing empire in the west, comparable to New York City in the empire state back east.

The purpose of this chapter is to examine the westward movement of empire into the southern antebellum frontier.[3] I focus specifically on three territories: Missouri, Arkansas, and Texas. All three states were the "wests" of their time. As Thomas Hart Benton, editor of the *St. Louis Enquirer*, wrote in 1819, "it is time that western men had some share in the destinies of this Republic."[4] The southwestern frontier was, like other parts of the country, a society with capitalism. As one commentator put it, "The farmers of the West are independent in feeling, plain in dress, simply in manners, frank and hospitable in their dwellings, and soon acquire a competency by moderate labor."[5] But this population quickly intersected with mining and railroad companies, and others seeking out western space for profitable use. As the same writer explains, western settlers tended to emigrate in three waves; first, pioneer families would occupy land and build log cabins, secondly, settlers who purchased the land built more sophisticated dwellings and cleared the land, and third, "The men of capital and enterprise come. The 'settler' is ready to sell out, and take the advantage of the rise of property—push farther into the interior, and become himself, a man of capital and enterprise in turn."[6] In other words, these territories emerged in an era in which the logic of capital was gradually coming to increasingly organize human social life and continued to push against non-capitalist frontier relations.

This chapter aims to explore these complexities on the southwestern frontier of white-settler colonialism. Rather than focusing on the more commonly discussed slave states such as Mississippi, by concentrating on the complexities of Missouri, Arkansas, and Texas, the chapter provides a lens to understand the ways "the south," a complex social formation, was both an empire of slavery and something more multi-layered than regional generalizations based solely upon the deep south might account for.

The French and Spanish eras

The fur trade was a central vanguard of North American white expansion.[7] Demand for North American furs, particularly beaver felts which provided material for European hats, linked the frontier back-country to the Atlantic world market. By 1673, when Jesuit Father Jacques Marquette and trader Louis Jolliet made their venture to Missouri territory, the fur trade, along with missionary activity, had pushed explorers west.[8] From the start of European settler expansion, French merchants were the dominant white influence in the territory that became the state of Missouri, often times living in a middle ground with native peoples, such as the Missouris, Sac and Foxes, and the Osages. French settlement shaped both the commercial orientation of early settlements and property and production patterns.

French expansion into Missouri was driven by a combination of motives: the fur trade, the search for precious metals, exploration for the fabled Northwest Passage, religiously civilizing the supposedly savage peoples, and interimperialist rivalry as the English increasingly took control of the eastern part of the continent.[9] And like much of French exploration and trade, the colonizers inserted themselves in preexisting and in-motion relations with native peoples, transforming the natives' ways of living as they incorporated European goods—perhaps most influentially weapons and alcohol—into their modes of production, altering them without fundamentally transforming them in a capitalist direction. For example, French traders quickly allied with the Osages, trading guns and other goods in return for skins and furs, and sometimes native slaves and horses. Osages responded by raiding western natives to acquire slaves and horses for further trade. Pushed by demand to acquire more trade goods, they also extended the length of their hunting season and the territory covered, and even altered marriage and kinship patterns as men took on more wives to take care of chores and cleaning furs, and hunting brought young warriors increased presence and prestige.[10]

Following these initial expeditions, French Canadians soon began to build villages in the first decades of the eighteenth century. They organized landholdings into fee simple land. Villagers owned strips of land (incidentally called "commons") which they farmed, and beyond this, villages were surrounded with collectively controlled commons which they used to graze livestock and collect wood and resources. By a 1732 census, 471 people lived in what was considered Illinois County. The census also recorded 164 people of African heritage, and by 1737, 314 slaves lived in the region.[11] While slavery in Missouri never reached such proportions as, say, in Mississippi, it did shape the social structure from the start. French capitalists were also interested in the region from an early time. For instance, the French Company of the West saw the territory as potentially profitable in the early 1700s: "A Company, incorporated with such ample rights and privileges, did not fail to draw upon it the attention of the speculative, or to enlist the aid of the enterprising capitalists of the French metropolis."[12]

In November 1762, France ceded the territory to Spain, but it was not until over three years later, in March of 1766, that Spanish administrators began to arrive. By that time Missouri had two primary settlements, Ste. Genevieve and St. Louis. For Spain, though, control of Louisiana was less about settlement, and more about politics. They continued the tradition of giving gifts to natives, set up several forts, and attempted to limit British fur trader incursions into the territory. But throughout the Spanish period, American settlers gradually began to flow into the region. The conclusion of the American Revolution and end of British limits on expansion past Trans-Appalachia meant Americans were free to migrate west, no matter what populations inhabited the land they wanted. Spain's initial reaction was one of hostility towards Americans. In 1784, for example, they closed the Mississippi River to Americans. But realizing they could not stop the population inflow, the Spanish soon changed their course. They began to allow Americans to sell goods down the river, for a duty, and built settlement policies, hoping that, by allowing Americans to settle, they could turn them into subjects of the Spanish Crown.[13] The Spanish offered Americans land grants to *pobladors* (populators) with the hope that they would build communities in the territory. And by the time of the Louisiana Purchase, around 6,000 Americans lived in the region.[14]

Famously in 1803, the United States purchased Louisiana from France, effectively doubling the size of the country, although at the time, the borders of the purchase were still relatively undefined. The purchase resulted from the failure of the French to control the Haitian Revolution.[15] Having lost France's most profitable Caribbean colony, Napoleon agreed to sell Louisiana to the Americans for $15 million, $3.75 million of which went to pay off French debts to the United States after attacks on travel and trade in the 1790s. Although the federal budget was $10 million a year, the Americans could not pass up the offer.[16] Of course, there was one small problem with this: when the Spanish agreed to transfer Louisiana with the Treaty of Saint Ildefonso on October 1, 1800, they did so with the agreement that France would not alienate the territory to another power. Nevertheless, Napoleon made the decision and the Spanish were in no position to successfully contest it. Thus, the formal political arrangements were put in place to expand the American Empire halfway across the continent.

Social relations in the west

When Schoolcraft traveled around Missouri territory in 1818–19 it was still very much the frontier era. His travels brought him between scattered white settlements and cabins and Native American controlled territory. In his encounters with frontier settlers, he was quickly surprised by the gender relations he encountered. For instance, while traveling he stopped at the home of a settler family and found

> The owner of the cabin was not himself in when we first arrived, but his wife very readily gave us every information respecting the direction of the trace, the streams we were to cross, the game we might expect to find for our subsistence, and other particulars, evincing a perfect acquaintance with the subject.[17]

Schoolcraft was surprised by this.

> She told us, also, that our guns were not well adapted to our journey; that we should have rifles; and pointed out some other errors in our dress, equipment, and mode of travelling, while we stood in astonishment to hear a woman direct us in matters which we had before thought the peculiar and exclusive province of men.[18]

On visiting another family he wrote,

> In the course of the evening I tried to engage our hostess and her daughters in small-talk, such as passes current in every social corner; but, for the first time, found I should not recommend myself in that way. They could only talk of bears, hunting, and the like. The rude pursuits, and the coarse enjoyment of the hunter state, were all they knew.[19]

The women he encountered defied eastern standards of femininity as he found rugged and strong frontier women adjusted to the conditions of their settlements as opposed to the dainty, white middle class women of the east. As he put it,

> They have ruddy complexions, but, in other respects, are rather gross, as they live chiefly on animal food. Being deprived of all advantages of dress, possessed by our fair country-women in the east, they are by no means calculated to inspire admiration, but on the contrary disgust; their whole wardrobe, until the age of twelve, consisting of one greasy buckskin frock, which is renewed whenever worn out.[20]

Meanwhile, frontier settlement reproduced masculinity, for example,

> Hunting is the principal, the most honourable, and the most profitable employment. To excel in the chace procures fame, and a man's reputation is measured by his skill as a marksman, his agility and strength, his boldness and dexterity in killing game, and his patient endurance and contempt of the hardships of the hunter's life.[21]

Throughout Trans-Appalachia, three general forms of agriculture predominated: "subsistence agriculture, surplus agriculture, and staple crop agriculture."[22] Most American settlers in Missouri would practice some form or combination of the first two of these in the early settlement years. As a traveler put it in the early 1800s, "By far the greater proportion of the population was engaged in agriculture; in fact, it was the business of all, since the surplus produce of the country was too inconsiderable to be depended upon."[23] Often times the first settlers to head west were frontier families, clearing land and building temporary cabins, barely living above subsistence and separated, for the most part, from market relations. As more settlers came, market relations deepened, and over time interacted with the development of increasingly capitalist productive relations in early western industries. As one advice for emigrants book from the 1830s put it, "Of new comers, there are two tolerably distinct classes: the one comprising farmers, mechanics, and indeed all those who calculate on obtaining a subsistence by manual industry; and other is composed of professional men, tradesmen, and adventurers of every description."[24] The settlement of Missouri represented this variety of relations as, gradually, incorporation into the world market and the development of capitalist production relations articulated through each other. And while the French organized themselves into villages, Americans preferred to settle in more scattered homesteads and clusters.[25] Settlers headed into unknown territory, carrying guns, axes, and basic foods, locating properties which they cleared and built cabins on. They hunted, fished, and grew crops, most importantly corn.

Many emigrants came to obtain competency. They were driven west by the abundance of relatively cheap, fertile land, and often came through family networks. More generally, as the population increased and land was decreasingly available and more expensive, patriarchs brought their families west to earn competency and obtain land, which, on death, could be parceled out to children to earn competency themselves.[26] In Perry County, for example, as late as 1850, farmers were living with relative self-sufficiency.[27] Like most Missouri yeomen, the staple of their diet was corn and hog, although they produced a variety of other crops including wheat, oats, peas, beans, barley, potatoes, and so on, and raised sheep, hunted, and engaged in other activities to reproduce the household. One reverend, for instance, encountered a family on the outskirts of the Ste. Genevieve District he referred to as "a specimen of the squatter race found on the extreme frontiers."[28]

But while some lived outside the market, more commonly, settlers practiced an economy that "was neither fully capitalistic or subsistence, but situated somewhere between these two forms of production."[29] As late as the 1840s, for instance, farmers in the Ozarks, one of the more isolated and subsistence farming-based parts of the state, regularly purchased fabrics and clothes, food, coffee, whiskey, salt, gun powder, and other goods.[30] As Walter Schroeder discusses, the territory developed around space and social forms in an uneven way:

> at the core were the large cities of the East where goods were consumed, business transactions made, strategy laid out, and wealth

> transferred. Surrounding the core was intensively used land of high value that provided products for direct sale in the cities, including more perishable products. Successively outward were zones of land use of correspondingly less intensively used land, because the value of land, in general, diminished with the distance from the core. Beyond was unoccupied and little-used land, viewed as part of this centralized economic system.[31]

In this sense, it is difficult to categorize the early settlement of Missouri as purely capitalist or non-capitalist; rather, it was a system of integrated relationships with gradations of capitalist behavior, from more capitalist urban centers to less capitalist rural petty-commodity producers.

While some settlers came for independent competency, others came for profit through, most significantly, mining. Schoolcraft, for example, also surveyed possible profitable deposits of metals for potential capitalists. He wrote that information regarding the geography and resources of the west was of interest to both the "man of business" and the "man of science" as the space of empire was mapped to chart the course of future investment. Towns such as Ste. Genevieve, Herculaneum, (most symbolically) Potosi, Mine á Breton, and St. Michael were quickly built up around the lead mining industry in particular.[32] By 1720 black slaves were being used to mine the main metal located in the region: lead.[33] And Moses Austin obtained a concession from the Spanish authorities to mine lead in Mine á Breton in 1797.[34] By the 1830s organizations such as the state chartered Missouri Iron Company built sophisticated corporate systems with large capital stock.[35] So while frontier settlers moved west organizing patriarchal frontier households, this went hand-in-hand with businesses seeking to profit by exploiting the natural resources of the country.

These complexities were also apparent in the way the social property relations of land developed. On the one hand, the state reinforced land as commodified private property, and allowed capitalist speculators to profit from land purchases and sales. On the other, the commodification of land provided a space for patriarchal households to own fee simple land, in doing so reproducing the patriarchal household mode of production. By the end of 1820 about 55,000 acres of government land were sold, a decade later that number was around 7 million and continued to grow.[36] Just as a variety of people came to Missouri, from German farmers to American speculators, so different classes of people used the land in different ways. While a farmer might obtain land with the purpose of raising a family and providing for future generations, for speculators land was a form of capital.[37] One example of this came out of the New Madrid earthquakes of 1811–12. As a result of these quakes, in 1815 the New Madrid Act was passed to compensate settlers whose land and property were damaged by the quakes. Claimants were given the right to claim public land elsewhere in the state, as long as it was the same size as their damaged land, up to 640 acres. Yet the majority of claims ended up in the hands of speculators: out of 516 certificates, 385 ended up owned by St. Louis speculators and only 4 percent of all grants were redeemed by the original recipients.[38] Many of these claims were also used to obtain land in the most profitable parts of the state, such as Boon's Lick County, and were opposed by squatters who were waiting for preemption rights on settled land.

The question of land claims was also complicated by the legacy of Spanish land grants. In the Spanish era, large sections of land were granted to settlers through networks of personal, political relationships. The borders of these claims were often unclear and much larger pieces of land were granted than their owners could profitably use. And some claims themselves were fraudulent. In general, it was found, in some cases, that land concessions were backdated, which landowners used to increase the size of the holdings they claimed to own. To address this problem, in 1805 a Board of Land Commissioners was formed, and by 1812 it confirmed 1,340 claims out of 3,340 in five previously Spanish districts.[39] For decades to come, the legal question of Spanish land grants continued to be debated, particularly as landholders feared registering their land as their claim might be rejected.

The most capitalistic behavior formed around the area most geographically connected to the world market, "little Dixie" on the Missouri River, particularly the counties of Clay, Lafayette, Saline, Cooper, Howard, Boone, and Callaway. Here, slaves rebuilt the ecology of the region by clearing land, growing corn, tobacco, and hemp, and eventually building railroads. For instance, one of the first settled areas was termed "Boon's lick" due to its abundant salt resources. By 1814, around 526 white males lived in this area, and that year settlers petitioned Congress to remove native titles to the land, which was accomplished the following year. The population quickly increased, and by 1820 around 12,000 people lived in the region. The main reason settlers preferred this region was its fertile soil and access to commercial markets. And, besides patriarchal farmers, capitalists and potential capitalists also moved into the area in the 1810s and 1820s. In some cases, businessmen focused on smaller business, such as taverns, and others on profits from trade. But in other cases, merchant capitalists invested in industry. For example, in the 1820s William Lamme, a highly successful merchant, opened a tobacco factory in Franklin.[40] Others opened gristmills and sawmills, and soon the region developed an uneven combination of relations that are not easy to characterize as fully capitalist, as much of production was still organized by patriarchal families, but in which families articulated with especially urban capitalist relations, linked through the Missouri and Mississippi Rivers to New Orleans and the world market.

State formation was also central to the creation of the space in which capitalism could develop. The state played a role, for example, via the Board of Internal Improvements, reconnoitering and mapping the land in a way "as may be considered useful to the citizen, or tending to the development of the resources of the state."[41] And a "factory" system was put in place in Missouri. Factories were set up on the frontier so that government trading posts and privately licensed traders could deepen the commercial integration and political alliances with natives, particularly the Osages, as their population could not so quickly be removed.[42] Of course, as the American population increased in Missouri, the factory system was replaced by the policy of removing the indigenous people from Missouri altogether.[43] At the same time that the American Fur Company was exploring Upper Missouri in the early 1820s, the Santa Fe Trail was taking off, driven initially by American merchant capital. In 1825 George C. Sibley was appointed by the federal government to lead a survey from Fort Osage to Santa Fe. As one author suggests, "the Santa Fe Trail was as a result arguably the most successful of the early nineteenth century federal road-building programs, which sought to expand commerce and integrate distant regions into the national market economy."[44] In other words, the making of the Santa Fe Trail represented a clear example of the importance of the federal government in helping produce a link between the expansion of state space and the space of capital accumulation.

Slavery in Missouri

When Missouri applied to become a full-fledged state, it had about 10,000 blacks, 16 percent of the population, similar to New York's slave population in the colonial era. And just as northern whites readily adopted the ideology of black inferiority, much of the national debate over Missouri was less about abolition than it was about sustaining a political balance between southern and northern states. Northerners worried that adding another slave state, under the three-fifths clause, would offset the balance in favor of Slave Power. And Tallmadge's amendment threatened southerners for the same reason, and, perhaps more importantly, because it would have outlawed slavery in the state all together: the foundation of the southern social order. Even southerners who were mildly dissatisfied with slavery supported slavery in Missouri for reasons of diffusion. The argument was if slavery was further diffused throughout the region, it would be a long-term step towards abolition.[45]

The outcome of these debates was the Missouri Compromise: Missouri entered the Union as a slave state, slavery was banned north of the 36°30′ latitude, and Maine entered the United States as a free state. This solidified the state in Missouri as a producer of potentially capitalist space; in this case, capitalist slavery. But slavery in Missouri tended to be different than slavery in the deep south. While the centers of slavery, such as the Mississippi cotton industry, relied on large plantations, slavery in Missouri took on a smaller character. While, for example, the most slave intense parts of Louisiana, Alabama, Georgia, South Carolina, and Virginia had populations comprised of as much as 50 percent slaves, Missouri's slave population in 1850 was 12.9 percent. Additionally, the median average number of slaves owned that year was 20.6, but only 8.6 in Missouri, second only to Delaware.[46]

The highest concentration of slaves was in little Dixie. In contrast to the rest of the state, counties in this region contained slave populations ranging from 22 to 37 percent in 1860. And while some became large planters holding dozens of slaves, the average slaveowner in little Dixie held 6.1 slaves, as opposed to 12.7 overall, and 7.7 in the upper south.[47] Larger slaveowners focused on producing tobacco and hemp for the world market, in addition to the more commonly produced corn and livestock. Missouri tobacco made it as far as Europe, as did Missouri hemp which was made into bags and rope used to store and transport cotton.

But while slaveowning capitalists focused on producing for local, regional, and world markets, some small slaveowners functioned less in a capitalist manner than through a patriarchal household mode of production which incorporated slavery. Many immigrants to the region came from the upper south, and were slaveowners, or potential slaveowners, of limited wealth: plain folk rather than planters.[48] This was partly because of the climate. Cotton was difficult to grow in the region due to a relatively short growing season, discouraging large planters from immigrating to Missouri. And slaveowners may have been reluctant to transport their valuable commodities to a region surrounded by non-slave states, for fear of escape.[49]

Many of these yeomen small slaveowning farmers organized their relations into a patriarchal household mode of production that included slaves. Thus,

> the marriages and family lives created by many small slaveholders ... in many ways better resembled the experiences of yeomen farmers than of planters. Whether they lived in the low country of South Carolina, the Nanticoke Valley of New York, or the prairies of Sugar Creek, Illinois, antebellum farm families hoped to ensure the economic sustainability of their households before they heavily entered into the commercial marketplace.[50]

A household might own a slave, or even three or four slaves, and still focus on composite and safety-first farming, rather than something closer to "pure" capitalist farming. In other words, while the south was organized around capitalist slavery, not all slavery was necessarily capitalist. Yeomen slaveowners did produce for the market, selling tobacco, hemp, corn, wheat, and livestock down the river. And it was not unusual for profits from this market activity to be used to expand production, and perhaps even more slaves. Generally, the closer to the Missouri and Mississippi Rivers, the denser slavery became, and the degree of market production tended to increase. But many producers were less large-scale capitalists, although yeomen contained the potentiality to become so, then independent property owners, patriarchal household producers with a slave or two.[51]

Urbanization, industrialization, and incorporation into the world market

Missouri entered into the Union as a state becoming capitalist, in an empire becoming capitalist, in a world becoming capitalist. From the rise of industrial capitalism in the east, to the Santa Fe Trail, to the California gold rush, the state found itself in the middle of a capitalist transformation, and gradually deepened its own capitalist tendencies. And the capitalist revolution went along with revolutions in both communications and transport: most importantly, steam power, the telegraph, and railroads. Daniel Walker Howe's monumental study highlights the ways that these technological transformations opened up new avenues for the United States, although he neglects to discuss the ways that this "annihilation of space by time" takes on particular characteristics due to its capitalist organization.[52] As David Harvey discusses, capitalism is characterized by "time-space compression."[53] Capital has a tendency to produce capitalist space, and speed up time, and in American history the communication and transportation revolutions reflected this. Specifically, the technologies developed by capital and for capital sped up the pace of accumulation, and quickening this pace broke down previous spatial barriers to capital's circulation. This was also supported by the state which commodified and sold land along rational, grid patterns and invested in infrastructure to hasten flows of capital.

The most important example of this before the railroad was the steam engine. Steam power connected Missouri to New Orleans, and to the world market, hastening and deepening its integration into an increasingly capitalist world. Through articulations with the world market Missouri's own social relations were remade through these interconnected social processes operating at different levels. In other words, Missouri did not become capitalist due to its articulation in a broader world-system, nor because of relatively autonomous social transformation within the state, but because of the complex ways that these forces articulated through and transformed each other. The steam engine annihilated space by time by revolutionizing the pace in which commodities circulated up and down the Mississippi River. The steamboat industry itself was also organized along capitalist lines. Steamboat owners invested and operated for a profit, drawing surplus value from the many slaves and laborers who worked on the boats themselves.[54] The first steamboat docked in St. Louis in the summer of 1817, and two years later as many as thirty-one boats ran between Louisville and New Orleans. By the 1830s, much of Missouri was linked to the world market through commodity chains organized around networks of steam powered transportation. From the War of 1812 to this time, the prices of goods moving up river declined by 90 percent, and the prices of commodities such as sugar, coffee, and tea fell from half to 75 percent.[55] Steamboats deepened the market integration of much of the state as farmers and urban dwellers could more easily market their own goods, and more cheaply purchase commodities to improve their lives.

As steamboats and later railroads deepened Missouri's market relations, industrial development also began to take off, and by 1860 St. Louis was the country's eighth largest city, producing $27 million a year in manufactured goods.[56] The city developed a variety of industries including sugar refining, meat packing, beer brewing, soap making, candle making, and ironworks. At the same time, population increases meant that less good land was available for cultivation, particularly land near major commercial centers. As a response, families sent their boys and girls into the city to work. For instance, boys would be sent to work in brick plants, or girls to work as nursemaids or in kitchens. With new market opportunities, farmers also began to devote larger portions of production to the market. This is also reflected in that rural stores began to show a much greater diversity of goods sold, as products such as whiskey, butter, or candles that were previously produced at home were instead purchased.[57]

Just as the path of expansion led to the crisis over Missouri statehood, similarly, in 1854, the expansion of the American frontier, and debate over what social form it should take, erupted again with the Kansas-Nebraska Act. These tensions, of course, led to the Civil War. While it might be an overstatement to consider Missouri a fully capitalist political economy by this time, Missouri was on its way to becoming so. Capitalist industry was expanding, and a larger proportion of the population was finding itself drawn into both market relations and capitalist relations, particularly as younger generations moved to cities such as St. Louis to work, as the patriarchal mode of rural production became increasingly difficult to sustain, and became increasingly marketized.

Arkansas

In the sixteenth century the first Spaniards arrived under Hernando de Soto, who explored the greater region in search of wealth from 1539 to 1543.[58] And while some French *coureurs de bois* traversed the region, even starting a trading post in 1686, the first serious attempt at colonization came in 1720 after the territory was given to the *Compagnie d'Occident* in 1717, directed by Scottish financier John Law.[59] Less than a hundred white settlers went to Law's colony, which failed after he went bankrupt, but it started a process of settlement, built around the Arkansas post, which was the primary colonial settlement up to post-Louisiana Purchase American colonization.[60]

By 1814, the state had perhaps close to 1,600 people, but following the end of the War of 1812, as in much of the west, the colonizing population expanded greatly, to 14,273 by 1820, 1,613 of them slaves.[61] Through the 1810s, Arkansas territory was brought into what the Speaker of the House of Representatives Robert Bean called "this remote part of the American empire."[62] And as in the case of Missouri and other states, much of the early colonization was driven not by capitalism, but hunters and relatively self-sufficient patriarchal households. Early on, many settlers lived in a middle ground with Indians, often considered more "savage" than "white." Schoolcraft wrote, observing the region, "in manners, morals, customs, dress, contempt of labor and hospitality, the state of society is not essentially different from that which exists among the savages."[63] More generally, even decades later, Arkansas was plagued with a stereotype as a rough and lawless place. One traveler, for instance, said the state was populated by a "race of semi-barbarians" while others wrote of the lack of morality and law in the region.[64] This reputation was secured through, among other events, a fight that broke out in 1837 between the Speaker of the House John Wilson and State Representative Joseph J. Anthony in which Wilson killed Anthony with a knife on the House floor.[65]

The territory that became the state of Arkansas developed as a dual economy.[66] Frontier families and squatters came to find patriarchal independence, and although not as inviting as other southern climates, social relations were shaped around ecological relations as in the upcountry regions the land proved to be less fertile, but the climate healthier for poor settlers. In the low country, the land was swampy but more fertile, and with some work could be made into cotton growing country. More generally, antebellum Arkansas was a patriarchal social order, and patriarchy drove imperialism. Particularly for the planter class and elite, masculine honor was central to the social order.[67] Richard Slotkin argued that the history of American expansion is one of "regeneration through violence," and this could well be said of masculinity in Arkansas. Dueling was common practice, especially in the first decades of settlement. Violence, potential and actual, could be a method of masculine rejuvenation. In 1836, for example, planter and lawyer Absalom and his rival Albert Pike both put together private militias and demonstrated in Little

Rock, although neither took their armies to the frontier. More significantly, Pike, among others, organized companies to fight against Mexico in 1846 and joined Zachary Taylor's army in the battle of Buena Vista in 1847.[68] In this case, the war to expand the American frontier was, for the men involved, a personal quest to demonstrate one's masculinity and honor. As one traveler discovered, Arkansas was settled by

> *Gentlemen*, who had taken the liberty to imitate the signatures of other persons; *bankrupts*, who were not disposed to be plundered by their creditors; *homicides*, *horse-stealers*, and *gamblers*, all admired Arkansas on account of the very gentle and tolerant state of public opinion which prevailed there in regard to such fundamental points as religion, morals, and property.[69]

White-settler colonialism in Arkansas

To include Arkansas in white-settler colonization, the middle ground between natives and colonists was gradually undermined. This was due to forces from above and from below. On one side, the increasing white population pushed against native control of territory. On the other side, state Indian removal policies solidified the dispossession of natives through the 1820s and 1830s. By the end, Arkansas was left open to be incorporated into the white patriarchal American structure.

Throughout the 1820s tensions remained between the state, native populations, and white settlers. For example, in one case the government tried to remove several thousand settlers from territory the latter believed was public domain but in which the government had decided (although quickly to renege) would be granted to the natives. The settlers resisted, as in one observed case in 1825,

> about two hundred men assembled at Inglish's for the purpose of making an attack on this post, the principle ringleaders, so far as I can learn, were William Brice, John Bowman and a man by the name of Pennington; I am not much versed in the law, but I should think, that it would at least, amount to an attempt to levy war against the United States, for which those three persons should be prosecuted.[70]

While the Quapaws had traditionally held the territory, Indian removal further east had pushed other Indian groups into Arkansas, including the Osages and Cherokee. As whites pushed forward, in 1816 Governor James Clark from Missouri sent representatives to warn settlers against infringing on Quapaw land. But by 1818, both politicians and settlers were increasingly in favor of removing them altogether. That summer, the Quapaw signed an alliance in which it was recognized they owned 2 million acres of land. In exchange, they gave up rights to 30 million acres that they had previously used as hunting land. Seven years later the Quapaw were fully removed to Oklahoma.[71]

The Cherokee had also been pushed into the region. They were known as the most supposedly "civilized" of the native groups, having, for example, encouraged Protestant missionaries to set up a mission, the first school in Arkansas, in 1820. Many claimed to be Christian, and additionally they wore white style clothing, a significant portion had white blood, and some even owned slaves. They also had law, police, and courts.[72] In this sense, they were the "whitest" of the Indians, but they never reached a status of honorary white to the extent that they would be free from the expanding white colonization process. In 1828, they too were pushed into Oklahoma.

Through this period the Cherokee and Osages continued to battle. In 1817, for instance, the Cherokees killed sixty-nine Osages, and took 100 prisoners after the Battle of Claremore Mound. Conflict between natives also posed a threat to the stability of the white man's country, as did conflict between natives and settlers, for example, Osages occasionally attacked white hunters. But before and during the 1830s, Arkansas was effectively cleared of Indians as the Creek, Choctaw, Cherokee, and Seminole were all forced into present day Oklahoma, along with the Osages and Quapaw.[73]

Cleared of natives, Arkansas provided a space for immigrants to settle. The majority of settlers came from the south, three-quarters from Tennessee, Missouri, Kentucky, and Mississippi before 1850. After 1850, particularly as the Arkansas slave plantation cotton boom began to take off, a higher proportion of settlers came from states such as Georgia and Alabama. Generally, these settlers went to the low country to produce for a profit, in contrast to earlier settlers from the upper south who tended to come more to pursue independence rather than profits. In general, by the end of the 1850s, the population was evenly divided between upland and lowland, with the lowland population surpassing the upland in approximately 1858.[74] This was also pushed by relatively easy land laws. In 1840 the Arkansas Land Donation Act promised land to anyone who agreed to pay taxes in the future. And the homestead laws put in place the next decade provided settlers with 160 acres per family member, not just per head of family.[75]

Sojourning through the territory in the 1840s, G.W. Featherstonhaugh found a scattered society of log cabins and dirty, uncivilized people which clashed with his British and northeastern American ideals of social life. The women of the country, for instance, lacked femininity. In one case, "On going into the house we were made acquainted with a person called Mrs. Meriwether, but who from her great height, which was six feet two inches, an extraordinary dark, bony, hairy face, and trimmings to match, I should have taken for some South American grenadier in women's clothes."[76] Her husband, said to be one of the earliest settlers in the territory, "got along as well as he could by hunting, and trading, and raising a patch of corn."[77] Elsewhere, he came across a settler who "was a squalid, half-negro looking, piratical ruffian from Louisiana, living in a wretched, filthy cabin, with a wife to match, and a Caliban-looking negress and her two children, who were his slaves."[78] And in another case,

> Mr. Barkman we did not see, but I shall certainly not forget his lady soon, as I have never seen any one, as far as manners and exterior went, with less pretensions to be classed within the feminine gender … She chewed tobacco, she smoked a pipe, she drank whiskey, and cursed and swore as heartily as any backwoodsman, all at the same time.[79]

These frontier settlers lacked standards of civilized cleanliness as he

> found the Judge living in one of the most dirty and unprovided holes we had yet got into, in addition to which his children and himself too were just recovering from the malaria. I pitied them, for, bred up in dirt, it was evident they knew not what cleanliness meant.[80]

In the dual society, most yeomen and small planters went to live in the cheaper, less fertile, but healthier climates of the upcountry. "The settler in these wild countries plants to live, and not to take to market."[81] Far from the market,

> These worthy people think, if you are not looking for land to settle, that you must be pedlars: there are no markets or shopkeepers in the

> country for them to go to, and therefore the markets come to them—pedlars to sell goods, and tailors to cut out and make new clothes.[82]

The Ozarks, for example, developed a reputation as a land of "hill folks." Up until 1828 the Ozark region was formally in the hands of the Cherokee, but some whites had settled by then. After the Cherokees were removed, whites flooded in, so by 1840 around 20,000 people lived there, including some slaves, such as 1,515 in the most populous area, Washington County. As many as half of these came from Tennessee, and perhaps 20 percent from Missouri.[83]

Settlers also clashed with speculators who saw "the agency of the almighty dollar, a superabundance of which being a substitute for other virtues, stands in place of all distinction. Wealth, therefore, since it implies virtue of every imaginable kind, must be had at any cost."[84] Those who saw the land as a space of profit clashed with those who viewed it as useful, and preemptively squatted on the land. Settlers, for example, outbid settlers for land—even on that which they had already settled and improved—and after bidding up the value, delayed payment so that the value of the land decreased to low government rates at which they purchased it before the settlers could.

According to Brooks Blevins, the census of 1840 reveals a society of mostly self-sufficient farmers. They owned horses, mules, cattle, sheep, and hogs, and grew small amounts of wheat, oats, tobacco, and cotton beside their main staple, corn. For example, that year farmers grew 1,105,652 bushels of corn, and only 59,618 pounds of tobacco and 133 bales of cotton. As time went on, these farmers tended to deepen their market interactions, as did slaveowners who, although a minority, did produce for profit. For instance, in 1859 the Ozarks produced 450,000 pounds of tobacco, and in 1860 produced 75,000 cattle, 190,000 hogs, 56,000 sheep, and 30,000 mules and horses.[85] Overall, this suggests that between 1840 and 1860 the degree of market integration in the region greatly increased, as larger amounts of agriculture and livestock were produced to supplement family and kinship relations of production.

By 1860, according to census tax records, about 10 percent of the population was dispossessed, 70 percent yeomen (owning 80 acres and a small amount of livestock), 17 percent slaveholding yeomen, and 3 percent large planters. About 10 percent of the population controlled 70 percent of the taxable wealth.[86] Arkansas yeomen lived similarly to yeomen elsewhere in the country, organized in a way in which, as one author puts it, "women had no political rights, and educational and occupational opportunities outside the home were almost nonexistent."[87] And like settlers elsewhere, most started by building a one-room log cabin, to which they gradually tended to expand, for example, adding second rooms for sleeping or cooking. Overall, yeoman life was organized into a patriarchal household mode of social reproduction.

Slavery and capitalist development in Arkansas

The most significant element of antebellum capitalist development in Arkansas occurred during the last two decades before the Civil War when, increasingly, settlers migrated from the lower south to the Arkansas low country to reproduce the plantation slavery system of the black belts of the old south. Slavery in the territory went back to the French colonial era and by 1798, 56 slaves lived amongst 393 people in total. It picked up in the twenty years before the Civil War, and by 1860, 111,115, or 26 percent of the population, were slaves.[88]

Arkansas' slave code was legislated in 1837, a year after statehood was gained. It drew from regulations in the territorial era, along with slave codes from other southern states.[89] As throughout the plantation south, slaves were restricted in virtually all aspects of social life. Of course, the slave code represented the problem of slave capital: black slaves were both capital and human. Much of the code restricted their movement, as, like elsewhere, slaves were prone to resist their masters and, in some cases, run away. In other cases, slaves attacked and killed their masters. J.W. Calvert, for example, had a brother murdered by a slave named Matilda. And, to take another example, as Donald McNeilly notes, the *Arkansas State Gazette* discussed a Mr. Henry Yerby who was killed by two of his slaves.[90]

But most slaves likely saw large-scale rebellion as futile, and instead opted to try and make the best of their conditions by obtaining concessions from their masters. Slaves insisted on masters providing for their basic needs of proper food and shelter, and beyond this challenged their master's discipline by, for instance, slowing down and controlling the pace of work. They also complained of cruel overseers, under which they lowered their rate of production. And they negotiated free time to work on their own gardens, tend livestock, hunt and fish, and even marry and build families, as much as they could, given constraints. Slaves bargained for rights to visit their spouses (not legally sanctioned) on other nearby plantations, and developed kinship relations both within and between plantations.[91] But because Arkansas was new to slave culture, many families were ripped apart as slaves were brought to the territory, and so, it is likely that the nuclear slave family was less common in Arkansas than elsewhere.[92]

As in Missouri, in some parts of the state slaves were owned more by yeomen farmers than big planters. In these cases, slaves were incorporated into the patriarchal mode of production. For instance, Hardy Banks who lived in Yell County owned four slaves, who worked alongside his wife and two boys. They produced mainly for the household, while growing small amounts of cotton to supplement this mode of life, and occasionally selling horses on the market.[93] Most slavery in the state, though, came in the late antebellum period with the slave population doubling between 1850 and 1860.

Plantation slavery in Arkansas developed around two primary regions: the eastern part of the state on the Mississippi River, and by the Red River in the southwest, although it also developed to a lesser degree elsewhere. Overall, the amount of cotton production increased from 6 million pounds in 1840 to close to 150 million by 1860.[94] Slaves often were the first to work on raw land, and in doing so it was slaves that remade the ecological conditions for expansion by clearing the land and preparing it for cultivation.[95] And, as elsewhere in the cotton kingdom, masters tended to organize their slaves into gangs, although most plantations also assigned some proportion of slaves to task labor, as most plantations contained some variation of both forms of labor discipline.

By the Civil War, capitalism was gradually developing in Arkansas, with capitalist plantation slavery taking the lead, but overall much of the state was in the hands of yeomen farmers gradually in the process of integrating more deeply into market relations. In particular, in the decade before the war, capitalist development in the state greatly accelerated with, for example, the monetary value of farms rising six times. But industrial development was slow to take off. By this time, only Oregon had less railroad than Arkansas. Manufacturing was valued at a total of $3 million, well behind states with urban industrial centers, such as St. Louis, Missouri. This may be in part because the institutional infrastructure necessary for capitalist development was also lacking in Arkansas. The only significant attempt to build a stable banking system took place in the 1830s. After a legislative meeting in 1836, lawmakers agreed to start both a state bank and a real estate bank. The state bank would hold state funds, print money, sell bonds, and give loans to promote business development. The real estate bank was designed also to promote capital accumulation by selling bonds, and by selling stock to be purchased with land or crops. Shareholders could use this stock to borrow up to one-half the share value. But these banks failed for a variety of reasons. First, corruption was rampant as large loans were, in some cases, given out even higher than the overall value of borrowers' assets. More importantly, following the crisis of 1837, which reached Arkansas by 1839, land and crop prices dramatically dropped and the banks soon closed. Following this, the legislature amended the state constitution to disallow the state from incorporating banks.[96]

Without a banking system, Arkansas capitalists had little credit to draw on for capitalist development. In addition to banking, the state did little to promote public works. The state did sponsor geological surveys with the explicit goal of locating resources that could profitably be invested in:

> But in how great an abundance these may be found and how profitably the capitalist may invest his means for their development, can only be determined and made known in a manner to command the confidence of the public at home and abroad, and by a careful survey by the state.[97]

Arkansas did pass a public roads act in 1836, requisitioning men to work twelve days a year for the state building roads and bridges, and putting signs at crossings. But it appears that this act was never taken seriously. And education in Arkansas was also well behind other states, and the state did not have a university until after the Civil War.[98] Overall, by 1860, capitalist development had occurred around the plantation slavery regions of the state, and market incorporation was increasing in pace elsewhere, but Arkansas still had some way to go before it might be considered "fully" capitalist. Meanwhile, other white colonialists were bypassing Arkansas for Texas.

White colonization in Texas

In 1844, Sam Houston, President of Texas, speaking to state congress, said, "the Pacific alone will bound the mighty march of our race and our empire."[99] And in 1863, E.H. Cushing wrote, "Texas is an empire in itself."[100] Texas, from the early age of white-settler colonialism through its integration into the United States, was viewed by locals as an empire, or an empire within an empire.

As with much of the country, the territory that became the state of Texas was populated by natives, then later incorporated, to some degree, into the Spanish Empire. By 1519 the Spanish made it to the coast of Texas, and by 1528 they made the first recorded contact with the natives.[101] As with most Spanish colonization, the goal of Spanish imperialists was to conquer rather than colonize. Missionaries gradually made their way up through Mexico to Texas, as did adventurers in search of riches, but by the 1821 census—the year of Mexican independence—Texas had a little over 3,000 settlers.[102] Of course, the natives had lived in Texas for centuries. By the time the Spanish arrived, the Apaches, Wichitas, Caddos, Tonkawas, and Karankawas were all in Texas, and around 1700 the Comanches also migrated there.[103] Each of these groups also had their own modes of living, complicating any potential idea of an "Indian mode of production."[104] While some groups were more itinerant, Wichitas and Caddos, for example, were productive farmers, raised mules and horses, and produced hides and jerky from buffalo. Native groups also regularly traded with each other, recirculating corn, clothes, and animals between groups that had excesses or lacks.

As elsewhere, natives were also devastated by European diseases. For instance, while there were an estimated 40,000 Comanches in the 1780s, by the 1840s there were perhaps 12,000. Overall, in 1820, approximately 30,000 natives lived in Texas.[105] Additionally, as the American frontier expanded to the west, natives from the east were also pushed into Texas territory. As Gary Clayton Anderson summarizes it:

> Texas soon became a place like no other in North America. Its lands harbored a growing Indian ethnic milieu after 1820. Pressing from the east were Anglo-Americans, mingling with a few Tejano inhabitants who remained. Crossing into Texas from Arkansas were immigrant Indians possessing many of the same hopes and desires as their southern Anglo counterparts. To the west and in central Texas were Comanches, Wichitas, and Caddos concerned about their homeland and prepared to defend it. And in the south, mostly, were pockets of Tejanos ... hoping without much hope to reestablish a prosperous Texas.[106]

On March 21, 1801, the Spanish killed an American adventurer named Philip Nolan. Initially with Spanish approval, Nolan ventured into Texas to collect wild horses to sell in the New Orleans market. Following his initial explorations, in 1800 Nolan visited at the time of Vice President Thomas Jefferson, after which the Spanish removed approval fearing that, with Jefferson's support, Nolan may have been planning for conquest for the United States. Nolan returned to Texas anyway, but was killed around what is today Blum, Texas.[107] Nolan was the first recorded American adventurer in Texas, setting the basis for American advance into the territory and the violence this created.

By the start of the 1820s, independent Mexico, controlling the lightly populated territory of Texas, began to allow white settlers into Texas under the *empresario* system. *Empresarios* were given land by the state, with the agreement that they would bring hundreds of settlers, loyal to Mexico, and formally (although not in practice) Catholic, to settle. This would set the basis for what Fehrenback calls "folk imperialism."[108] Bottom-up white-settler folk imperialism, rather than the monarchical imperialism of the Spanish, would be the driving force behind the white colonization of Texas. It was eventually incorporated into the United States when folk imperialism, linked with the democratic imperialism of James K. Polk, came together in empire building from the bottom up and top down.

The most well-known and influential *empresario* was Stephen Austin. Austin's father, Moses Austin, a leader of the development of the Missouri mining industry at Mine á Breton, was ruined by the economic depression of 1819. Picking up his feet, Moses traveled to Béxar in the fall of 1820. Austin arranged a meeting with the governor, and, upon admitting he was American, the governor, wary of American filibusters, told Austin to leave that night or be arrested, regardless of the fact that Austin had Spanish citizenship papers. But by chance, after leaving the meeting, Austin ran into an old friend: Baron de Bastrop. With Bastrop's influence, Austin was able to obtain *empresario* rights in Texas, based on the idea that, given the lack of Spanish and Mexican colonization, and the native threat, Americans loyal to the Spanish Crown might provide a buffer.[109]

But Moses Austin died at the beginning of 1821, never living to see his project flourish. It was taken up by his son Stephen, who was a businessman, and there is no doubt that part of his motivation was to acquire a profit from the *empresario*. He quickly received hundreds of requests for white settlement on the land; 297 grants were given, in some cases to farmers, in other cases to potential plantation owners seeking after a profit. Austin's colony tended to discourage settlement by rugged frontiersmen, instead bringing over middle and upper class whites in search of cheap land and profits. By 1825 Austin's colony had 1,347 whites and 443 slaves.[110]

Following the Mexican Revolution, Mexico continued to grant *empresarios* to American settlers. In 1822, for example, under the leadership of Robert Leftwich, the Texas Association was formed. The association itself tended to be comprised of doctors, lawyers, and merchants, rather than the farmers and artisans of Austin's grant. Many of those involved were interested in profits from speculation, rather than settlement, seen in that, by 1830, only six out of seventy who had signed on to the association went to Texas.[111] Overall, from 1823 to 1835, forty-one *empresarios* were granted with Mexico, although not all succeeded. This was also made possible by the Colonization Law of 1824, which was removed six years later as tensions between Mexico and white American settlers developed.[112]

Violence, dispossession, and the Republic of Texas

In 1835–36 colonists struggled against the government of Mexico, and in victory established the decade-long Republic of Texas. This came after fifteen years of policy changes, coups, and transitions within the Mexican government that had implications for the settlement of Texas. The direct causes of the Texas Revolution itself were multiple, including taxes and political control. One of the issues involved, also, was the question of slavery. As one author puts it, "the Mexican leaders found it extremely difficult to choose between the revolutionary ideal of liberty and the practical need to protect property interests and encourage settlement of their nation."[113] In other words, while Mexican authorities were critical of slavery, their policies vacillated from banning it to allowing it to grow with hesitation, and even during periods in which legal authority went against it, colonists found ways to circumvent the law.

The first Colonization Law was passed in January of 1823.[114] Article 30 of the law stated that slaves brought into the territory may not be bought or sold, and children, at the age of 14, would be set free. This law was annulled the next month after Emperor Iturbide was removed from power, but under a new government in August of 1824 a new Colonization Law was passed, followed by a new constitution. While this law did not discuss slavery, tacitly allowing it, the debate over slavery in Texas was not over. In 1827, for example, a law was put forward in which no one would be born a slave, and after six months, the introduction of slaves was illegal. Settlers responded by continuing to bring slaves into Texas, but making a legal change, calling them indentured servants rather than slaves. In other words, simply by altering the wording, the institution continued to grow.[115]

On April 6 of 1830, under President Bustamante, Mexico issued a decree against allowing further immigration from the United States. This would stop settlers from coming in who were, as Mexico saw it, violating the Colonization Law. It was also a key moment in drawing further support away from Mexico towards rebellion against Mexico. In addition to banning immigration, the law called for duties and troop garrisons in Texas, and American-Texans were resistant to Mexican tax collection from the start. They began to hold conventions to repeal the laws. Finally, in January 1835, under President Santa Anna, soldiers went to Galveston Bay to support duty collection. With tensions continuing to rise, in October of that year fighting finally broke out as Texans argued war was the only way to defend the rights of the white-settler colonists.[116]

The revolution against Mexico created the space for the development of capitalism in Texas in several ways. First, it legalized slavery, and plantation slavery became the leading force of capitalist development in Texas. Secondly, on a more general level, the state that formed after the revolution put in place a legal and institutional regime, led by merchant capitalists that allowed for the commodification of land and expansion of capitalist social property relations. The American dominated Texas also set the basis for the dispossession of Tejanos. David Montejano notes that along the Rio Grande in the mid-nineteenth century, the Tejano social structure was organized around patriarchal lines with landlords at the top. Land was owned according to ancestry and family, rather than individually. In this sense, the social order was not organized around profit, but the reproduction of hierarchical kinship-based social relations. Starting before, and continuing after the Civil War, American merchants and lawyers worked to dispossess the Tejanos through fraud and coercion. For instance, the state taxed land grants, and when the grant holder could not pay, the sheriff sold a portion of the land to cover the debt. In other cases, the Mexicans were simply pushed out through force.[117] On top of this, dozens of Mexicans were killed by gangs of white settlers on, for example, the San Antonio-Goliad highway where they worked transporting freight, with the state unwilling to arrest anyone.

The incorporation of Texas into the American Empire also spurred debate regarding slavery, race, and empire. As one commentator put it, the "Addition of slave territory at the south-west has been our '*Course of Empire*.'"[118] Thus,

> The American race was planted in the western world not merely to clear forests, dig canals, construct railroads, plant cotton, grow sugar and amass wealth. For higher and nobler objects were, we fondly hope, the foundations of this vast empire laid. To hold up to the world the spectacle of a great, free self-governed country, bearing for its motto equality and justice, a refuge for the oppressed of the old world, a warning to tyrants, and an incitement for the brave and good of every age.[119]

For those opposing expansion, "Who will wish again to curtail the limits of this great republican empire, and again to dismember the glorious valley of the West?"[120]

Some of those opposed to slavery saw the incorporation of Texas into the United States as being fundamentally about the perpetuation of slavery. Benjamin Lundy, for instance, said:

> *It is susceptible of the clearest demonstration, that the immediate cause, and the leading object of this contest, originated in a settled design, among the slaveholders of this country, (with land speculators and slave-traders,) to wrest the large and valuable territory of Texas from the Mexican Republic, in order to re-establish the* SYSTEM OF SLAVERY; *to open a vast and profitable* SLAVE MARKET *therein; and ultimately to annex it to the United States.*[121]

And another commentator said, "The veil is rent, and fortunately rent in time—Texas is to be annexed, for the sole and only object of perpetuating slavery."[122] Orville Dewey also wrote,

> What is the precise question before us? Not whether it is right to hold the slaves we have, but whether it is right to accept as a component part of our social and political State, another body of slaves. Not whether it

> is right to adhere to a compact with regard to slavery already existing, but whether it is right to legalize slavery anew.[123]

The roots of the war itself were also seen in racial terms as "it was, thus, reserved for the Mexicans, whose blood is mixed with that of an Arab ancestry, to exhibit the spectacle of continual domestic broils, and, latterly of a positive warfare against a nation whose friendly hand was the first to summon them into the pale of national independence."[124] This contrasted with Americans as "such a country naturally attracted the attention of the people of the United States, numbers of whom are always ready, with the adventurous spirit that characterises our race, to seek new lands and improve their fortunes by emigrating from the crowded places of their birth."[125] In this regard, white Americans were to build a new, more racially pure empire as "it was left for the Anglo-American inhabitants of the Western Continent to furnish a new mode of enlarging the bounds of empire, by the more natural tendency and operation of the principles of their free government."[126]

Finally, it was said,

> That Texas would add much to the geographical perfection of this Republican Empire, is certain; that it is a great and valuable country no less true; that it is likely to consitute a part of this Union, at a future day, may easily be believed; but a little reflection will show, that its *immediate* annexation as a slave State, will of necessity and rapidly revolutionize the commercial condition of the present slave States, and tend to impoverish them.[127]

This was on top of the more general ethnic cleansing of Texas away from native peoples, a war that lasted half a century until the Comanches and Kiowas were defeated in 1874–75. Overall, it was through this use of violence that white settlers could continue to flood into the state as the population boomed from tens of thousands in the 1830s to 160,000 by 1845, and 600,000 on the eve of the Civil War.[128]

Slavery and yeomen in Texas

By the time of the Civil War, Texas was a society with capitalism on its way to becoming a capitalist society. While still very much a territory of yeomen, this class was increasingly pulled into market relations and, at the same time, plantation capitalism spread from the lower south into Texas.

By 1860, few whites lived beyond the eastern two-fifths of the state. And within this section of Texas, different settlement patterns shaped around different ecological conditions. Lowe and Campbell, for example, delineate four social-ecological zones. In the east, hilly uplands and mixed forests prevailed. On the southeast coast, rich alluvial soil predominated. West of this were more prairie and planes with less rainfall, and in the north was the drier and cooler region of prairie counties.[129] And like elsewhere in the south, social relations and land prices formed around these ecological conditions. Along the coast and in the more fertile eastern regions, for example, most of the plantation slave population lived, whereas in the drier northern regions, yeomen predominated and slaveholding was much less common.

In Texas about one-third of all farmers owned slaves on the verge of the Civil War, and within this only a small portion could consider themselves planters. For example, 11.2 percent of the farm population controlled over $10,000 in personal wealth, or 64.4 percent. And within that, 8 percent of the population controlled 55.1 percent of the wealth.[130] Texas plantation owners migrated primarily from the lower south, and went into the state in search of cheap land and profits generated from surplus value produced by black slaves. Most slaves likely immigrated with their owners, but some came in through the slave market. Cities such as Houston and Galveston, similar to cities in Louisiana, developed permanent slave marts and auctions, and a mayor of Galveston named J.P. Sydnor was even a commission merchant and auctioneer himself.[131]

Slave life on a Texas plantation was no different from plantations throughout the south. Slaveowners acted to reproduce the value of their slave capital and profit from the labor of slaves through the management of the plantations. Slaves were seen as lazy, childlike, and in need of supervision. One plantation owner, for instance, on his instructions to overseers, wrote, "Negroes lack the motive of self-interest to make them careful & diligent, hence the necessity of great patience in the management of them."[132] In other words, slaves did not naturally act in their own self-interest to maximize their market conditions, as neoclassical economic theory suggests all humans do, but had to be forced to understand self-interest through careful management and, if needed, the whip. Capitalist time discipline and work habits had to be imposed with violence. As elsewhere, slaves tried to build lives and families in the conditions they were forced into. And class struggle also shaped the social relations on plantations as, if pushed too hard, slaves would fight back or flee. Most slaves were expected to work five and a half days per week, from sunrise to sunset. On some plantations slaves were given their own plots of land to garden, and even, with the master's permission, allowed, in some cases, to sell their produce on the market.[133]

Before the Civil War slavery in Texas was profitable and expanding. In 1846, Texas had 30,505 slaves. By 1860 that number was, according to tax roll data, 160,467, or 182,556 by census data. Even in the five years before the Civil War the slave population increased by 50 percent, as slavery was not a static or frozen system, but an expanding, dynamic one. Overall, between 1850 and 1860, the slave population increased by 200 percent. It was also profitable. Through Texas' slave era, the price continued to increase even as the population did; the average price rose from approximately $345 in 1843 to $765 by the start of the war. And it was not unusual for even small slaveowners to receive a 6 percent average return on their investment, with relatively higher rates tending to go to larger slaveowners; those with over fifty slaves averaged as much as 12.35 percent by 1860.[134]

Slave productivity also tended to rise in this era, as larger amounts of relative surplus value were extracted from the energy of slaves. For example, between 1850 and 1860 productivity in the cotton industry (bales of cotton produced per slave) rose significantly, from 1.2 bales per slave to 2.52 bales, or 110 percent. This was also divided by scale, as smaller farmers averaged a 77 percent increase, and owners of 20–49 slaves 141 percent.[135] In general, slavery was a dynamic, productive, expanding mode of capitalist production, which would have continued to spread west had it not been for the Civil War. Slavery also persisted due to the lack of wage labor. "We have employed both slave and free labor, and are well satisfied that, where it can be procured, the latter is decidedly cheaper to the small farmer than the former. The only drawback is the extreme scarcity of the latter."[136]

But, as noted, two-thirds of families did not own slaves. And even a portion of those who did owned very few. Thus, "during the whole antebellum era Texas was still a log cabin frontier."[137] Another early settler wrote of traveling across Texas and finding scattered settlements. In some cases, families combined their efforts to organize their travel and early communities, as for example, "on our arrival at the settlement we found five or six families … they were engaged in building cabins."[138]

Not all came as families though, as the immigrant records soon after coming across several men: "none of them had any white family, Wilson had a few negroes."[139] Another commentator noted,

> it must be conceded that the most independent station in life is that of the man who is free from debt, and who owns the soil that he cultivates. Trade may desert a man, money may take to itself wings, and the most accomplished financier may fail: but the attentive farmer, on the rich lands of Texas, will indeed seldom, if ever, fail to produce a sufficiency to serve the purposes of his family.[140]

And one advertiser suggested: "A competency may be easily acquired; and affluence is at the command of those who aspire to it. He who keeps his speculations within a laudable compass, cannot fail, ultimately, of rising to independence and wealth."[141] These settlers were also seen as inferior to the whit*er* whites back east, for instance,

> But it sometimes happens that a white man from the *States*, who has become some what decivilized, (to coin a word,) is substituted. The dress of these hunters is usually of deer-skin; hence the appropriate name of *Leather Stocking*. Their generic name, for they form a distinct class, is *Frontiers-men*.[142]

Early settlers lived in dog-run wood cabins (generally with two rooms connected by a covered corridor) and produced little beyond subsistence. Mary Rabb, one of Austin's original 300, provides a clear example of early white-settler life. She left with her husband and baby from Arkansas in October 1823, bringing along over a dozen cattle and six horses, although some of the animals did not survive the trip. With local help, John Rabb built a log house in a week, their first house in Texas. They began to work to clear the land, but after conflicts with natives, decided to look elsewhere. Later they settled near Bernard River, and built another house, growing corn, raising livestock, and living little beyond subsistence. As early as April 1826, Mary Rabb records her husband selling corn in Brazos, but, as was the case with the patriarchal household mode of life, the Rabbs practiced safety-first agriculture.[143]

Mary Helm, whose husband founded Matagorda, Texas, in 1829, tells a similar story. What exchange did occur in this mode of living was not about profit, but taking care of basic needs. Helm records, for example, trading five cows and calves for hewed logs they could use to build their home. She also notes that, with little money in circulation, cows served as a form of currency, with one cow and calf equaling about $10.[144] Mathilda Wagner's story, part of the German immigration, is also similar. Her family settled in Texas where the local men contributed their labor by constructing a two-room home. The division of labor was structured around kinship and gender with the community, more broadly, contributing to larger scale tasks such as raising a house. Her father cleared the land and farmed, while the women made clothes, prepared food, and did other household tasks. Practically everything was produced in the household. Wagner notes, for example, that there were shoemakers in Fredericksburg, but often yeomen and their families went barefoot or crafted their own shoes: most could not afford to purchase such a luxury.[145]

While a small amount of sugar was produced in antebellum Texas, the primary crop Texan plantation owners grew for the market was cotton. Additionally, between 1850 and 1860 it appears that an increasing portion of farmers were producing cotton, suggesting that market integration was deepening, even for small farmers, in the decade before the Civil War. For instance, while in 1850 around three-quarters of the farm population grew no cotton, a decade later 60 percent did not. This suggests that, overall, Texans were increasingly participating in market activity. That being said, 90 percent of cotton was grown by that one-third of the population owning slaves, suggesting that, as throughout the south, plantation slavery was the vanguard of capitalism, and many yeomen farmers were yet to be dominated by the law of value.[146]

By the middle of the 1800s visions of empire—whether it be one of capitalist slavery or patriarchal competency—drove white settlers across the southern section of North America. But as a different form of capitalism began to dominate in the north, and as the northwest and northeast deepened their economic relations, so different views as to the shape of empire began to take hold of the American imagination. And up until the eve of the Civil War it was not the weakness of slavery that was the issue at hand, as has been suggested, but its strength.[147] Slavery was a dynamic, expanding form of capitalism that sought out more room to generate profits. And, as the next chapter will discuss, it was tensions over empire's form that led to the Civil War.

6
The Consolidation of American Capitalism

Up to this point, this book has charted a pathway of the uneven development of American Empire gradually transforming from a society with capitalism into a capitalist society. It has traced an interpretation of this story by focusing on the histories of settlement and development in particular states. This chapter moves forward to attempt to locate the moments in which capitalism and expansion converged in space and time and deepened their relationship. This chapter, in this regard, moves to a broader level of abstraction to link the particular uneven history of development into a broader picture. I do so by arguing that the period from approximately the 1850s to 1870s was an era of the consolidation of American capitalism. To say that capitalism consolidated does not mean that the society emerging out of the Civil War and Reconstruction was "purely" capitalist. Rather, by consolidation I mean the national imperial order was remade in a way that essentially meant that capitalism would fundamentally dominate American society and, most significantly for the purposes of this book, expansion itself would be driven primarily by the power of capital.

To present this argument, the chapter explores several main themes. First, it examines the extent to which, in a general sense, by 1860, the United States was becoming an increasingly capitalist country. Secondly, it looks at the relation between these developments and the origins of the Civil War. Here I argue that it was not a division between northern capitalism and southern non-capitalism that the war was rooted in, but competing pathways of capitalist imperialism: one in slave capitalist form, the other in an increasingly industrial capitalist form, linked with the northwest of the country's agrarian and increasingly capitalist development.[1] It was, then, a war over the form the American frontier would take. Third, the chapter looks at Reconstruction. To answer the question: was the Civil War a bourgeois (or capitalist) revolution(?), it is necessary not to focus just on the causes of the war but, more importantly, the results: how did the war, and the remaking of social and political relations across the country, set the basis for further capitalist development? Finally, I end the chapter by looking at the new south, and the ways that it was restructured in order to fit into an expanding capitalist state dominated by the increasingly industrial capitalist north.

Late-antebellum capitalism

Capitalism is a system of labor control. It is experienced personally, as workers labor under bosses who command them, and abstractly, as forces of price dictate what workers might, or might not, decide to spend their money on, and linked to a broader chain of valuation stretching to fluctuating abstract valuations on a global scale. Either way, the uniqueness of capitalist relations of production stems not simply from market relations, but the ways that social relations are organized and articulated through market relations. By 1860, these relations were coming to define the American north. While, as discussed, southern capitalist slavery continued to expand west, into Texas and elsewhere, in the north capitalism was both expanding and deepening, and taking on an increasingly industrial form.

This is seen in the making of an American labor market. Between 1800 and 1860, the percentage of wage workers as a part of the total labor force (the south included) rose from around 12 to 40 percent.[2] At the same time, the population laboring in agriculture declined from perhaps 75–83 to 52–55 percent, give or take, depending on the estimate.[3] Thus, the antebellum era was also the epoch of the "initial proletarianization" of the United States.[4] This trend continued after the war, with one estimate suggesting that by 1870 as many as 67 percent of American workers were fully market dependent laborers.[5]

As Norman Ware discussed in the 1920s, and "new" labor historians would later emphasize, the making of the American working class was a story in which a rising capitalist system stripped workers of control of the means of production, and pressed upon them an alien capitalist force, in which new forms of abstract value production structured into, and ruled over, the practices of everyday life.[6] Artisans spoke in terms of prices rather than wages; in other words, it was not their labor power that was valued but the products they produced.[7] And "journeymen subscribed to traditional conceptions of social improvement. As late as midcentury, they spoke alternatively of achieving independence or securing competencies, not of the constant accumulation of wealth."[8] Many early labor organizations, termed "associations" and "societies," were reflective of the pressures of this social—capitalist—revolution as artisans organized to hold on to the rights they had to control their own labor against the rising pressures of an emerging capitalist order.[9]

While journeyman strikes, called "turn outs," occurred in the colonial period, the first continuous organization of wage workers appears to be the Federal Society of Journeymen Cordwainers which started in Philadelphia in 1794. And the first general trade union that brought different craftsworkers together seems to be the Mechanics' Union of Trade Associations, also in Philadelphia.[10] Using a type of labor theory of value, the association did not engage in union politics in the sense of battling over labor's share of the profits, for example, but, "they thought of themselves as the real producers, in contrast to the emerging parasitic capitalists who neither toiled nor benefited society."[11] Many of these early labor organizations represented a response to the rising pressures of capitalism and the desire of workers to hold on to control over their labor and lives. Labor leader Thomas Skidmore, for example, criticized the rising capitalist order, arguing, "whoever looks at the world as it is now is, will see it divided into two distinct classes; proprietors and non-proprietors; those who own the world, and those who own no part of it."[12] For Skidmore, the solution was to redivide property so that "then will everyone understand that he has full liberty to use the materials of which, during his life-time, he is the master, in such a manner as, in his judgment, shall promote his own happiness."[13] Rather than a world of capital and labor, then, for Skidmore, among others, the ideal world to fight over, as workers of this era did, was one in which the worker was his own master (and, given the patriarchy of the time, perhaps also master of wife and children).

As David Montgomery discusses, the desire of workers to control the organization of production continued through the industrial era. Workers in the Columbus Iron Works in Ohio, in the mid-1870s, for instance, organized their labor around a moral code in which "those who held fast to the carefully measured stint, despite the curses of their employers and the lure of higher earnings, depicted themselves as sober and trustworthy masters of their trades. Unlimited output led to slashed piece rates, irregular employment, drink, and debauchery, they argued."[14] But over time, workers gradually lost control to capital, as bosses and managers organized the rhythms of labor, rather than workers. Thus, to make a relatively reliable working class, capital had to remake the culture of labor.[15] This also entailed a movement from "customary" to "industrial" time, in which workers' habits and behaviors were strictly regulated by clocks, and labor was organized to maximize profit, rather than reproducing the "competency" of workers.[16]

Along with the stripping away of workers' control came increased dependence on market relations for every aspect of social reproduction. This occurred both rurally and in urban locations as the American population decreasingly produced its own means of social reproduction, and increasingly specialized in market production to purchase the necessities of daily life.[17] For example, in the making of the middle class, patriarchal culture meant that new consumer standards developed to fit the emerging increasingly capitalist class and gender structure. In places like New England in the 1830s and 1840s a variety of changes occurred and "these include improved lighting, more on-the-road vehicles, greater segregation of sleeping from daytime living facilities, and elements of the parlor culture associated with the cult of domesticity—window curtains, wallpaper, carpets, clocks, musical instruments, sofas, heating stoves, and the like."[18]

The making of an American wage labor class was further developed by a large influx of immigrants. Through the late antebellum period immigrants continued to flood into the United States, including those fleeing the Irish potato famine and Germans following 1848. Between 1845 and 1855, for example, about 3 million immigrants arrived.[19] And as David Roediger, among others, famously discussed, Irish immigrants were often not considered white, but something closer to blacks as immigration increased racial tensions and racial divisions within the working class.[20] And just as early American industry, such as the Lowell factories, drew from women's labor, so Irish women also became an important component of the American working class as, by 1855, perhaps more than half of American industrial textile workers were Irish women.[21]

While in cities, capitalist development tended to consist of the gradual transformation of "artisans into workers," as Laurie put it, in the countryside it took a different path.[22] Social relations of production in the northern countryside, between the American Revolution and Civil War, gradually were remade from what Charles Post discusses as "independent household-production" into "petty-commodity production."[23] During the Revolutionary War itself, state governments and the military purchased supplies from yeomen farmers for high prices, increasingly drawing them into market relations as farmers themselves borrowed from stores. Along with debts, higher taxes also pushed yeomen farmers to specialize more in market production. This increased market deepening was a slow process, though, and by the 1820s and 1830s perhaps 30 percent of farmers' production in places such as the Ohio Valley was production for the market.[24] But

> by 1860, north-western farmers were selling approximately 60% of their total yield, well over the 40% that usually marked the transition from "subsistence" to "commercial" agriculture. In other words, these farmers were marketing not only their "surplus" product, but a major proportion of their "necessary" product, necessitating the purchase of elements of their subsistence, and making them increasingly dependent on the sale of commodities for their economic survival.[25]

As Elizabeth Blackmar shows, credit relations and probate courts also deepened yeomen family market incorporation. Traditionally, social reproduction expanded as farmers owned land and upon their death distributed it customarily and legally to widows and heirs. The eldest son often got double the share, with younger sons getting outlying properties, widows gaining a portion of the property, and daughters getting a portion of the non-landed property.[26] But a variety of complications arose, particularly because farmers often died in debt. Thus, "from the 1790s to the 1840s, the judiciary took charge of disciplining customary practices of probate. In the process, courts brought commercial reasoning and accounting into the affairs of households and communities accustomed to informal arrangements and personal prerogatives in managing family property."[27] Against the customary pattern of property distribution upon death, courts valued the property and settled with creditors. It also became more common for the land to be sold and the proceeds divided equally among heirs. And through mortgages, farmers' estates were also incorporated into the financial system, deepening their integration into the more advanced eastern urban capitalism. Companies such as the Massachusetts Hospital Life Insurance Company and New York Life Insurance and Trust Company, beginning in the 1820s and 1830s, invested in mortgages and profited from interest, paying dividends to stockholders, as "such institutions in effect siphoned off a share of family property to corporate investors."[28]

While deepened market integration and incorporation into eastern financial markets did not immediately transform the way production itself was organized for patriarchal yeomen households, it did provide a starting point for the remaking of these relations along increasingly capitalist lines. But over time, especially after the Civil War, the social reproduction of non-capitalist (or proto-capitalist) agrarian relations were increasingly outpaced by the development of capitalist agriculture.

And to create a working class from below, of course, also meant the creation of a top layer; a capitalist class. By the 1850s the modern corporate institution began to take form. Of course, different capitalist institutional forms had been developed and practiced much earlier than this, from port merchants building up profitable networks stretching across the Atlantic to Almy & Brown that in 1790 began the first significant cotton mill in the country, to the Lowell factory system, and beyond.[29] As state and capital shape each other's forms so, as early as 1809 for Massachusetts and 1811 for New York, general acts to allow for manufacturing corporations were passed.[30] The number of corporations per 100,000 people rose from one to twenty-three from the late eighteenth century through the first twenty years of the nineteenth century as the United States started on its way to be the world's original "corporate nation."[31] And the United States continued on this path as, between 1845 and 1859, Louisiana, Iowa, New York, Illinois, Wisconsin, California, Michigan, Massachusetts, Maryland, Ohio, Indiana, Minnesota, and Oregon all passed general incorporation laws in their state constitutions.[32]

The modern corporate form emerged most significantly through the railroad industry in the 1850s. Nationally, the miles of railroad tracks during this part of the "transportation revolution" increased from 8,879 in 1850 to over 30,000 by 1860.[33] Stretching across the landmass, railroad companies had to deal with practically countless details as companies used complex organizations of managers, assistant managers, superintendents and salaried workers, and so on. Each played a role in the large-scale division of management labor that constituted a central part of the modern corporate form further creating a division between ownership and control.[34] The scale of these firms dwarfed previous textile mills, the most significant type of corporate form in the earlier era of American capital. For example, the scale of accounting dramatically increased. While textile mills might have four or five different types of accounts, companies such as the Pennsylvania Railroad had, in 1857, 144 sets of accounts.[35]

The Civil War and southern modernity

As slavery expanded west in the south, and industrial capitalism increasingly took root in the north, so political tensions shaped by social and economic conditions deepened leading to war. The causes of the Civil War itself are still debated to this day. Was it an "irrepressible conflict," or unnecessary, caused by a "blundering generation"? To what extent was the war caused, socially, by two different forms of society—slavery and capitalism—in contrast to the contingency of politics? What roles did culture and ideology play?[36]

My goal here is not to definitively suggest any overarching causal account, as in the most general sense perhaps all that can be said is that the war was structured around shifting social and economic relations that were interpreted and triggered politically, resulting in secession and war. My aim here is simply to emphasize the extent to which the conflicts that led to the war were primarily conflicts over what to do with the expanding western space. It was not the existence of slavery in itself that the war was rooted in, but the expansion of slavery. As Eric Foner has suggested, "there was no purely economic reason why the North could not continue to coexist for many years with a slave-economy in the south."[37] After all, the "lords of the loom" and "lords of the lash" had co-existed in harmony for decades. What was at stake was whether or not western territory would allow for slavery or not; in other words, it was a conflict over the social order of the west and the right of slavery to expand.

Explaining the war this way also means looking at it not as a battle between capitalist and slave modes of production, but of two increasingly "modern" forms of capitalism that pushed different imperial strategies and politics. To reiterate an earlier theme discussed, the slave south was not frozen in time nor a product of an earlier era, but a key part of capitalist modernity, and itself modern and capitalist. The argument that the south was not modern or productive emerged out of northern, Republican, abolitionist, and new south ideology.[38] In many respects, it developed to view slavery and forced labor as less progressive than the emerging modern capitalist system, and in doing so functioned—as it does today—as a form of liberal ideology, which a historical materialist perspective that sees capitalist history as practically always organized around racial, class, and gendered violence can view more accurately.

As Brian Schoen summarizes, southern slave society was modern in a wide variety of ways. "The size and scope of larger operations, including the estimated 46,000 planters who in 1860 possessed upwards of twenty slaves, almost certainly approximated Northern factories or merchant houses more closely than urban artisan shops or family farms."[39] Planters developed complex, scientifically managed systems of agriculture organized around clock time; capitalist time discipline, and used techniques such as "overwork" (rewarding slaves who worked beyond the required time) to increase output; to suck more value out of their slave capital. They reacted to changing market conditions by altering their production, such as in the expansion of King Cotton. They fought for state policies to support their economic positions, such as tariffs for lower south sugar planters, or less tariffs, as in the case of cotton producers. They also invested in technologies such as steam exhaust vacuums to produce sugar, conveyer belts, thermometers, steam-driven thrashers, and so on besides, as discussed in an earlier chapter, investing in industry and more productive modified seeds.[40]

That being said, there is no doubt that southern farmers, practicing shifting cultivation, tended to use and improve less land than northerners. While planters in Virginia and South Carolina, for instance, typically cultivated one-third of their farmland at a time, northerners tended to cultivate half.[41] While northern farmers might use land for fodder crops or clover, for example, after a regular cultivation period, southerners would let this land lay fallow. This occurred for a variety of reasons including more fertile, nutrient-rich and less acidic northern soils, a southern climate which made livestock more difficult to raise due to diseases, fodder crops had a more difficult time adjusting to the warmer southern climate, and fertilizers were less common.[42] But some southern planters aimed to reform southern agriculture, perhaps the most well known being Virginian planter Edmund Ruffin. Reformers, publishing in a variety of trade journals, pushed for southern planters to move from shifting cultivation, use more fertilizers, advocated for state support to subsidize scientific agricultural developments, professorships, and geological surveys as, "in their calls for state action, reformers combined scientific reasoning, economic rationalism, and romantic imagery."[43] But reformers ultimately failed for one main reason: the reforms suggested were, from planter-capitalist perspectives, not clearly profitable. For example, fertilizer had to be shipped and was expensive to obtain, and it was not clearly profitable for planters to invest in this, particularly if they could continue to profit through shifting cultivation. Overall, reform did not seem profitable enough to be adopted en masse.

Another aspect of the south's modernity was the rush to construct railroads in the 1850s. Of the total 22,000 new miles of railroad tracks built nationally in this decade, 8,300 miles were in the south.[44] Much of this was in the western, expanding part of the south, linking the region together. Railroad companies were themselves modern capitalist corporations and regularly used and owned slaves; these companies employed over 10,000 slaves in the 1850s and particular companies owned slaves themselves. Companies tended to use both slave and Irish wage labor, in some cases giving wage workers the more dangerous parts of the job (after all, it was a more expendable, dismissible form of labor. What capitalist would want to risk their big investment in a slave, when temporary wage labor that could easily be replaced could be used for dangerous work?).[45] Railroad construction in the south also demonstrated the southern states' interests in economic development. Much of southern railroad building was state-funded and southern states spent over $128 million building railroads.[46]

The imperial road to the Civil War and birth of the Republican Party

Perhaps more than anything else, the political struggles that led to the Civil War were determined by competing pathways of imperialism. Both the north and the south were driven by expansionary social forces. Small farmers desired land while land speculators, railroad companies, and slave planters pushed to increase the space for profits. This was solidified by the ideology of Manifest Destiny and racism, used to purge the land of Native Americans and expand the frontier.

Tensions over slavery were foreshadowed as early as the Constitutional Convention of 1787 with the three-fifths compromise and Northwest Ordinance, and tensions over slavery were most substantially rekindled during the Missouri Crisis. The battle over Missouri was not a question of slavery itself, but slavery's expansion. It was a conflict over the social form that the western part of the United States would take. It began when New York congressman James Tallmadge introduced two amendments to a bill that would allow Missouri to enter the Union. One banned new slaves from entering the state and the other said all slaves in Missouri born after the state was admitted would be free at the age of 25. Initially, voting was sectionally split over the amendments. The amendment preventing new slaves from entering Missouri passed the House 87-76 with most northerners for it and most southerners against. And the other amendment passed 82-78, with most northerners for it and most southerners, again, against the measure. But the amendments went on to be defeated in the Senate, which had a higher proportion of southern representatives.[47] The result, after much wrangling, was the so-called compromise in which slavery would be prohibited above 36°30′ for future states entering the Union, Missouri would become a slave state, and Maine a free state. But this was not a compromise on which both parties agreed, so much as a strategically developed political move in which the bills were taken individually, rather than as a whole, in order to develop the support needed to pass them in total. First, when the Tallmadge amendments returned to the House, fourteen northerners in the House voted against it and four abstained, although most continued to support it. And 39 out of 76 southern congressmen in the House—and a higher proportion in the Senate—agreed to the banning of slavery above the compromise line.[48] Thus, while a compromise, with many exceptions, was passed, overall the Missouri Crisis demonstrated a wide sectional division between north and south that would be rekindled several decades later as sectional politics developed into total war.

Sectional tensions would also escalate in the Nullification Crisis. The crisis arose as South Carolina's economic pressures—with 56,000 whites and 30,000 blacks leaving in the 1820s—came into conflict with northern industry's push for higher tariffs. In 1828, the tariff on imported goods was raised to 50 percent. For South Carolinians, this meant that the north was pushing upon them a higher price for imported goods, while giving them nothing in return. And while tariffs were reduced to, on average, 25 percent in 1832, they remained as high as 50 percent on some key goods such as wool, cotton, and iron. As a result, the "Nullification" Convention in South Carolina declared the tariffs unconstitutional, not to be enforced in the state. Eventually, though, the Calhoun-Clay compromise in 1833 agreed to keep the 50 percent rates in place that year, and slowly lower them after at a rate of one-tenth until they would get to 20 percent in 1842. This passed with the Compromise Tariff and Force Bill on March 1, 1833, with the Force Bill adding the stipulation that the federal government could use force to prevent nullification in the future.[49]

This was followed by the Gag Rule controversy, the next significant sectional conflict. Northern abolitionists, still a small minority, decided to send anti-slavery propaganda to Congress, given that mailing southerners themselves did not seem a successful tactic. But for southerners like James Henry Hammond, even this seemed a threat and he petitioned on December 18, 1835 that the mail be gagged before even being taken in. Eventually, supported by Calhoun and others, gagging the mail altogether failed to obtain support, and the result was the passing of Henry Pickney's resolution which stated that abolitionist literature might be accepted in, but would immediately be tabled, and while some northerners and southerners continued to protest, it passed the House 117-68.[50]

While the Nullification Crisis and Gag Rule battles may have been debates more over slavery and sectionalism within the Union, soon another major debate arose over the future of expansion with the annexation of Texas. Throughout the 1830s and 1840s, population expansion west continued to grow. Between 1830 and 1840 while the eastern seaboard population increased by 17 percent, the population of Trans-Appalachia grew by 73 percent.[51] As discussed, some of this growth occurred into Texas, which became independent in 1836. Initially, Jackson delayed annexation due to both domestic and international pressures. If annexed, opposition in the north might prevent his successor, Martin Van Buren, from winning the next election. He did not recognize Texas independence until his last day in office.[52] Additionally, Mexico might desire revenge for the loss of Texas, and annexation could provoke war.[53] Thus, the question of Texas annexation stayed open for nearly a decade.

But things changed due to the continued American desire to annex, along with Texas President Sam Houston's own political maneuvers. By 1844, Whig President John Tyler, expansionist democrats in the south and midwest, and southern rights supporters continued to push annexation.[54] At the same time, Houston began to look towards Britain as a solution to the Texas predicament.[55] Houston, open to the idea of disallowing slavery in Texas in return for British loans and support, traveled to London at the beginning of 1843 with the goal of using Britain to broker a peace with Mexico. From Houston's perspective, the outcome could be either succeeding at this, or else forcing the United States to annex Texas to prevent British influence in the territory. Houston's tactics succeeded and on April 12, 1844 Texas and the United States signed an annexation treaty, which was passed by the House on January 25, 1845 and the Senate on February 27, with a joint resolution passed the next day inviting Texas to formally become a part of the United States.[56] At the same time, the pressures of democratic imperialism pushed for annexation. James K. Polk defeated Henry Clay in the 1844 election.[57] Polk's platform was centered on the "re-annexation of Texas" and "re-occupation of Oregon." Polk finally signed the official bill bringing Texas into the United States at the end of 1845, and in February of the next year Texas officially became part of the United States. Meanwhile, its population continued to expand, to 102,961 whites and 38,753 blacks by the first census in 1847.[58]

Besides triggering a war with Mexico over disputed territory along the Rio Grande, the annexation of Texas also rekindled the issue of the form new parts of the American state would take. This was seen most significantly with the introduction of the Wilmot Proviso. The proviso was introduced on August 8, 1846, and stated that slavery and involuntary servitude be outlawed in any territory received from Mexico. Although Congress expired before the bill could pass, it signaled American politics increasingly dividing along the geographical lines of north and south; those who voted in favor were primarily northerners, those against southerners.[59] Overall—over the question of empire—sectional politics increasingly took shape.

The debate over the politics of westward movement resulted in the so-called Compromise of 1850. It was "so-called" because, as David Potter points out, it was not a compromise all parties agreed to, so much as a series of bills which passed because each, on its own, had enough support. First, under Henry Clay's leadership, an omnibus bill linking the elements of the compromise together failed. Next, Stephen A. Douglas picked up the pieces as

> where Clay depended upon the existence of a majority in favor of compromise, and hence lumped the several measures together ... Douglas was astute enough to recognize that there was no workable majority in favor of compromise. But there were strong sectional blocs, in some cases northern, in other southern, in favor of each of the measures separately, and there was a bloc in favor of compromise.[60]

The final result of the bills was Texas becoming a slave state with the government taking over a substantial portion of Texas' debts in return for Texas relinquishing its claims to New Mexico which became a territory, California became a free state, Utah a territory, the slave trade in the District of Columbia was abolished, and the fugitive slave bill passed. With the exception of New Mexico, which received support from a significant portion of northern senators, each vote was passed along sectional lines.[61]

Four years later the debate over the form American expansion would take—slave or non-slave—reemerged with "Bleeding Kansas" and, two years later, "Bloody Sumner." On May 22, 1854, the Kansas-Nebraska Act was finalized with a "popular sovereignty" clause, meaning it would be up to the population of the states to decide whether slavery would be legal or not. The result was a small-scale civil war in Kansas. A month before the bill passed, Eli Thayer organized the Massachusetts Emigrant Aid Company to bring free settlers into the area. On the other side, on July 29, the Platte County Self-Defense Association formed in Missouri. These two organizations represented the tensions the act created. From the point of view of anti-slavery northerners, bringing Kansas in as a slave state would upset the Missouri Compromise. For slaveholders in Missouri, being trapped between non-slave states would threaten the stability of slavery in the state.

The laws of the new territory qualified anyone in the territory who might be eligible (that is, white men) to vote. In response, pro-slavery Missourians flooded into Kansas to vote, and through an election with much ballot fraud, elected a pro-slavery legislature.[62] The new government prevented those opposed to slavery from holding office, from criticizing slavery publicly, and sitting on juries on slavery-based cases.[63] Soon after another government formed in the state. While the pro-slavery government sat in Lecompton passing the "Lecompton Constitution," in Topeka another government formed attempting to outlaw slavery.[64] Violence also broke out, perhaps most famously in the pro-slavery "Sack of Lawrence" and rebuttal in the Pottawatomie Massacre in which John Brown convinced seven others, including four sons, to travel to the cabins of several settlers, including Allen Wilkinson who was a member of the territorial legislature, and slaughter about half a dozen people.[65] Violence also spread to Congress when, on May 22, 1856, South Carolina representative Preston Brooks attacked and greatly injured Charles Sumner of Massachusetts in the Senate chamber.[66]

The Dread Scott decision and John Brown's famous attack on Harpur's Ferry further, famously, polarized north and south. The former stated both that blacks could not be citizens and the federal government did not have jurisdiction to regulate slavery.[67] And the latter, given the support Brown received from the north as a martyr, further deepened distrust between north and south.[68] And more generally, by the late 1850s, while both abolitionists and sectionalists were radicals in their own societies, northern fear of "Slave Power" and southern fear of anti-slavery continued to increase as the politics of the country realigned around the slavery issue.

Tensions would continue to escalate. In part, this was due to deepening economic connections and development within the north. On the one hand, right up until the war, a segment of northern capital supported concessions to the south to hold the Union together. Particularly, northeastern merchant capital had a stake in the profits of slavery, and many merchants, although not all, did not desire to see it abolished.[69] New York capitalists such as Charles Morgan built their own personal empires of capital through shipments of slaves and the products they produced.[70] On the other hand, though, increasingly the northern midwest and northeast came together as a regional economic bloc. Canals and railroads linked states like Ohio and Illinois—and cities such as Cincinnati and Chicago—with the northeast, the midwest producing grains and livestock in exchange for northeastern industry. This emerging economy clamored for more improvements, but when Polk vetoed the Harbor and River Bill in 1847, thousands—perhaps tens of thousands—of people met in Chicago for the Northwestern Rivers and Harbors Convention in July of that year, as northerners increasingly saw their own economic development blocked by southern politicians.[71] Tensions also increased as southern politicians, initially half supportive, pushed against the Homestead Act (eventually passing in 1862 after the war began) and northerners and southerners fought over the route of a transcontinental railroad.[72]

Finally, the birth of the Republican Party as an alliance of anti-slavery politicians further deepened the sectional divide. The party itself was the result of debates over the course of expansion. It emerged in the wake of the Kansas-Nebraska dispute and the collapse of the Whigs, bringing together a wide variety of different social groups with varied political interests, but all, to some degree, opposed to the expansion of slavery. As noted,

> the new party was an amalgam of many northern elements: Free Soilers, who were antislavery but also frequently anti-black; supporters

> of the "American" or Know-Nothing Party, which was anti-immigrant and anti-Catholic; some remnants of the old Whigs; along with abolitionists, women's rights advocates, and friends of temperance and other reform groups. They all agreed only that the south and slavery "must be contained."[73]

The idea of a "Republican" party emerged out of meetings called by the Free-Soil Party in early 1854. In February of that year, for example, Alvin E. Bovay wrote a letter to Horace Greeley, editor of the *New York Tribune*, proposing such a party. And by that summer, political conventions in states such as Wisconsin and Michigan were beginning to use the idea of a Republican Party. At the same time, the Know-Nothing Party also emerged on an anti-immigrant platform, particularly in reaction to increased German and Irish Catholic immigration. By the time elections came in November of 1854, the political alignments of the north were highly complex. In Massachusetts, the Know-Nothings dominated, in Wisconsin and Michigan, the Republicans, elsewhere Fusionist parties sprang up. While it was clear that the Democrats had lost support in the north, as they increasingly became the sectional party of the south, it was not clear which party or parties would dominate the north in the coming years.[74] Some Democrats became Republicans, as did some Whigs, Free-Soilers, and nativists, while other Whigs attempted to continue to hold their banner, but as Holt points out, they linked together through a, "lowest common denominator of opposition to southern whites and their northern Democratic allies, whom Republicans always portrayed as lackeys of and surrogates for the Slave Power."[75] Specifically, it was not just Slave Power, although, especially early on, Republicanism contained some abolitionist elements, but opposition to slavery's expansion that united the Republican Party.

Yet through the late 1850s up until the election of 1860, the Republican Party was not completely accepted as the leading party in the north. Other names such as the Union, Anti-Administration, Independent, or, most prominently, the People's Party, were used, for example, in 1860, Lincoln was on a People's Party, rather than Republican, ticket in New Jersey and Pennsylvania.[76] And oddly enough, for the election which triggered secession, Lincoln, in part increasing his reputation through the 1858 debates with Stephen Douglas, was chosen as the candidate particularly because of his moderation. Possible candidates such as William Seward and Salmon P. Chase seemed too divisive within a divided party.

Lincoln, on the other hand, had a moderate but clear position on slavery (opposed to it in the long run, but not an abolitionist and viewed blacks as racially inferior to whites) and, "like a good politician, Lincoln had refrained from public comment on such diverse issues as temperance, nativism, and the Fugitive Slave Law."[77]

While the party represented a diversity of interests opposed to Slave Power, it also reflected the worldview of an increasingly capitalist society. Some Republicans may have maintained the idea, as Eric Foner famously discussed, that the Republican Party was the party of "free labor."[78] Thus, "for Republicans, 'free labor' meant labor with economic choices, with the opportunity to quit the wage-earning class. A man who remained all his life dependent on wages for his livelihood appeared almost as unfree as the southern slave."[79] But views on labor and capitalism in the party may have been more of a spectrum than this alone. While some Republicans, Lincoln himself included, may have had a definition of free labor as Foner suggests, other Republicans, including some supporting the Homestead Act, were more uncomfortable with wage labor, even if temporary, while others increasingly defined American "freedom" as the ability to labor for a wage: that wage labor and free labor were compatible, if not the same thing.[80] Nevertheless, some Republicans increasingly developed an ideology that, with variation, accepted capitalism as American freedom, fundamentally different from the earlier view of American freedom as freedom from dependence, including wage labor.

Southern imperialism and the road to war

In many respects, the election of James Buchanan was a last desperate attempt to hold together the conflicting paths of imperialism within the expanding United States that led to the Civil War. As William Freehling put it, "Buchanan was a northern man with southern principles, if one means a Border North man with Border South principles."[81] He grew up on the edge of Pennsylvania, 10 miles from Maryland, and his politics reflected a borderland mentality. For example, in 1834 he bought two female slaves ages 5 and 22. Immediately he signed papers to manumit the older one in seven years and the younger one in twenty-three years. In the meantime, they would serve as household servants. His politics reflected these types of borderland relations. Thus, he stood as the Democratic candidate due to his position as a moderator, whose main platform was saving the Union.[82]

Buchanan was also an ardent imperialist during an era in which public opinion was shaped around an ideology of democratic imperialism. To be elected president during this era one had to be an imperialist. Buchanan—the great expansionist James K. Polk's Secretary of State—was such a person. While not supportive of unconditional expansion—he believed that it needed to be done through legal methods, rather than strictly aggressive violence—in his personal records in 1859, for example, he wrote that it was "the destiny of our own race to people and assimilate to themselves the whole of North America before the close of the present century."[83] Buchanan, then, was a supporter of the racialized imperialism of his time, and his politics reflected this. And as an advocate of the Monroe Doctrine, among other things, throughout his administration he pushed for Congress to grant him the right to use force to hold transit routes throughout Central America, and against natives and Mexicans in the southwestern border, although Congress prevented him from sending troops across the border. He also pushed to acquire more of Mexico, including Baja, northern Chihuahua, and Sonora, and sent agents to attempt to acquire Cuba from the Spanish. Congress also gave Buchanan funds to attack Paraguay in reaction to Paraguay attacking a US steamer in the country on a scientific exploration, the *Water Witch*, and pushed for an "open door" policy towards China in which the United States would have an equal stake with the European imperial powers.[84]

While Buchanan was a relative moderate, other southerners pushed for imperialism as a solution to increased tension and sectionalism. In particular, it was seen as the destiny of the United States to acquire islands in the Caribbean and territory in Central America. To attempt to turn this imperial dream into reality, several filibusters developed. As both Polk and Buchanan failed to buy Cuba from the Spanish, others began to believe a war of conquest would solve the issue. Most prominently, Narciso López led several filibuster expeditions to conquer Cuba. While initially receiving much support from exiled Cubans in New York City, he eventually looked to the south for support following an initial attempt in 1849 that was stopped by US officials. Receiving help from southerners including cotton capitalist and former US Senator John Henderson, López made another attempt the following year with an army of 600, mostly Americans. They made it to Cuba, but failed to generate support locally for the filibuster, and retreated back to the Key West, barely dodging Spanish and American authorities. Finally,

López again made it to Cuba in 1851 with 400 troops, but this time was defeated and killed.[85]

The movement for Cuba continued, its next major filibustering attempt led by John Quitman, New York born-turned southern plantation owner, military man, and politician. As Robert May puts it, "to Quitman, annexation of Cuba was a means of strengthening the South and states' rights within the union, given the unwillingness of the southern states to secede in 1850."[86] Quitman was an ardent imperialist who saw expansion as a way to preserve the slave structure (through the ideological lens of "states rights") of the south. In 1854, Quitman obtained support from Cuban exiles in New York, who previously supported López, and they agreed to sell bonds up to a total of $800,000 to fund the mission; in effect, trying to get support for capital with the idea that expansion would be profitable. Quitman also received support from the south as southern soldiers volunteered to participate in imperialism as a way to prove their manhood. But Quitman failed for a variety of reasons. For one, the federal government's non-support for filibustering made it difficult to obtain funds, and investors could not be sure that expansion was profitable, and some even began to ask for their money back by late 1854. After much pressure, Quitman resigned as leader of the Junta on April 20, 1855. The Pierce Administration continued to attempt to persuade Spain to sell Cuba, but it became increasingly difficult after the "Ostend Manifesto," which implied that the United States might pursue war against Spain if the Spanish did not sell, further spoiled this possibility.[87]

The final major attempt to expand the American frontier south was led by William Walker of Tennessee. Within the growing American country, Nicaragua was increasingly seen as a route to California, where the gold rush had taken off, as dreams of personal capitalist empires coalesced with dreams of continental conquest. Cornelius Vanderbilt, in particular, obtained a contract from Nicaragua in 1851 for his Accessory Transit Company to transport people across the country. In this sense, the battle between Vanderbilt and Walker that developed was a battle over the form of expansion. While Vanderbilt preferred informal empire—securing economic profits through deals with other "formally" sovereign states—Walker preferred the formal empire of conquest. And when one struggling side of a civil war in Nicaragua invited Americans to support them, Walker saw his chance. Walker and his men made their way from San Francisco Bay to Nicaragua and soon after he became President of Nicaragua, although deposed in 1857. Walker received much support from the American south, legalized slavery within the country (in part to obtain this), and his minister to the United States, Padre Vigil, was even recognized as legitimate by President Pierce.[88]

In 1860, Walker was killed in Honduras as he made another attempt to expand the southern part of the United States. And with Lincoln's election that year, and the secession of the lower south, led by South Carolina, followed by the upper south after the attack on Fort Sumter (but never the border states of Missouri, Kentucky, Maryland, and Delaware), the attempt to use imperialism to save southern slavery ultimately failed.[89] In fact, the only truly successful case of 1850s southern border expansion was the Gadsden Purchase in 1854, in which a part of Mexico in present day Arizona and New Mexico was purchased by capitalist James Gadsden who dreamed of a southern route for a transcontinental railroad.[90]

Economics of the Civil War in the north and remaking of the American state

The war itself is sometimes considered the first industrialized "total war," resulting in the deaths of 600,000–750,000 people, depending on the estimate. And it resulted in the abolition of southern formal slavery.[91] It also gave the Republican Party unprecedented power to consolidate and remake the laws and social relations of the country. If the Civil War was a "bourgeois revolution," it was so precisely because of the ways politics and power were reshaped during the war and after in the era of Reconstruction and making of a "new south."

By 1860, the Republican Party, although still more of an alliance of different political groups than a cohesive institution, was increasingly both a party of expansion and capital. In the 1860 election, a phrase, "westward the star of empire takes its way" was used as a campaign slogan.[92] Thus, the party that would go on to create a more centralized state during and after the war, protecting the interests of capital against labor, was also a party that embraced the idea of American Empire.

Economically, much changed during the war. Decades ago economic historians debated the effects of the war upon the development of American capitalism.[93] In a classic article by Thomas C. Cochran the author argued that, in fact, the war slowed economic growth and industrial development in the north. The rate of growth of the production of commodities such as pig-iron, copper production, railroads, and cotton textiles dramatically decreased during the war.[94] Cochran's conclusions were further developed by, for instance, Saul Engelbourg who examined a wide variety of industries, including guns and ammunition and boots and textiles which, it might be thought, advanced during the war due to war production. In the small arms industry, for example, it seems that while the machine-based production of small arms with interchangeable parts continued, the industry itself was not revolutionized. In some cases, even, to increase output and lower costs, less advanced industrial methods were used. Similarly, while the explosives industries grew, its largest company, Du Pont, increased output without expanding its overall number of employees, instead relying on overtime work. In other industries, there were more drastic changes, for example, wood paper increasingly replaced cotton paper and the wool industry grew. But even in the boot and shoe industry output per worker did not significantly increase during the war, as new, more efficient methods of production did not take off.[95]

Within the north, though, during the war farmers increased their market integration and some took on more capitalistic production. For example, hay prices dramatically increased, and farmers reacted by selling hay on the market to the military. Additionally, farmers chopped down trees to sell firewood to the military. And as demand for wool for soldiers' uniforms greatly increased, farmers raised more sheep. The eight leading wool producing states in the north, for example, increased their overall production of sheep from 22.5 million in 1860 to 28.6 million by the start of 1865 as wool prices increased during the war. The production of cattle and hogs decreased, for example, in Ohio from about 1.779 million cattle and 1.918 million hogs in 1860 to 1.244 million cattle and 1.455 hogs in 1865. Agriculture became increasingly industrialized as the reaper and mower industries, already growing before the war, continued to expand; in 1860, there were seventy-three producers with a capitalization of $3,516, whereas in four years there were 187 plants with 60,000 workers and machines valued at $15 million.[96] Overall, agricultural production in the north grew in some ways and did not grow in others, but in general the war increased farmers' economic integration into capitalism.

But more importantly than the increasing or decreasing of output was the remaking of the American state to further the development of American capitalism. One part of this was the regulation of the working class and suppression of labor radicalism during the war. While, on the one hand, many workers, and particularly skilled artisans, filled with national ambition to protect the Union, volunteered for the cause, on the other hand, for most workers the war was a disaster. Wages lagged behind prices, greenbacks created inflation, and taxation fell upon them.[97] The result was increased labor militancy as strikes broke out across the Union. As a result, states passed anti-labor legislation. For example, Montgomery points out that laws around the coal fields of LaSalle Illinois, the "LaSalle Black Laws," as they became known, were passed in a bipartisan manner, making it illegal to prevent a person from going to work, to organize against the lawful use of an owner's property, and to enter a coal mine with the purpose of convincing others to strike. Other states proposed similar legislature, with Ohio passing a law preventing a person from stopping another from going to work.

And besides legislation, military violence was also used to control workers. When workers at R.P. Parrott Works, Cold Springs, New York, struck, martial law was declared and two army companies came to town, putting several labor leaders in prison. Similarly, in Pennsylvania 300 soldiers, in addition to the sheriff's own army, put down a strike by workers in the Fall Brook Coal Company, only to later rehire the workers at half wages and an oath not to join a union. This was followed by legislation allowing companies to evict employees from their company houses for going on strike. And most famously, after the state attempted to institute the draft in New York City in 1863, riots broke out which sprawled out to become race and class riots as whites murdered blacks they found and attacked and looted the homes of the wealthy.[98]

With the Democrats out of the way and in wartime circumstances, the Republicans also remade the American state during the war in a way that, in the long run, created an infrastructure supportive of capitalist development. As one author puts it,

> they were the party of economic growth and development. They passed the laws that helped create the Gilded Age, an age symbolized not by Lincoln but by Ulysses Grant and his cronies, by bearded, overweight men in dark suits, smoking cigars at lavish banquets, eating ten-course meals while their minions crushed strikes, swindled farmers, and displaced workers. The Robber Barons threatened to eclipse the railsplitter.[99]

For example, Jay Cooke used the war to become one of the country's leading capitalists. Cooke and his team sold over $1.5 billion in war bonds over the course of the war, as Cooke made a hefty profit for himself while developing personal relationships with the Republican leadership.[100]

A Union monetary system was also created during the war. Before the war, banks issued their own currencies, based on their ability to honor the paper in circulation. With the Legal Tender Act that became law on February 25, 1862, the Union now had a national currency: greenbacks. And the first National Banking Act of 1863 (other national banking acts were also passed in the following years), while not outlawing individual banks from printing currency, made it increasingly difficult by requiring new banks to put one-third of their capital stock into union bonds, in return for a national currency that was redeemable in greenbacks or specie. Additionally, taxes were placed on banks' own currencies to discourage the use of independent bank currencies instead of union currency.

The Morrill Tariff Bill, initially introduced in 1860 but shot down in the Senate, became law on March 2, 1861 after southern senators left the government during the war. The Republicans dominated the north, and with southern Democrats no longer in their way, also greatly raised tariffs to protect domestic industry. The first national taxation system was also put in place after, in March 1862, a bill was passed imposing a 3 percent tax on domestic manufactures and created a new institution—the Internal Revenue Bureau—to enforce collection. By 1864, domestic taxes were seen as a legitimate instrument of government, and income taxes were passed in which incomes of $600 to $5,000 were taxed at 5 percent, $5,000 to $10,000 at 7.5 percent, and over $10,000 at 10 percent.

In addition to currency, taxes, and tariffs, the earlier much debated Homestead Act was also passed in 1862, along with the creation of a Department of Agriculture, Land Grant College Act, and 1864 Immigrant Act to promote workers to come to the north.[101] The Homestead Act was supposed to offer any eligible citizen over the age of 21 up to 160 acres of public land, but in fact, in conjunction with other land acts, was, at best, moderately successful. It has been estimated that from 1860 to 1900, perhaps 400,000 families obtained land with the act which they kept.[102] For one, it was not easy for workers without agricultural skills to suddenly live off the land. At the same time, the continued expansion of "the west" provided a great space for speculators to acquire large amounts of land, as expansion and profit shaped the west. And other acts also prevented the previous pattern of the expansion of the patriarchal household mode of production, most significantly railroad grants;

from the antebellum period up through 1900, about 183 million acres were given as grants to railroad companies.[103] Overall, land policies put in place did more to allow capital to develop the west after 1860 than they did to continue the earlier tradition of the not-entirely-but-partly self-sufficient farm household.

James McPherson has suggested that "as for [the Republicans] becoming the 'party of big business,' that too may require some modification. Republicans could not have won all the elections they did in the North without support from many workers and farmers, who after all vastly outnumbered the Robber Barons."[104] But Republicans becoming the party of capital does not just mean they controlled the state: after all, the state is not simply an "instrument" to be wielded by one class over another, so much as a class space structured around capital's legal dominance backed by police force. In this case, the hegemony of the Republican Party and creation of a deeper and more expansive "relatively autonomous" state during the war produced a structure in which capital accumulation could expand after the war.

Reconstruction and the consolidation of American capitalism

With the Thirteenth, Fourteenth, and Fifteenth Amendments, American society was revolutionized. No longer slaves, blacks were now legal citizens with the right to vote (although the right to vote could be limited through literacy tests, education tests, and property).[105] Overall, though, the social order based around racialized slavery was fundamentally transformed. Ideas that seemed radical even a decade before suddenly became law.

On the other hand, as generations of scholars have shown, for African Americans Reconstruction was, ultimately, a failure. Rather than liberating southern blacks, many of them found themselves, once again, working on plantations, this time as sharecroppers rather than slaves, but in conditions similar to slavery. And southern Democrat "redeemers" once again took control of southern states.[106] By the end of the 1870s, the "retreat from Reconstruction" was complete.[107] A "new" south was born in which blacks would remain in legal bondage, subject to "black codes" and the Jim Crow laws which remained in place for a century after the Civil War.

Debates over why Reconstruction failed to do more for southern blacks have a long history, and covering the entire debate would be outside the scope of this book. That being said, this section aims to emphasize the roles of capitalism and slavery in the retreat from Reconstruction. I want to suggest two important reasons why Reconstruction failed. First, in a sense, it was not a failure for northern Republicans. With the exception of the radical wing of the party, their aim was less to liberate blacks than to reestablish national capitalism and re-proletarianize slaves as workers. Secondly, imperialism remained a constant in American history, and American troops were brought from the south to the west as expansion took precedent over southern Reconstruction. In other words, Reconstruction and its retreat set the basis for the consolidation of capitalism, at the expense of both black and Native American freedom and life.

As Eric Fonor discusses in his magnum opus, the goal of northerners was to create a free labor society in the south. But "as Northern investors understood the term, 'free labor' meant working for wages on plantations; to blacks it meant farming their own land, and living largely independent of the marketplace."[108] Without masters, former slaves who obtained land tended to become relatively self-sufficient farmers. In the well-known case of the Sea Islands, for instance, they destroyed the former property of their masters, and grew crops like corn and potatoes to feed themselves, but expressed little interest in growing cotton.[109] Elsewhere, similar stories prevailed. In Davis Bend in the Mississippi Valley, for example, existed "the largest laboratory in black economic independence."[110] Here, free blacks even went so far as to self-organize their own type of commodity production, producing cotton for the market and earning $160,000.

But—as it continues to today—the fear of black independence sent shivers down the spines of most whites. And it was in this context that Reconstruction policies were organized. The central organization in this was the Bureau of Refugees, Freedmen, and Abandoned Lands, generally termed the Freedmen's Bureau. The goal of the bureau was not to support black independence and autonomy, but remake the south in the image of northern free labor ideology. As Michael Fitzgerald puts it, "the Bureau's basic policy was to induce planters and freedmen to sign annual labor contracts at standard rate of wages; the object was to school both planters and their ex-slaves in the ways of free labor while monitoring their outcome."[111] Initially, in 1865, the military pushed for blacks to return to plantations and kept in place racialized laws, such as making it illegal to travel without passes, which went along with the "black codes" southern states put in place, such as vagrancy laws, forcing blacks back to plantations. The Freedmen's Bureau continued these traditions, in many respects, as their goal became not land redistribution, "40 acres and a mule," but returning blacks to plantations. This went along with the redistribution of land back to its original owners, half of which was returned by the middle of 1866, and more afterwards.[112]

By the late 1860s, then, on the one hand, Reconstruction policies aimed to put black labor back in the hands of plantation owners and, on the other, blacks pushed against this system to obtain autonomy. The result of this racialized class struggle was the sharecropping system.[113] This prevailed on cotton plantations by the early 1870s, and remained the primary labor system on southern capitalist plantations for decades. Sharecropping itself also took different forms. Legally in states such as South Carolina, for example, technically sharecropping was a type of wage labor in which dispossessed working families obtained their means of survival by working for the landlord who essentially owned the means of production, and were paid an indirect wage in the form of a share of the production.[114] Under sharecropping, farmers, owning no implements, rented equipment, land, and often houses, from plantation owners. In return they were required to give generally one-half of their production (in some cases one-third or one-quarter) to the capitalist. By contrast, tenant farmers technically rented the land in return for a portion of their crop or a cash rent.[115] That being said, as Edward Royce notes, "however clearly established in law, the distinction between sharecropping and tenancy tended to break down in practice; this distinction, furthermore, was not clearly recognized or acted upon by landlords and laborers."[116] And not all ex-slaves became sharecroppers.[117] Some became wage laborers, in which a very small proportion were able to obtain their own land, albeit often times in less fertile regions. Nevertheless, overall, sharecropping became the predominant form of agricultural life replacing the old south slave system. Sharecropping, in the general sense of free ex-slaves lacking access to their basic means of survival, were forced into variations of the sharecropping system which replaced the plantation south. And as Aiken discusses, this was part of the broader "resubjection of blacks" as an entire legal structure was put in place to control black labor for the profits of southern capital. This included passing lien laws to fortify the sharecropping and tenancy systems and laws preventing blacks from voting, for example, by 1910 less than 10 percent of southern blacks registered to vote.[118] And this, was, of course driven by violence against blacks, seen more prominently with the rise of the Ku Klux Klan.

This also raises a question as to the extent to which the new south was "capitalist" or not. On the one hand, it seems that sharecropping may have been a step backward for capitalism. Former slaves regained some of their dignity and control over their own lives by working for themselves as sharecroppers rather than slaves (although in some cases sharecroppers remained directly supervised by landowners). Their control over their own means of production was greater than previously. On the other hand, they remained formally subsumed to the power of capital. Under the credit lien system which prevailed, croppers were indebted to merchants and landowners (who themselves were often in debt) or in some cases merchant-landowners, thus had to focus on for-market commodity production so that someone else would profit from their labor. And this led to, for example, an explosion of credit rating agencies in the postbellum era.[119] Thus, while it might be tempting to say sharecropping was not really "capitalist," I might suggest it was, in the sense that dispossessed former slaves who asserted their power against becoming simply wage laborers still remained subordinated to capitalists under whom they labored so that the latter could profit.

William Gillette, in *Retreat from Reconstruction*, saw the period as, primarily, a political failure. A divided, relatively weak northern Republican government, along with a decentralized political tradition, reinforced with rampant racism, blocked Reconstruction from going further.[120] But framing the Reconstruction's retreat simply in terms of politics and race misses the important question of capitalism. Du Bois saw this eighty years ago, arguing:

> this control of super-capital and big business was being developed during the ten years of Southern Reconstruction and was dependent and consequent upon the failure of democracy in the South, just as it fattened upon the perversion of democracy in the North. And when once the control of industry by big business was certain through consolidation and manipulation that included both North and South, big business shamelessly deserted, not only the Negro, but the cause of democracy; not only in the South, but in the North.[121]

In this sense, when asking whether Reconstruction failed, the question is: for whom? For the white American north, Reconstruction was, apart from radicals and abolitionists, not a failure. Their goal was to develop and expand American capitalism, and in this sense, Reconstruction was as successful as it needed to be. As Richardson has put it, "Northerners wanted the South to develop an economic system that was compatible with the North quickly so that the nation could boom."[122] This meant viewing former slaves as "good workers" and potential free wage laborers (as wage labor became increasingly defined as compatible with American freedom). And for some northern capitalists, concerned with profits rather than equality, the post-war south was seen as a space to invest their capital. In particular, the ecology of the south was seen as potentially exploitable by northern capitalism as, in the 1870s, northern capital went south. Woodward notes, for example, a northern congressman who purchased 111,188 acres in Louisiana, Chicago capitalists who purchased 195,804 acres, a Michigan company for land brokers that purchased close to 700,000 acres, a capitalist in Grand Rapids who bought 126,238 acres, and so on. Overall, forty-one northern groups purchased 1,370,332 acres in Louisiana alone.[123]

But it was not just the Republican Party that transformed. In the elections of 1868 the Democratic Party campaigned with the slogan "new departure," as they also became a party of capital in its post-war form. Northeastern American capital, for example, had always been somewhat reluctant to embrace the cause of the north as they had a long history of profiting from the slave trade and its products, most significantly cotton which went in northeastern ships to England.[124] At the same time, while some southern capitalists found their fortunes destroyed by the war, many southern planters reestablished themselves as Reconstruction and Andrew Johnson's pardons restored their property.[125] For capital, the politics of north and south were less important than the politics of profit, and, like the Republican Party, Democrats shifted accordingly. As Camejo puts it, "the Democratic Party was becoming an alternate expression of the same class interests as the Republicans."[126] By the 1872 elections, the Democrats ran with the slogan "acceptance of the results of the war," against the corruption and radicalism within the Republican Party. They also supported Liberal Republican, rather than traditionally Democratic candidates, as many previously Republican members split with the party in 1872, opposed to Ulysses Grant's perceived corruption and found themselves fusing with the Democrats, including Charles Sumner, Horace Greeley, George W. Julian, and Lyman Trumbull. In 1876, for example, the Democrats ran Samuel J. Tilden, a New York lawyer, for president, signifying the extent to which the parties were no longer sectional, but variations of a party of national capitalism.[127]

For the most part, then, the period after the Civil War might be thought of less as the failure of Reconstruction than as the success of racialized capitalism. While the economy and culture of the south would continue to be shaped by the legacy of slavery—as it is to this day—and the "new" south remained relatively economically weak compared to the north, overall the Civil War and Reconstruction successfully further established the hegemony of American capitalism. The final phase of continental empire building was to be forged, principally, by the power of capital.

Conclusion: Capital and the Conquest of Space

By the 1870s, from the standpoint of capital, the west was a vast garden ripe for exploitation. And the extraction of western natural resources, along with the creation of the nation's breadbasket, would also provide the United States with the capacity to propel itself further on to the world stage. Unlike previous eras of expansion, which were comprised of more complex articulations between capitalist and not-so-capitalist social relations, the incorporation of the great and far west was primarily driven by the forces of capital. This was not just a national capitalist project though. From British capital investing into the burgeoning railroad industry to Chinese workers digging in the mines of California, the making of the capitalist west was a globalized process.

David Harvey defines the uniqueness of capitalist imperialism as "a contradictory fusion of 'the politics of state and empire.'"[1] For capitalists, territory and political power are not so much important beyond the sense that they encourage capital accumulation through time and space. For politicians, augmenting state power against other states and questions of territory are central. While this distinction may risk underplaying the extent to which capital and state are not separate, but tend to be merged (as often the same people running the state are the capitalist elite), by the era of Reconstruction, in the United States, the politics of state and expansion, and the logic of capital's growth were, essentially, fully merged. Space itself would be territorially incorporated into empire to generate profit. Of course, capitalism is never "pure," and the Homestead Act did allow for the continuation, to a limited degree, of independent household production, but overall, this became increasingly secondary in relation to the political economic dominance of capital.

The continued opening of the west after the Civil War created a vast space for capital accumulation.[2] As William Robbins discusses in what remains the most significant work that links imperialism and capitalism in the west, by the 1870s, expansion was no longer about pioneers and small farms, but capital and industry. As he argues, "to a significant degree, then, the emerging western industrial program was an extension of capitalist relations in eastern North America and in Europe where surpluses had accumulated."[3] Central to this was the rise of Chicago as the nodal point between east and west. By mid-century it appeared that all roads led through Chicago to New York City and back again. And as New York's rise came from its commercial orientation from the start, so Chicago was very much started as a capitalist project. As William Cronon discusses in his definitive study, early Chicago development was a product of the speculative mania of the 1830s that culminated in the panic of 1837. As the US government "removed" native populations in the region by 1833, so capitalists who viewed western space as a land of profit flooded into Chicago.[4] The state also played a key role in transforming Chicago into the empire's western thoroughfare by organizing and investing in internal improvements. Following the lead of the Erie Canal, first, the legislature supported the construction of the Illinois and Michigan Canal. Secondly, it established a Board of Fund Commissioners and a Board of Public Works along with an internal improvement fund. As the harbor was dredged and roads and railroads were built, so the state played a key role in developing capitalism in Chicago.[5]

By 1836, Chicago is reported to have exported a total of $1,000.64 worth of goods from its port. By 1840 that number was $328,635.74.[6] By the mid-1850s Chicago was said to be perhaps the world's largest grain port, with total exports for the year 1855 as high as 12,902,310 bushels of grain and with over 100,000 hogs packed and 23,691 cattle slaughtered as the meatpacking industry formed. By this year the population had risen from 12,088 in 1845 to 83,509 a decade later.[7]

As Chicago arose as a trade and manufacturing center of power, so elsewhere in the capitalist west mining and agribusiness took off. The government additionally paved the way as the American state also began to develop more of an interest in incorporating the west as a space for capital accumulation. In the 1850s, for example, the US Army Corps of Topographical Engineers conducted large railroad surveys, and surveys continued after the war with the government sponsoring Clarence King, Ferdinand V. Hayden, George M. Wheeler, and John Wesley to further survey the west. These surveys, and the eventual establishment of the US Geological Survey, opened the way for capital by locating the potentially profitable geography of the west.[8] This was explicit as shown, for example, in the introduction to the 1871 annual report of the Commissioner of Mining Statistics which states the report is "likely to be of use to miners, metallurgists, capitalists, and legislators."[9] Thus, the state-led sciences of mapping, statistics, and so on became central to providing investors with key information to make the west profitable. This went hand-in-hand with a renewed interest in the study of geography itself, as concerns over mapping and controlling space and territory to subject them to capital's will became of greater concern both for mining and agriculture.[10]

States such as Colorado also rapidly developed due to the mining industry. Incorporated as a territory in 1861, by 1863 the population was estimated to be 45,000 settlers along with 15,000 Native Americans.[11] Capital in search of profits and workers in search of higher wages flooded in, as by the late 1870s it was suggested that over 60,000 mines had been discovered. Additionally, soon after agriculture began to take off; in 1877, the state exported about $9 million worth of gold, silver, copper, and coal and perhaps 1.5 million head of livestock and 1,750,000 bushels of wheat, among other commodities.[12] Colorado's capitalist development was also a broad-scale process as Denver quickly became the territory's main commercial center and by the late 1860s, 400 Chinese laborers were even recorded to have been imported.[13] Montana's history tells a similar story. While some settlers may have come as homesteaders, many came for the mines. It was estimated that $600,000 worth of precious metals were exported in 1862 alone, and by 1878 that number was $5,867,000.[14] Similarly, in the 1870s prospectors began to flood into the Black Hills of Dakota as the native Sioux were pushed out of the region. Cities such as Deadwood sprung up, driven by the mania for gold and minerals. Mining companies from California and Colorado came in and developed towns fundamentally based around mining as early sorts of company towns formed. The Homestake Mining Company, for example, was one of many corporations incorporated (in this case in California in 1877) to explore the riches of the Black Hills. With a capital stock of $10 million divided into 100,000 shares (a relatively common amount for these large investment projects)[15] the company was soon processing thousands upon thousands of tons of ore and set up a machine shop, carpenter's shop, offices, homes, and so on as settlement was strictly built in the name of capital.

As extractive mining drove the capitalist west from Nevada's Comstock Lode to Arizona copper and beyond (not to mention the California gold rush) so the midwest rose to become the breadbasket of the west. By the late 1870s, for instance, Nebraska was said to be "full in the pathway of empire, on the great highway of the nations."[16] While by

1870, 1,848,000 bushels of wheat were grown, in 1877 that number was 8,759,319.[17] While petty-commodity producing homesteaders came into the state, much land was also swallowed up by capital, particularly that near railroad lines. This land was farmed under contract at established rates for crops as speculators monopolized and profited from the land with easiest market access.[18] And other commodities such as oats, rye, and so on along with corn have a similar story: "the total corn crop of Nebraska for 1877 was greater, by a good margin, than the combined corn crops of all New England, New York and New Jersey for 1876."[19] Stock raising for profit also quickly developed as by this time 250,000 cattle grazed in western Nebraska.[20] And Omaha itself was in many ways started as a for-profit enterprise by William D. Brown who started the Lone Tree Ferry across the Missouri River in the spot where Omaha would grow.[21] Brown then organized a variety of other investors to start the Council Bluffs and Nebraska Ferry Company in 1853. As treaties were made with the native peoples, including the Omahas themselves, the Ferry Company surveyed the land as capital directed frontier urbanization.[22] Meanwhile in Kansas, for instance, one commentator wrote, "the American people are about, then, to inaugurate a new and immense order of industrial production—pastoral agriculture."[23] Throughout the great west, agriculture would develop at an industrial pace as it "filled its appropriate place in the general economy of our industrial empire."[24] And the destiny of Kansas City was to be "one of the most substantial depots of this extensive empire."[25] While by 1875 the yearly dollar value of the combined production of major agricultural commodities for eleven combined states in the northeast amounted to around $383,421,397, for twelve combined western states it was around $715,824,075.[26]

The development of California, perhaps more than anything else, is demonstrative of the consolidation of American capitalism. And perhaps the gold rush more than anything symbolizes the mid-century mania for riches. Following the discovery of gold at Sutter's Mill at the end of the 1840s, the population rose from 25,000 in 1848 to 865,000 in 1880.[27] Native populations were pushed out and in some cases themselves employed to mine for gold.[28] Additionally, laborers came up from as far south as Chile and Peru and contracted out as far across the ocean as China as California developed through a global capitalist process.[29] And through this globalization San Francisco emerged as the central key point for the movements of commodities and labor across the state. Additionally, as in other cases, it was also quickly found that the soil—if irrigation systems were put in place—was highly bountiful.[30] Not only grains, but fruits grew in abundance as (along with Florida) California became the nation's fruit basket.[31]

As Bruce Cumings puts it, "California agriculture differed dramatically from the Jeffersonian ideal from the beginnings—in its industrial scope, its high-tech machines, and its employment of masses of cheaply paid labor in a milieu of rank exploitation."[32] From its relatively late development onward, always with an eye to the markets of the east, California developed into a capitalist powerhouse. As of 2016, for instance, California, ranked by GDP, was only topped by five *countries*.[33] California's development, resulting in Hollywood and Silicon Valley, emerged not only from its ecological resources, but from its position at the western edge of the continental American Empire. It provided not only a powerful state economy, but a ledge from which American power could expand.

In 1854 the Gadsden Purchase of the bottom part of Arizona and southwestern corner of New Mexico was the last piece of the continental empire the United States would acquire, not including "internal" colonization through the continual dispossession of Native Americans. And it was the result, basically, of a capitalist process. Eastern capitalists had long been pushing for the construction of a transcontinental railroad and this dream was taken up by James Gadsden, President of the South Carolina Railroad Company.[34] In an attempt to prevent revolution in Mexico, and desperately seeking funds, Santa Anna finally agreed to the treaty which provided Mexico with $10 million in return for the land.[35]

By 1870, the first transcontinental railroad had been completed, and three decades later five railroads ran across the continent. Railroads made the transportation of goods and peoples to incorporate the west into capitalism possible, and were a profitable industry in themselves. And a significant amount of capital came from Britain, as between the Civil War and First World War, 34 percent of Britain's overseas portfolio investment went to the United States. Effectively, it was not just western-oriented companies building the railroads, but British capital, transferred to New York City banks, then flowing to the west that developed the western capitalist frontier.[36]

Of course, as with the entire history of American expansion up to this point, there was one major obstacle to expansion: the fact that the land was populated by native peoples. During the Civil War itself southerners continued to see it as their own Manifest Destiny to continue expanding west as, for example, from autumn 1861 to summer 1862, 2,700 soldiers transported thousands of animals, and, of course, themselves, west from Texas to New Mexico. And under Henry Silbey, in 1862 Texas troops traveled west to Glorieta Mesa, outside of Santa Fe, where they were attacked by soldiers from Colorado at the Battle of Glorieta Pass, after which they were forced to retreat.[37] And under the leadership of Christopher "Kit" Carson, Indian wars continued in the southeast against, among other tribes, Mescaleros and Navajos. After a campaign against the Navajos, for example, the natives were finally coerced to go to Bosque Redondo, New Mexico, and on their 300-mile march 300 were reported dead, 200 escaped, and several children stolen (as Hispanos and Pueblos appear to have raided them). And more generally, while 10,000 were said to have made the journey, only 8,000 arrived, their whereabouts unknown, whether enslaved, killed, or escaped.[38]

Further north, wars with indigenous peoples also continued through the Civil War. The Sioux rose up against Americans in Minnesota in 1862, and war with various native groups broke out again in 1864. Led by John Evans and John Chivington, American soldiers waged a campaign of cleansing against the Cheyenne in Colorado. At Sand Creek Village on November 29, 1864, while men were out hunting, 700 soldiers attacked, killing over 100 women and children. In response, Sioux, Cheyenne, and Arapaho attacked American stations and ranches in the era, triggering a broader war in the South Platte area.[39]

After the Civil War the last wave of ethnic cleansing continued. From the Mexican-American War to 1892, according to the War Department, thirty-four wars were fought with natives, and between 1866 and 1876 alone, 200 military engagements occurred.[40] Among other figures Americans continue to glorify, in 1868 General Custer and his troops killed 103 indigenous people near the Washita River in Kansas, and, although it turned out that these were not hostile natives but friendly Cheyenne, he considered it a noble battle. And "Buffalo Bill," William F. Cody, killed over 4,000 animals as, between 1872 and 1874, over 6 million buffalo were killed in the great plains, mostly by whites, as the natives' modes of production were destroyed.[41] Yet today, figures such as these are memorialized as American heroes for paving the way for the expansion of the great white country.[42]

The reservation system also became increasingly used after the Civil War. As natives were forced into reservations, and, in some cases, do-gooding whites set up native schools to supposedly "civilize" them, they continued to lose their land. From 1881 to 1900, for example, the amount of land natives held went down from 155,632,312 acres to 77,865,373 acres. And finally, at the Battle of Wounded Knee, the indigenous peoples were, essentially, fully subordinated and defeated by the United States. The roots of the war went back to the discovery of gold in South Dakota's Black Hills in the middle of the 1870s, after which, through a decade and a half of war, the natives were cleansed so that the whites could turn the land and resources into profits.[43]

Imperialism ad infinitum

This book has examined the history of how the rise of capitalism transformed the shape of American Empire over two and a half centuries. The narrative began with the international development of capitalism in Europe. It was through the formation of European capitalism and Europe's globalizing links with the rest of the world that white-settler colonialism reached the shores of New England and Virginia. And, while in each case a joint-stock company provided the investment so potential settlers could realize their dreams, the social relations that developed in the early colonies differed drastically both from each other and were somewhat unique from the land the colonists came from. The forms these settlements took, then, went on to shape the pathways of empire in the north and south. From the submission of capitalist tendencies to the moral economy in the north, to the violence of slave capitalism in the south, the first colonies set the course of future empire.

From here, the story moved west as the American settler population grew, fueled both by the expanded reproduction of colonial society and the continual influx of European immigrants and African slaves to the so-called New World. Of course the land that became the United States was far from unsettled. Although colonialists may have viewed the early western frontier as an empty space to conquer, the narrative told here has also discussed the ways this involved the dispossession and destruction of native populations who continually resisted the force of empire. And this powerful, complex social force also shaped, and was shaped by, the forms of racism and patriarchy that developed in the colony-into-independent empire. Expansion west was pushed by both the political economy of colonialism and by the reproduction of masculinity through "independence" expressed through imperialism as, generally, the ever-expanding frontier was built by white men who brought their families and slaves further and further west.

The argument made here has also suggested that plantation slavery was central to the history of capitalism. In a sense, it was an especially powerful form of capitalism, as capitalists did not simply buy the temporary labor time of the wage laborer, but had total bodily control over the life of the unpaid, violently controlled slave. But I have also suggested that while plantations were essentially capitalist institutions, not all slavery was necessarily capitalist, as small farmers in some cases incorporated slaves into a patriarchal household mode of social reproduction, similar to the frontier yeomen of the north.

Throughout the story the book has also emphasized the continual usage of the imagery of empire by Americans. Not only were white colonialists building an empire, they were highly self-aware that they were as the term "empire" was regularly used to triumphantly describe the society they were creating. But while this language fell out of use by the latter part of the 1800s, particularly as "imperialism" became criticized publicly, by the end of the nineteenth century the United States was essentially a dominant capitalist empire, and ready to establish its place as the premier power in an increasingly capitalist global order. But in many ways this was only the beginning of the story of American Empire. The raw materials and resources made available by the spatial capitalist conquest of the west would allow the United States to propel itself to the world stage.[44] By the end of the century, Hawaii would be incorporated into the empire as a result of American sugar planters taking control of the islands and overthrowing the indigenous government, and the Spanish-American War would further extend the grasp of America's capitalist empire. And, to this day, the United States is setting its sights on the conquest and control of the next frontiers: cyberspace and outer-space.[45] The end of the imperial vision is yet to be in sight.

Notes

On the Prospect of Planting Arts and Learning in America

1. George Berkeley, "On the Prospects of Planting Arts and Learning in America," in *Library of the World's Best Literature, Ancient and Modern, Vol. 4*, ed. Charles Dudley Warner (New York: R.S. Peale and J.A. Hill, 1897).

Introduction: The Embrace of Empire

1. Emanuel Gottlieb Leutze, "Westward the Course of Empire Takes Its Way" (Washington, DC: Architects of the Capitol, 1862), accessed January 15, 2017 at www.aoc.gov/capitol-hill/other-paintings-and-murals/westward-course-empire-takes-its-way.
2. Smithsonian American Art Museum, "Westward the Course of Empire Takes Its Way (Mural Study, U.S. Capitol)" (Washington, DC: Smithsonian Art Museum, 2012), accessed February 13, 2017 at http://americanart.si.edu/collections/search/artwork/researchNotes/1931.6.1.pdf.
3. Edwin C. Manning, ed., *The Big Blue Union* (Marysville, KA, 1866); Jerry L. Wallace, *Remembering Edwin Cassander Manning: The Founder of Winfield, Kansas* (Winfield, KA: Cowley County Historical Society, 2010), accessed January 29, 2017 at www.cchsm.com/resources/research/wallace/manning.pdf.
4. For a thorough discussion of the ways that early Americans embraced the idea of empire culturally and politically also see: Edward Larkin, *The American School of Empire* (New York: Cambridge University Press, 2016).
5. Joseph John Gurney, *A Journey in North America, Described in Familiar Letters to Amelia Opie* (Norwich: Josiah Fletcher, 1841), 34.
6. Henry R. Schoolcraft, *A View of the Lead Mines of Missouri; Including Some Observations on the Mineralogy, Geology, Geography, Antiquities, Soil, Climate, Population, and Productions of Missouri and Arkansaw, and Other Sections of the Western Country* (New York: Charles Wiley & Co., 1819), 4.
7. This distinction is a play on the terms "society with slaves" and "slave society" which historians of slavery, most significantly in the American case, Ira Berlin, have elaborated upon. See: Ira Berlin, *Many Thousands Gone: The First Two Centuries of Slavery in North America* (Cambridge, MA: Belknap Press of Harvard University, 1998).

8. Francis J. Grund, *The Americans in their Moral, Social, and Political Relations Volume II* (London: Longman, Rees, Orme, Brown, Green, & Longman, 1837), 1.
9. Grund, *The Americans*, 60–1.
10. William Appleman Williams, *Empire as a Way of Life* (New York: Ig Publishing, 2007).
11. For a survey of the literature through the 1980s see: Anthony Brewer, *Marxist Theories of Imperialism: A Critical Survey* (New York: Routledge and Kegan Paul, 1987). For a discussion of the revival of debates over imperialism in the early and mid-2000s see: Vivek Chibber, "The Return of Imperialism to Social Science," *European Journal of Social Science* 45 (2004): 427–41.
12. James Parisot, "Expanding Geopolitical Economy: A Critique of the Theory of Successive Hegemonies," in *Theoretical Engagements in Geopolitical Economy (Research in Political Economy, Volume 30A)*, ed. Radhika Desai (Bingley, UK: Emerald, 2015), 155–74.
13. Perhaps the most path-breaking work in the US historical context in this regard has been: Amy Kaplan and Donald E. Pease, eds., *Cultures of United States Imperialism* (Durham, NC: Duke University Press, 1993).
14. Fernand Braudel, "History and the Social Sciences: The *Longue Durée*," *Review (Fernand Braudel Center)* 32, no. 2 (2009): 171–203.
15. Immanuel Wallerstein has useful insights here in his criticisms of the ways that the existing "structures of knowledge" are based upon liberal, nineteenth-century assumptions that incorrectly separate politics, economics, "the social," and so on. For Wallerstein the solution is to embrace the idea of the "world-system" as a whole. But this is also problematic in that the idea of an all-encompassing world-system is, essentially, an abstraction imposed on history. By contrast, the methodology used in this book attempts to develop a more open and reflexive approach to the theory-history question. See, for example: Immanuel Wallerstein, *Unthinking Social Science: Limits of Nineteenth-Century Paradigms* (Philadelphia, PA: Temple University Press, 2011); Immanuel Wallerstein, *World-Systems Analysis: An Introduction* (Durham, NC: Duke University Press, 2004).
16. William Henry Drayton, *A Charge on the Rise of the American Empire* (Charlestown: David Bruce, 1776).
17. Grund, *The Americans*, 50–1.
18. Richard Koebner, *Imperialism: The Story and Significance of a Political Word 1840–1960* (New York: Cambridge University Press, 1964), 1 (emphases in the original).
19. Ray Kiely, *Rethinking Imperialism* (New York: Palgrave Macmillan, 2010), 2; Bernard Semmel, *The Liberal Ideal and the Demons of Empire: Theories of Imperialism from Adam Smith to Lenin* (Baltimore, MD: Johns Hopkins University Press, 1993), 5.
20. Emmeline, "Letter to the editor," *Morning Herald*, New York, November 11, 1837.

21. A Texan Lady, "History of Texas," *New-York Daily Tribune*, New York, vol. IV, no. 99, August 1, 1844.
22. "France," *National Intelligencer*, Washington, DC, July 6, 1848.
23. "Seven Days Later from Europe," *Evansville Daily Journal*, Evansville, IN, July 10, 1848.
24. Giuseppe Mazzini, *The Sentinel*, Winnfield, LA, August 27, 1859.
25. "The Presidents Interpretation of the Monroe Doctrine," *The Daily Phoenix*, Columbia, SC, December 16, 1865.
26. "Liberalism and Imperialism," *The Daily Evening Telegraph*, Philadelphia, PA, June 29, 1869.
27. "A Republican Aristocracy," *Nashville Union and American*, Nashville, TN, April 15, 1874.
28. "The Fifteenth Amendment. A Blow at the Organic Structure of the States and in the Interests of Imperialism," *The Democratic Press*, Ravenna, OH, May 6, 1869.
29. "Imperialism of the Grant Administration," *Nashville Union and American*, Nashville, TN, July 30, 1873.
30. "Hancock to the Front," *The St. Tammany Farmer*, Covington, LA, March 27, 1880.
31. Joseph Pulitzer, "What is Imperialism?" *The Newberry Herald*, Newberry, SC, September 29, 1880.
32. J.H. Tyndale, "Letters to 'Greenboy,'" *The Courier*, Lincoln, NE, October 28, 1899.
33. "An Honest Imperialist," *The Commoner*, Lincoln, NE, December 13, 1901.
34. Norman Etherington, *Theories of Imperialism: War, Conquest, and Capital* (Kent: Croom Helm, 1984), 10.
35. Walter LaFeber, *The New Empire: An Interpretation of American Expansion, 1860–1898* (Ithaca, NY: Cornell University Press, 1998).
36. Charles A. Conant, "The Economic Basis of 'Imperialism,'" *The North American Review*, 167, no. 502 (1898): 339.
37. Etherington, *Theories of Imperialism*, 31.
38. H. Gaylord Wilshire, *The Problem of the Trust* (Los Angeles, CA: B.R. Baumgardt & Co., 1900).
39. Cited in Etherington, *Theories of Imperialism*, 32.
40. Karl Marx, *Capital Volume I* (New York: Penguin Books, 1990), 256.
41. For some examples of work breaking down the free-unfree binary see: Marc W. Steinberg, "Capitalist Development, the Labor Process, and the Law," *American Journal of Sociology* 109, no. 2 (2003): 445–95; Jairus Banaji, *Theory as History: Essays on Modes of Production and Exploitation* (Chicago, IL: Haymarket Books, 2011); Carolyn Brown and Marcel van der Linden, "Shifting Boundaries between Free and Unfree Labor: Introduction," *International Labor and Working-Class History* 78 (2010): 4–11; Genevieve LeBaron, "Unfree Labour Beyond Binaries: Insecurity, Social Hierarchy and Labor Market Restructuring," *International Feminist Journal of Politics* 17, no. 1 (2015): 1–19.

42. The literature on Marxism, feminism, and social reproduction is voluminous. For some useful sources see: Lydia Sargent, ed., *Women and Revolution: A Discussion of the Unhappy Marriage of Marxism and Feminism* (Boston, MA: South End Press, 1981); Rosemary Hennessy and Chrys Ingraham, eds., *Materialist Feminism* (New York: Routledge, 1997); Lise Vogel, *Marxism and the Oppression of Women* (New Brunswick, NJ: Rutgers University Press, 1987); Leopoldina Fortunati, *Arcane of Reproduction: Housework, Prostitution, Labor and Capital* (Brooklyn, NY: Autonomedia, 1996); Silvia Federici, *Caliban and the Witch* (Brooklyn, NY: Autonomedia, 2004); Sue Ferguson and David McNally, "Social Reproduction Beyond Intersectionality: An Interview," *Viewpoint* 5 (2015), accessed October 25, 2017 at www.viewpointmag.com/2015/10/31/social-reproduction-beyond-intersectionality-an-interview-with-sue-ferguson-and-david-mcnally/; Michelle Murphy, "Reproduction," in *Marxism and Feminism*, ed. Shahrzad Mojab (London: Zed Books, 2015), 287–304.
43. For a discussion of the concept of "violent abstraction" see: Derek Sayer, *The Violence of Abstraction: The Analytic Foundations of Historical Materialism* (Oxford: Basil Blackwell, 1989).
44. Jean-Paul Sartre, *Search for a Method* (New York: Vintage Books, 1968), 37.
45. E.P. Thompson, *The Poverty of Theory and Other Essays* (New York: Monthly Review Press, 2008), 62 (emphasis in the original).
46. Banaji, *Theory as History*, 6. In this sense, the perspective offered here differs from both world-systems analysis and political Marxism. See: Immanuel Wallerstein, *The Modern World System: Capitalist Agriculture and the Origins of the European World-Economy in the Sixteenth Century* (New York: Academic Press, 1974); T.H. Aston and C.H.E. Philpin, eds., *The Brenner Debate: Agrarian Class Structure and Economic Development in Pre-Industrial Europe* (New York: Cambridge University Press, 1995).
47. For some main representative works of this trend see: Charles Grier Sellers, *The Market Revolution: Jacksonian America, 1815–1846* (New York: Oxford University Press, 1991); John Lauritz Larson, *The Market Revolution in America: Liberty, Ambition, and the Eclipse of the Common Good* (New York: Cambridge University Press, 2010).
48. For some examples of this position, each with their own variations, see: Eugene Genovese, *The Political Economy of Slavery; Studies in the Economy and Society of the Slave South* (New York: Pantheon Books, 1967); John Ashworth, *Slavery, Capitalism, and Politics in the Antebellum Republic Volume I: Commerce and Compromise 1820–1850* (New York: Cambridge University Press, 1995); Charles Post, *The American Road to Capitalism: Studies in Class-Structure, Economic Development and Political Conflict, 1620–1877* (Chicago, IL: Haymarket Books, 2012).
49. For some works that view slavery as a type of capitalism see: Robert William Fogel, *Without Consent or Contract: The Rise and Fall of American Slavery* (New York: Norton & Co., 1989); Alan Olmstead and Paul Rhode,

"Biological Innovation and Productivity Growth in the Antebellum Cotton Economy," *Journal of Economic History* 68, no. 4 (2008): 1123–71; Walter Johnson, *River of Dark Dreams: Slavery and Empire in the Cotton Kingdom* (Cambridge, MA: Harvard University Press, 2013); Caitlin Rosenthal, "From Memory to Mastery: Accounting for Control in America, 1750–1880," *Enterprise and Society* 14, no. 4 (2013): 732–48; Calvin Schermerhorn, *The Business of Slavery and the Rise of American Capitalism, 1815–1860* (New Haven, CT: Yale University Press, 2015); Sven Beckert, *Empire of Cotton: A Global History* (New York: Alfred A. Knopf, 2015); Edward Baptist, *The Half Has Never Been Told: Slavery and the Making of American Capitalism* (New York: Basic Books, 2016).

50. For a discussion of American Empire as manager of contemporary domestic and global capitalism see: Leo Panitch and Sam Gindin, *The Making of Global Capitalism* (New York: Verso, 2013).
51. For examples of transhistorical perspectives see: Michael Doyle, *Empires* (Ithaca, NY: Cornell University Press, 1986); Jane Burbank and Frederick Cooper, *Empires in World History: Power and the Politics of Difference* (Princeton, NJ: Princeton University Press, 2010), 23–42; Herfried Munkler, *Empires: The Logic of World Domination from Ancient Rome to the United States* (Malden, MA: Cambridge University Press, 2007), 5; Charles Maier, *Among Empires: American Ascendency and its Predecessors* (Cambridge, MA: Harvard University Press, 2006), 31; Robert Aldrich and Kristen McKenzie, eds., *The Routledge History of Western Empires* (New York: Routledge, 2014).
52. For the Marxist debate over imperialism in recent years see, for example: David Harvey, *The New Imperialism* (Oxford: Oxford University Press, 2003); Ellen Meiksins Wood, *Empire of Capital* (New York: Verso, 2003); Giovanni Arrighi, *The Long Twentieth Century* (New York: Verso, 2006); Alex Callinicos, *Imperialism and the Global Political Economy* (Cambridge: Polity, 2009); Panitch and Gindin, *The Making of Global Capitalism*.
53. For an example of this lacuna see: Ronald H. Chilcote, *Imperialism: Theoretical Directions* (Amherst, NY: Humanity Books, 2000).
54. W.E.B. Du Bois, *Darkwater: Voices from Within the Veil* (Mineola, NY: Dover Publications, 1999).
55. Du Bois, *Darkwater*, 24.

1. The Origins of Colonial Society

1. While there has been a tendency to view the origins of capitalism in the sixteenth century, whether in England specifically or as part of the origins of the modern world system, a variety of scholars have discussed evidence of the pre-sixteenth-century history of capitalism. See, for example: Henri Pirenne, "The Stages in the Social History of Capitalism," *American Historical Review* 19, no. 3 (1914): 494–515; Oliver Cox, *The Foundations of Capitalism* (New York: Philosophical Library, 1959); Maurice Aymard, "From Feudalism to Capitalism in Italy: The Case that

Doesn't Fit," *Review (Fernand Braudel Center)* 6, no. 2 (1982): 131–208; Fernand Braudel, *The Perspective of the World: Civilization & Capitalism 15th–18th Century Volume 3* (New York: Harper & Row, 1984); Janet Abu-Lughod, *Before European Hegemony: The World System A.D. 1250–1350* (New York: Oxford University Press, 1989); Eric Mielants, *The Origins of Capitalism and the "Rise of the West"* (Philadelphia, PA: Temple University Press, 2008); Henry Heller, *The Birth of Capitalism: A 21st Century Perspective* (London: Pluto Press, 2011). For a recent attempt to interpret the origins of capitalism through a non-Eurocentric lens also see: Alexander Anievas and Kerem Nişancioğlu, *How the West Came to Rule: The Geopolitical Origins of Capitalism* (London: Pluto Press, 2015). While their approach provides a space for understanding the international context out of which European capitalism could arise, it does not necessarily present a theoretical approach that can explain the social dynamics of the origins and rise of capitalism itself.

2. David Nicholas, *Medieval Flanders* (New York: Longman, 1992), 113.
3. Nicholas, *Medieval Flanders*, 203–5.
4. Jan Dumolyn and Jelle Haemers, "Patterns of Urban Rebellion in Medieval Flanders," *Journal of Medieval History* 31 (2005): 375.
5. Braudel, *The Perspective of the World*, 101.
6. Abu-Lughod, *Before European Hegemony*, 87.
7. Tim Soens, "Floods and Money: Funding Drainage and Flood Control in Coastal Flanders from the Thirteenth to the Sixteenth Centuries," *Continuity and Change* 26, no. 3 (2011): 342–5.
8. Peter Stabel, "Guilds in Late Medieval Flanders: Myths and Realities of Guild Life in an Export-Oriented Environment," *Journal of Medieval History* 30 (2004): 200.
9. Bas van Bavel, "The Medieval Origins of Capitalism in the Netherlands," *Low Countries Historical Review* 125, no. 2–3 (2010): 45–79.
10. Benedikt Koehler, *Early Islam and the Birth of Capitalism* (New York: Lexington Books, 2014), 172–6.
11. Gene W. Heck, *Charlemagne, Muhammad, and the Arab Roots of Capitalism* (Berlin: Walter de Gruyter, 2006), 218–19.
12. Koehler, *Early Islam*, 194.
13. Heck, *Charlemagne, Muhammad*, 227.
14. Giovanni Arrighi, *The Long Twentieth Century* (New York: Verso, 2006), 101.
15. Robin Blackburn, *The Making of New World Slavery: From the Baroque to the Modern 1492–1800* (New York: Verso, 1998), 106.
16. Immanuel Wallerstein, *The Modern World System: Capitalist Agriculture and the Origins of the European World-Economy in the Sixteenth Century* (New York: Academic Press, 1974), 326.
17. Blackburn, *The Making of New World Slavery*, 108–9, 137, 167–8.
18. Ellen Meiksins Wood, *The Origin of Capitalism: A Longer View* (New York: Verso, 2002).

19. Michael Merrill, "Cash is Good to Eat: Self-Sufficiency and Exchange in the Rural Economy of the United States," *Radical History Review* 13 (1977): 42–71; Robert Mutch, "Yeoman and Merchant in Pre-Industrial America: Eighteenth Century Massachusetts as a Case Study," *Societas* 7 (1977): 279–302; James Henretta, "Families and Farms: Mentalité in Pre-Industrial America," *The William and Mary Quarterly* 35, no. 1 (1978): 3–32; Robert Mutch, "Colonial America and the Debate about Transition to Capitalism," *Theory and Society* 9, no. 6 (1980): 847–63; Stephen Hahn and Jonathan Prude, eds., *The Countryside in the Age of Capitalist Transformation: Essays in the Social History of Rural America* (Chapel Hill, NC: University of North Carolina Press, 1986); Michael Merrill, "The Anticapitalist Origins of the United States," *Review: Fernand Braudel Center* 13 (1990): 465–97; Sue Headlee, *The Political Economy of the Family Farm: The Agrarian Roots of American Capitalism* (New York: Praeger, 1991); Elizabeth A. Perkins, "The Consumer Frontier: Household Consumption in Early Kentucky," *Journal of American History* 78, no. 2 (1991): 486–510; Allan Kulikoff, *The Agrarian Origins of American Capitalism* (Charlottesville, VA: University Press of Virginia, 1992); N.G. Osterud, "Gender and the Transition to Capitalism in Rural America," *Agricultural History* 67 (1993): 14–29; John Ashworth, *Slavery, Capitalism, and Politics in the Antebellum Republic Volume I: Commerce and Compromise 1820–1850* (New York: Cambridge University Press, 1995); Paul A. Gilje, "The Rise of Capitalism in the Early Republic," *Journal of the Early Republic* 16, no. 2 (1996): 159–81; Craig T. Friend, "Merchants and Markethouses: Reflections on Moral Economy in Early Kentucky," *Journal of the Early Republic* 17, no. 4 (1997): 553–74; Richard Lyman Bushman, "Markets and Composite Farms in Early America," *The William and Mary Quarterly* 55, no. 3 (1998): 351–74; Christopher Clark, *The Roots of Rural Capitalism: Western Massachusetts, 1780–1860* (Ithaca, NY: Cornell University Press, 1999); Amy Dru Stanley, *From Bondage to Contract: Wage Labor, Marriage, and the Market in the Age of Slave Emancipation* (New York: Cambridge University Press, 1998); Allan Kulikoff, *From British Peasants to Colonial American Farmers* (Chapel Hill, NC: University of North Carolina Press, 2000); Naomi Lamoreaux, Daniel Raff, and Peter Temin, "Beyond Markets and Hierarchies: Toward a New Synthesis of American Business History," *American Historical Review* 108 (2003): 404–33; Naomi Lamoreaux, "Rethinking the Transition to Capitalism in the Early American Northeast," *Journal of American History* 90 no. 2 (2003): 437–61; Donald J. Ratcliffe, "The Market Revolution and Party Alignments in Ohio, 1828–1840," in *The Pursuit of Public Power: Political Culture in Ohio, 1787--1861*, eds. Jeffrey Paul Brown and Andrew R.L. Cayton (Kent, OH: Kent State University Press, 1994), 99–106; Ginette Aley, "A Republic of Farm People: Women, Families, and Market-Minded Agrarianism in Ohio, 1820s–1830s," *Ohio History* 114 (2007): 28–45; John Ashworth, *Slavery, Capitalism, and Politics in the Antebellum Republic Volume II: The Coming of the Civil War 1850–1861* (New York:

Cambridge University Press, 2007); Jeff Bremer, "Frontier Capitalism: Market Migration to Rural Central Missouri, 1815–1860," in *Southern Society and Its Transformations, 1790–1860*, eds. Michelle Gillespie, Susan Delfino, and Lous Kyriakoudes (Columbia, MI: University of Missouri Press, 2011), 79–101; Gary Edwards, "Anything That Would Pay: Yeomen Farmers and the Nascent Market Economy on the Antebellum Plantation Frontier," in *Southern Society and Its Transformations: 1790–1860*, eds. Susanna Delfino, Michele Gillespie, and Louis Kyriakoudes (Columbia, MI: University of Missouri Press, 2011), 102–30; Charles Post, *The American Road to Capitalism: Studies in Class-Structure, Economic Development and Political Conflict, 1620–1877* (Chicago, IL: Haymarket Books, 2012); Michael Zakim and Gary John Kornblith, eds., *Capitalism Takes Command: The Social Transformation of Nineteenth Century America* (Chicago, IL: University of Chicago Press, 2012).

20. As Kupperman puts it, "Roanoke was intended to be parasitic; its reason for existence was the Spanish treasure fleet, which was in turn parasitic on the Indian peoples of Central and South America." Karen Ordahl Kupperman, *Roanoke: The Abandoned Colony* (Totowa, NJ: Rowman & Littlefield Publishers, 1984), 15.
21. Thomas Hariot, *A Brief and True Report of the New Found Land of Virginia* (New York: The History Book Club, 1951). Originally published in 1588.
22. Kupperman, *Roanoke: The Abandoned Colony*, 33–4.
23. Wesley Frank Craven, *The Virginia Company of London, 1606–1624* (Williamsburg, VA: Virginia 350th Anniversary Celebration Corporation, 2009).
24. Edmund S. Morgan, *American Slavery, American Freedom: The Ordeal of Colonial Virginia* (New York: W.W. Norton & Co., 1995), 72.
25. Allan Kulikoff, *From British Peasants*, 62.
26. Morgan, *American Slavery*, 84.
27. Morgan, *American Slavery*, 73.
28. Virginia Company, "A Note of the Shipping, Men, And Provisions, Sent to Virginia, by the Treasurer and Company in the Yeere 1619," in *The Records of the Virginia Company of London Volume III*, ed. Susan Myra Kingsbury (Washington, DC: Library of Congress, 1933), 115. Note from 1619.
29. Virginia Council and Company, "Letter to Governor and Council in Virginia," in *The Records of the Virginia Company* (September 11, 1621), 505.
30. To quote one example, "also that they wilbe pleased to allowe to the male children, of them and of all others begotten in Virginia, being the onely hope of posterity, a single share a piece, and shares for their issues or for themselves." John Pory, "A Reporte of the Manner of Proceeding in the General Assembly Convented at James City," in *The Records of the Virginia Company* (July 30–August 4, 1619), 160.
31. The full quote is: "for Powhaton and his Weroances it is Clere even to reason beside our experience that he loued not our neighbourhood

and therefore you may no way trust him, but if you finde it not best to make him yo[r] prisoner yet you make him yo[r] tributary, and all other his weroances about him first to acknowledge no other Lord but Kinge James, and so we shall free them all from the Tirrany of Powhaton." Virginia Council, "Instruccons Orders and Constitucons to Sr Thomas Gates Knight Governor of Virginia," in *The Records of the Virginia Company* (May, 1609), 19.

32. Virginia Council, "Instruccons Orders and Constitucons," 22.
33. Virginia Company, "A Note of the Shipping, Men, and Provisions, Sent and Prouided for Virginia," in *The Records of the Virginia Company* (1620), 240.
34. Virginia Council, "Instruccons Orders and Constitucons," 21.
35. Morgan, *American Slavery*, 82.
36. Morris Talpalar, *Sociology of Colonial Virginia* (New York: Philosophical Library, 1968), 54.
37. Nathaniel Claiborne Hale, *Virginia Venturer, a Historical Biography of William Claiborne, 1600–1677: The Story of the Merchant Venturers who Founded Virginia, and the War in the Chesapeake* (Richmond, VA: Dietz Press, 1951), 48.
38. Governor Argall, "Proclamations or Edicts," in *The Records of the Virginia Company* (May 18, 1618), 93.
39. For instance, their instructions to George Yeardley stated, "fifty other persons now sent and transported with you you place as tenants on the said Governors land and that all persons heretofore transported at the Common Charge of the Company since the coming away of S[r] Thomas Dale Knight late Deputy Governor be placed as Tennants on the said Companies Lands." Virginia Company, "Instructions to George Yeardley," in *The Records of the Virginia Company* (November 18, 1618), 99–100.
40. Talpalar, *Sociology of Colonial Virginia*, 67.
41. William E. Nelson, *The Common Law in Colonial America* (New York: Oxford University Press, 2008), 45.
42. Morgan, *American Slavery*, 94.
43. Morgan, *American Slavery*, 95–108.
44. For example, "one chiefe [error] whereof hath byn the excessive applying of Tobacco, and the neglect to plant Corne w[ch] of all other thinge is most necessarie for the increase of the plantation." Treasurer and Council for Virginia, "A Letter to Sir George Yeardley," in *The Records of the Virginia Company* (June 21, 1619), 147.
45. Pory, "A Reporte of the Manner of Proceeding in the General Assembly," 176.
46. "Auditor Wm. Byrd's Report on the Amount of Tobacco Pain to 'the Rangers' at the Heads of the Rivers for the Time they were in Service," in *Calendar of Virginia State Papers and Other Manuscripts, 1652–1781 Volume I*, ed. W.M.P. Palmer (New York: Kraus Reprint Corporation, 1968), 32. Originally published in 1692.

47. Sir Edwin Sandys, "A Letter to Sir Robert Naunton," in *The Records of the Virginia Company* (January 1619), 260.
48. David W. Galenson, *White Servitude in Colonial America: An Economic Analysis* (New York: Cambridge University Press, 1984), 11–12.
49. Kulikoff, *From British Peasants*, 51; Christopher Tomlins, *Freedom Bound: Law, Labor, and Civic Identity in Colonizing English America, 1580–1865* (New York: Cambridge University Press, 2010), 35.
50. Galenson, *White Servitude in Colonial America*, 13.
51. Tomlins, *Freedom Bound*, 38–40.
52. David Hackett Fischer, *Albion's Seed: Four British Folkways in America* (New York: Oxford University Press, 1989), 210.
53. Kulikoff, *From British Peasants*, 63.
54. Berkeley, Thorpe, Tracy, and Smith, "Agreement with Richard Smyth and Wife and Others," in *The Records of the Virginia Company* (September 1, 1620), 394.
55. James R. Perry, *The Formation of a Society on Virginia's Eastern Shore, 1615–1655* (Chapel Hill, NC: University of North Carolina Press, 2011).
56. Henry Hartwell, James Blair, and Edward Chilton, *The Present State of Virginia and the College* (Williamsburg: Colonial Williamsburg, Incorporated, 1940), 9. Originally written in 1697 and published in 1727.
57. Robert Beverly, *The History and Present State of Virginia* (Chapel Hill, NC: University of North Carolina Press, 1947), 104. Originally published in 1705.
58. Marion Tinling, ed., *The Correspondence of the Three William Byrds* (Charlottesville, VA: University of Virginia Press, 1977). For a broader discussion of these issues see: Charles J. Farmer, *In the Absence of Towns: Settlement of Country Trade in Southside Virginia, 1730–1800* (Lanham, MD: Rowman & Littlefield Publishers, 1993).
59. "The Petition of Philip Corven, a Negro, in all humility fhoweth," in *Calendar of Virginia State*, 10. Petition from 1675.
60. Edward Waterhouse, "A Declaration of the State of the Colony and a Relation of the Barbarous Massacre," in *The Records of the Virginia Company* (1622), 562.
61. "Petition of One Crawford," in *Calendar of Virginia State*, 19. Petition from 1685.
62. Winthrop D. Jordan, *White Over Black: American Attitudes Toward the Negro, 1550–1812* (New York: W.W. Norton & Co., 1977), 77.
63. Jordan, *White Over Black*, 79.
64. James Rice, *Tales from a Revolution: Bacon's Rebellion and the Transformation of Early America* (New York: Oxford University Press, 2012).
65. Gary B. Nash, *Red, White, and Black: The Peoples of Early North America* (Upper Saddle River, NJ: Pearson Prentice Hall, 2006), 167.
66. Beverly, *The History and Present State*, 271.
67. Hartwell, Blair, and Chilton, *The Present State of Virginia and the College*, 57.
68. Beverly, *The History and Present State*, 67.

69. Cotton Mather, *Magnalia Christi Americana, or, the Ecclesiastical History of New-England: from its First Planting, in the Year 1620, unto the Year of Our Lord 1698* (Hartford, CT: Silas Andrus & Son, 1855). Originally published in 1702.
70. Henry Seljins, "A Poem Concerning the Mighty Works of Jesus Christ in America Arranged in Seven Books By that Great and Most Learned Man, Mr. Cotton Mather," in Mather, *Magnalia Christi Americana*, 23.
71. George Offor, "Introduction," in Increase Mather, *Remarkable Providences Illustrative of the Earlier Days of American Colonisation* (London: John Russel Smith, 1856), x.
72. Lydia Marie Child, *The First Settlers of New-England, or, Conquest of the Pequods, Narragansets and Pokanokets: as Related by a Mother to her Children by a Lady of Massachusetts* (Boston, MA: Munroe and Francis, 1829), 158.
73. As she put it, "by indulgence of a disposition to tyrannize over the weak, we deprive ourselves of all those social and best affections, which were bestowed on us by the gracious Foundation of all good to promote the present and everlasting felicity of his creatures." Child, *The First Settlers*, iv.
74. Joseph A. Conforti, *Saints and Strangers: New England in British North America* (Baltimore, MD: Johns Hopkins University Press, 2005), 35–6.
75. Gloria Main, *Peoples of a Spacious Land: Families and Cultures in Colonial New England* (Cambridge, MA: Harvard University Press, 2001), 1.
76. Alan Taylor, *American Colonies: The Settling of North America* (New York: Penguin, 2001), 169.
77. Roger Thompson, *Mobility and Migration: East Anglian Founders of New England, 1629–1640* (Amherst, MA: University of Massachusetts Press, 1994), 23.
78. Fischer, *Albion's Seed*, 26.
79. Fischer, *Albion's Seed*, 27.
80. William G. Robbins, "The Massachusetts Bay Company: An Analysis of Motives," *The Historian* 32, no. 1 (1969): 83–98.
81. Frances Rose-Troup, *The Massachusetts Bay Company and Its Predecessors* (London: The Grafton Press, 1930).
82. Mark W. Crilly, "John Winthrop: Magistrate, Minister, Merchant," *The Midwest Quarterly* 40, no. 2 (1999): 190–1. Also see: Ronald Dale Karr, "The Missing Clause: Myth and the Massachusetts Bay Charter of 1629," *The New England Quarterly* 77, no. 1 (2004): 89–107.
83. "A Gen^{r}all Court At Mr Goff's House, on Monday, the Last Day of Novem^{b}, 1629," in *Records of the Governor and Company of the Massachusetts Bay in New England Vol. I*, ed. Nathaniel B. Shurtleff (Boston, MA: William White, Printer to the Commonwealth, 1853), 65. Record from 1629.
84. "A Gen^{r}all Court, on Wensday, the 25 of Novem., 1629," *Records of the Governor and Company* (1629), 63.
85. "The Charter of the Colony of the Massachusetts Bay in New England, 1628–1629," *Records of the Governor and Company* (1629), 17.

86. Max Weber, *The Protestant Ethic and the Spirit of Capitalism* (New York: Routledge, 2001).
87. William B. Weeden, *Economic and Social History of New England, 1620–1789* (New York: Houghton, Mifflin and Company, 1890), 49; Conforti, *Saints and Strangers*, 56–7.
88. For example, "the purpose, evidently, was not to make individual settlers rich in lands, nor even simply to dispose of land to those who would actually occupy and cultivate it all. But the resources of the company were to be used in building up a compact state of freeholders, covering a territory ample for the requirements of comfortable living—and nothing more." Melville Egleston, *The Land System of the New England Colonies* (New York: Evening Post Print, 1880), 18.
89. Egleston, *The Land System*, 37.
90. "A Generall Courte, held at Newetowne, the 17th of the 3rd M°, @ 1637, for Elections," *Records of the Governor and Company* (1637), 196.
91. Egleston, *The Land System*, 41.
92. See: "Att a Genr^{r}all Court, holden att Newe Towne, May 6th, 1635," *Records of the Governor and Company* (1635), 147; "Att a Genr^{r}all Court, holden att Newe Towne, Sept' 2, 1635," *Records of the Governor and Company* (1635), 157; "Att a Genr^{r}all Court, holden at Boston, September 8th, 1636," *Records of the Governor and Company* (1636), 147; "A Genr^{r}all Court, held at Newetowne, the 2nd Day of the 9th M°, 1637," *Records of the Governor and Company* (1637), 210.
93. "The 6 Marche, 1628," *Records of the Governor and Company* (1628), 33.
94. "Att a Genr^{r}all Court, holden att Newe Towne, Sept: 3, 1634," *Records of the Governor and Company* (1634), 124.
95. For example, "It was ordered, that carpenters, joyners, brickelayers, sawers, and thatchers shall not take aboue 2^{s} aday, nor any man shall giue more, vnder paine of x^{s} to taker & giuer; and that sawers shall not take aboue 4^{3} 6^{d} ye hundred for boards, att 6 scoore to the hundred, if they haue their wood felled & squared for them, & not aboue 5^{8} 6^{d} if they fell & square their wood themselues." "The first Court of Assistants, holden att Charlton, August 23rd, Ano Dm. 1630," *Records of the Governor and Company* (1630), 74.
96. Robert Keayne, *The Apologia of Robert Keayne*, ed. Bernard Bailyn (New York: Harper & Row, 1964), originally written in 1653; Archer, *Fissures in the Rock*, 80.
97. As one example put it, "Ordered, that noe mill^{r} shall take above the sixteenth pte of the corne hee grindes, & that euy millar shall have always ready in his mill, waights & scales pvided att his owne charge." "Att the Genr^{r}all Court, holden att Newe Towne, March 3, 1635," *Records of the Governor and Company* (1635), 168.
98. John Winthrop, *Winthrop's Journal "History of New England,"* ed. James Kendall Hosmer (New York: Scribner's Sons, 1908).

99. Robert Cushman, *The Sin and Danger of Self-Love Described in a Sermon Preached at Plymouth, in New England, 1621* (Boston, MA: Charles Ewer, 1846), 15. Originally written in 1621.
100. Cushman, *The Sin and Danger*, 25.
101. For instance, "It is further ordered, that noe pson, howse houlder or oth[r], shall spend his time idley or vnpffitably, vnder paine of such punishm[t] as the Court shall thinke meete to inflicte." "A Court, holden att Boston, Octob[r] 1st, 1633," *Records of the Governor and Company* (1633), 109.
102. "A Generall Court, holden at Boston, the 4th Day of the 7th Month, 1639," *Records of the Governor and Company* (1639), 274.
103. "A Generall Court, holden at Boston, the 4th Day of the 7th Month, 1639," 274.
104. "A Generall Court, held at Boston, the 7th Day of the 8th M[o], 1641," *Records of the Governor and Company* (1641), 344.
105. "A Court of Assistants, holden att Boston, Septemb[r] 6th, 1631," *Records of the Governor and Company* (1631), 91.
106. "A Quarter Court, held at Boston, the 3rd Day of the 7th Month, @ 1639," *Records of the Governor and Company* (1639), 269.
107. Winthrop, *Winthrop's Journal*, 147.
108. Eric Foner, *Free Soil, Free Labor, Free Men: The Ideology of the Republican Party before the Civil War* (New York: Oxford University Press, 1971); Jonathan A. Glickstein, *Concepts of Free Labor in Antebellum America* (New Haven, CT: Yale University Press, 1991).
109. Taylor, *American Colonies*, 172.
110. Archer, *Fissures in the Rock*, 128.
111. Archer, *Fissures in the Rock*, 129.
112. Taylor, *American Colonies*, 176–7.
113. Mather, *Magnalia Christi Americana*, 556 (emphases in the original). See also: Ibram X. Kendi, *Stamped from the Beginning: The Definitive History of Racist Ideas in America* (New York: Nation Books, 2017).
114. Maria Mies, *Patriarchy and Accumulation on a World Scale* (London: Zed Books, 1987); Osterud, "Gender and the Transition to Capitalism," 14–29; Wally Seccombe, *Weathering the Storm: Working-Class Families from the Industrial Revolution to the Fertility Decline* (New York: Verso, 1993); Wally Seccombe, *A Millennium of Change: Feudalism to Capitalism in Northwestern Europe* (New York: Verso, 1995); Silvia Federici, *Caliban and the Witch: Women, the Body, and Primitive Accumulation* (Brooklyn, NY: Autonomedia, 2004); Paddy Quick, "Feudalism and Household Production," *Science & Society* 74, no. 2 (2010): 157–83; Gary Blank, "Gender, Production and 'the Transition to Capitalism': Assessing the Historical Basis for a Unitary Materialist Theory," *New Proposals: Journal of Marxism and Interdisciplinary Inquiry* 4, no. 2 (2011): 6–28; Nicole Leach, "Transitions to Capitalism: Social Reproduction Feminism Encounters Political Marxism," *Historical Materialism* 24, no. 2 (2016): 111–37; Amy Dru Stanley, "Histories of Capitalism and Sex Difference," *Journal of the Early Republic* 36 (2016): 343–50.

115. Anne McClintock, *Imperial Leather: Race, Gender and Sexuality in the Colonial Context* (New York: Routledge, 1995).
116. Edward Said, *Culture and Imperialism* (New York: Vintage Books, 1994), 9 (emphasis in the original).
117. As Marxist feminists have shown, capitalism is not simply a mode of production but social reproduction. While the concept of a mode of production has tended to privilege the male-dominated industrial workplace and privilege men's labor over women's—and, for that matter, assume a heteronormative gender binary—to explain capitalism as a social totality means to examine *all* aspects of life under capitalism. Capitalism is not just a system defined by social class, or market relations, but by the way social norms are generated, the way power seeps into all aspects of social life, and the way gender relations are continually remade through the history of capital's expansion. Historical transitions to capitalism, then, meant transformation in production processes and the organization of labor, but also much more than this. It also meant the creation of new gender roles, and new conceptions of gender's spectrum, often viewed in terms of more or less strict notions of masculinity and femininity.
118. T.J. Gilfoyle, *City of Eros: New York City, Prostitution, and the Commercialization of Sex, 1790–1920* (New York: W.W. Norton & Co., 1992); Thomas A. Foster, ed., *Long before Stonewall: Histories of Same-Sex Sexuality in Early America* (Albany, NY: State University of New York Press, 2007). For another interesting case see also: Rachel Hope Cleaves, *Charity and Sylvia: A Same Sex Marriage in Early America* (New York: Oxford University Press, 2014).
119. Anne S. Lombard, *Making Manhood: Growing up Male in Colonial New England* (Cambridge, MA: Harvard University Press, 2003), 10.
120. Jeanne Boydston, *Home and Work: Housework, Wages, and the Ideology of Labor in the Early Republic* (Oxford: Oxford University Press, 1990), 4.
121. Kathleen M. Brown, *Good Wives, Nasty Wenches, and Anxious Patriarchs: Gender, Race, and Power in Colonial Virginia* (Chapel Hill, NC: University of North Carolina Press, 1996), 16; Mary Beth Norton, *Founding Mothers and Fathers: Gendered Power and the Forming of American Society* (New York: Alfred A. Knopf, 1996), 8.
122. William Fleming to Nancy Fleming, December 20, 1779, *Fleming-Edmonds Family Papers*, Filson Historical Society (emphasis in the original).
123. Lombard, *Making Manhood*, 27.
124. Richard Godbeer, *Sexual Revolution in Early America* (Baltimore, MD: Johns Hopkins University Press, 2002), 22.
125. Godbeer, *Sexual Revolution*, 45–50.
126. William Benemann, *Male-Male Intimacy in Early America: Beyond Romantic Friendships* (New York: Harrington Park Press, 2006).
127. Godbeer, *Sexual Revolution*, 123.
128. Letter from Patrick Henry to Annie Henry Christian, May 15, 1786, *Bullitt Family Papers Oxmoor Collection*, Filson Historical Society.

129. Letter from Annie Henry Christian to Anne Christian Fleming. Date unspecified, but likely late spring or summer 1786. *Bullitt Family Papers Oxmoor Collection*, Filson Historical Society.
130. Richard Taylor Jr. Letter, October 24, 1797, *Taylor-Hay Family Papers*, Filson Historical Society.
131. Kathleen Brown, "'Changed into the Fashion of a Man': The Politics of Sexual Difference in a Seventeenth Century Anglo-American Settlement," *Journal of the History of Sexuality* 6, no. 2 (1995): 176.
132. Brown, "Changed into the Fashion of a Man," 187–8.
133. Godbeer, *Sexual Revolution*, 79.
134. Greta LaFleur, "Sex and "Unsex": Histories of Gender Trouble in Eighteenth-Century North America," *Early American Studies: An Interdisciplinary Journal* 12, no. 3 (2014): 489.
135. Norton, *Founding Mothers and Fathers*, 222.
136. Mary Beth Norton, "The Evolution of White Women's Experience in Early America," *American Historical Review* 89, no. 3 (1984): 597.
137. Stanley, *From Bondage to Contract*, 10.
138. Alice Kessler-Harris, *Out to Work: The History of Wage-Earning Women in the United States* (New York: Oxford University Press, 1982), 12.
139. Kessler-Harris, *Out to Work*, 12.
140. Sharon Block, *Rape and Sexual Power in Early America* (Chapel Hill, NC: University of North Carolina Press, 2006), 6.
141. M.E. Kaan, *Taming Passion for the Public Good: Policing Sex in the Early Republic* (Albany, NY: State University of New York Press, 2013), 66.
142. Paula A. Treckel, *To Comfort the Heart: Women in Seventeenth-Century America* (New York: Twayne Publishers, 1996), 34.
143. Treckel, *To Comfort the Heart*, 38.
144. Godbeer, *Sexual Revolution*, 129.
145. J. Hector St. John Crèvecoeur, *Letters from an American Farmer, Describing Certain Provincial Situations, Manners, and Customs, and Conveying Some Idea of the State of the People of North America* (New York: Duffield & Company, 1904), 46–7. Originally published in 1782.
146. Carroll Smith-Rosenberg, *This Violent Empire: The Birth of an American National Identity* (Chapel Hill, NC: University of North Carolina Press, 2010), 7.
147. Godbeer, *Sexual Revolution*, 300.
148. M.E. Kaan, "Patriarchal Policing of Sex in the Early United States," *Politics & Gender* 7 (2011): 335–63.
149. Bruce Dorsey, *Reforming Men & Women: Gender in the Antebellum City* (Ithaca, NY: Cornell University Press, 2002), 39; Barbara J. Berg, *The Remembered Gate: Origins of American Feminism, the Woman and the City, 1800–1860* (New York: Oxford University Press, 1987); Janet Zollinger Giele, *Two Paths to Women's Equality: Temperance, Suffrage, and the Origins of Modern Feminism* (New York: Twayne Publishers, 1995).

150. Carolyn Eastman, "Fight Like a Man: Gender and Rhetoric in the Early Nineteenth-Century American Peace Movement," *American Nineteenth Century History* 10, no. 3 (2009): 253.
151. Nancy F. Cott, *Public Vows: A History of Marriage and the Nation* (Cambridge, MA: Harvard University Press, 2000), 50.
152. Stephanie Coontz, *The Social Origins of Private Life: A History of American Families 1600–1900* (New York: Verso, 1988), 224.
153. Francis J. Grund, *The Americans in their Moral, Social, and Political Relations Volume II* (London: Longman, Rees, Orme, Brown, Green, & Longman, 1837), 109.
154. Sally L. Kitch, *The Spectre of Sex: Gendered Foundations of Racial Formation in the United States* (Albany, NY: State University of New York Press, 2009).
155. Pauline Schloesser, *The Fair Sex: White Women and Racial Patriarchy in the Early American Republic* (Albany, NY: State University of New York Press, 2002).
156. Kathleen Brown, *Foul Bodies: Cleanliness in Early America* (New Haven, CT: Yale University Press, 2009), 340–1.
157. Melissa Stein, *Measuring Manhood: Race and the Science of Masculinity, 1830–1934* (Minneapolis, MN: University of Minnesota Press, 2015), 48.
158. Elizabeth Fox-Genovese, *Within the Plantation Household* (Chapel Hill, NC: University of North Carolina Press, 1988), 114.
159. Gilfoyle, *City of Eros*, 71.
160. Gilfoyle, *City of Eros*, 136.
161. Mary Ann Jimenez, "Madness in Early American History: Insanity in Massachusetts from 1700 to 1830," *Journal of Social History* 20, no. 1 (1986): 33.
162. Jonathan Ned Katz, *Gay American History: Lesbians & Gay Men in the U.S.A.* (New York: Penguin, 1992), 130–4.
163. Amy S. Greenberg, *Manifest Manhood and the Antebellum American Empire* (New York: Cambridge University Press, 2005); David G. Pugh, *Sons of Liberty: The Masculine Mind in Nineteenth-Century America* (Westport, CT: Greenwood Press, 1984).

2. The Expansion of Empire

1. The Marquis de Chastellux, *Travels in North-America, in the Years 1780–81–82* (New York, 1828), 34.
2. Chastellux, *Travels in North-America*, 34.
3. United States Bureau of the Census, *Historical Statistics of the United States Colonial Times to 1970* (Washington, DC: US Bureau of the Census, 1976), 1168.
4. United States Bureau of the Census, *Historical Statistics*, 89.
5. Will Mackintosh, "'Ticketed Through' the Commodification of Travel in the Nineteenth Century," *Journal of the Early Republic*, 32 (2012): 63.

6. William Amphlett, *The Emigrant's Directory to the Western States of North America; Including a Voyage out from Liverpool; the Geography and Topography of the Whole Western Country, According to its Latest Improvements; With Instructions for Descending the Rivers Ohio and Mississippi, also, a Brief Account of a New British Settlement on the Headwaters of the Susquehanna, in Philadelphia* (London: Longman, Hurst, Rees, Orme, and Brown, 1819), 67–8.
7. Amphlett, *The Emigrant's Directory*, 68–9.
8. Amphlett, *The Emigrant's Directory*, 69–70.
9. George Rogers Taylor, *The Transportation Revolution, 1815–1860* (New York: Harper & Row, 1951).
10. For the classic study on capitalist time discipline see: E.P. Thompson, "Time, Word-Discipline, and Industrial Capitalism," *Past and Present* 38 (1967): 56–97.
11. Gloria L. Main, "Rocking the Cradle: Downsizing the New England Family," *Journal of Interdisciplinary History* 37, no. 1 (2006): 42; Susan E. Klepp, *Revolutionary Conceptions: Women, Fertility, and Family Limitation in America, 1760–1820* (Chapel Hill, NC: University of North Carolina Press, 2009), 8.
12. Morton Owen Schapiro, "Land Availability and Fertility in the United States, 1760–1870," *Journal of Economic History* 42, no. 3 (1982): 577–600.
13. Benedict Anderson, *Imagined Communities* (New York: Verso Books, 2006).
14. For an insightful discussion of this see: Martin Brückner, "The Spectacle of Maps in British America, 1750–1800," in *Early American Cartographies*, ed. Martin Brückner (Chapel Hill, NC: University of North Carolina Press, 2011), 389–441.
15. Erwin Raisz, "Outline of the History of American Cartography," *Isis* 26 no. 2 (1937): 6; Library of Congress, "Mapping a New Nation: Abel Buell's Map of the United States, 1784," accessed May 22, 2017 at www.loc.gov/exhibits/mapping-a-new-nation/online-exhibition.html#obj005 or http://brbl-zoom.library.yale.edu/viewer/15637042.
16. Brückner, "The Spectacle of Maps," 418.
17. Karl Marx, *Capital Volume I* (New York: Penguin Books, 1990), 915.
18. Bernard Bailyn, *The New England Merchants in the Seventeenth Century* (Cambridge, MA: Harvard University Press, 1955), 10.
19. Rothenberg's study makes the point that the United States was never a non-market society; market relations existed, just as they did in different forms going back to antiquity. And she also acknowledges that modern market society is different than pre-modern. But while tracing price convergence may be an interesting symbolic way of understanding how market relations increasingly became more predominant over time, by suggesting that factors can be empirically tested through prediction and explicitly imposing a definition of the market economy from neoclassical economics onto American history, she is unable to provide an analysis of actual, concrete social relations and the ways they transformed over time.

Thus, she vaguely suggests but does not adequately define how a capitalist society may be different from a society with market relations. See: Winifred Barr Rothenberg, *From Market-Places to a Market Economy: The Transformation of Rural Massachusetts, 1750–1850* (Chicago, IL: University of Chicago Press, 1992). Additionally, the opposite of this, Rona Weiss has suggested, "class relations in seventeenth-century Massachusetts were largely noncapitalist." Rona S. Weiss, "Primitive Accumulation in the United States: The Interaction between Capitalist and Noncapitalist Class Relations in Seventeenth-Century Massachusetts," *Journal of Economic History* 42, no. 1 (1982): 77.

20. Kenneth A. Lockridge, *A New England Town: The First Hundred Years: Dedham, Massachusetts, 1636–1736* (New York: W.W. Norton & Co., 1970), 76. At risk of misrepresenting his argument, it should be noted that the non-Marxist author goes on to criticize "Marx's hopelessly idealized industrial proletariat."
21. Lockridge, *A New England Town*, 16.
22. Lockridge, *A New England Town*, 71–82.
23. Christine Leigh Heyrman, *Commerce and Culture: The Maritime Communities of Colonial Massachusetts, 1690–1750* (New York: W.W. Norton & Co., 1984), 48.
24. Heyrman, *Commerce and Culture*, 46–7.
25. Richard I. Melvoin, *New England Outpost: War and Society in Colonial Deerfield* (New York: W.W. Norton & Co., 1989), 132.
26. Melvoin, *New England Outpost*, 135–7.
27. Melvoin, *New England Outpost*, 172–3.
28. Marsha Hamilton, *Social and Economic Networks in Early Massachusetts* (University Park, PA: Penn State University Press, 2009), 30–1.
29. Hamilton, *Social and Economic Networks*, 42.
30. Daniel Vickers, *Farmers & Fishermen: Two Centuries of Work in Essex County, Massachusetts, 1630–1850* (Chapel Hill, NC: University of North Carolina Press, 1994), 91.
31. Vickers, *Farmers & Fishermen*, 98.
32. Vickers, *Farmers & Fishermen*, 161.
33. Francis J. Grund, *The Americans in their Moral, Social, and Political Relations Volume II* (London: Longman, Rees, Orme, Brown, Green, & Longman, 1837), 177, 178.
34. Crèvecoeur, *Letters*, 169.
35. George H. Moore, *Notes on the History of Slavery in Massachusetts* (New York: Negro Universities Press, 1968), 4. Originally published in 1866.
36. Christopher M. Spraker, "The Lost History of Slaves and Slave Owners in Billerica, Massachusetts, 1655–1790," *Historical Journal of Massachusetts* 42, no. 1 (2014): 113–15.
37. Elise Lemire, *Black Walden: Slavery and Its Aftermath in Concord, Massachusetts* (Philadelphia, PA: University of Pennsylvania Press, 2009), 16.

38. Gregory H. Nobles, *Divisions Throughout the Whole: Politics and Society in Hampshire County, Massachusetts, 1740–1755* (New York: Cambridge University Press, 1983), 108.
39. Nobles, *Divisions Throughout the Whole*, 112–19.
40. Christopher Clark, *The Roots of Rural Capitalism: Western Massachusetts, 1780–1860* (Ithaca, NY: Cornell University Press, 1990), 35.
41. Clark, *The Roots of Rural Capitalism*, 125.
42. Clark, *The Roots of Rural Capitalism*, 62.
43. Clark, *The Roots of Rural Capitalism*, 180.
44. Thomas Dublin, *Women at Work: The Transformation of Work and Community in Lowell, Massachusetts, 1826–1860* (New York: Columbia University Press, 1979).
45. Ritchie J. Garrison, *Landscape and Material Life in Franklin County, Massachusetts, 1770–1860* (Knoxville, TN: University of Tennessee Press, 1991), 65.
46. Garrison, *Landscape and Material Life*, 86.
47. Vickers, *Farmers & Fishermen*, 212.
48. Vickers, *Farmers & Fishermen*, 249–52.
49. Gerald F. Reid, "The Seeds of Prosperity and Discord: The Political Economy of Community Polarization in Greenfield, Massachusetts, 1770–1820," *Journal of Social History* 27, no. 2 (1993): 361–3.
50. Jonathan Prude, *The Coming of Industrial Order: Town and Factory Life in Rural Massachusetts, 1810–1860* (Amherst, MA: University of Massachusetts Press, 1985), 50.
51. Prude, *The Coming of Industrial Order*, 54.
52. Prude, *The Coming of Industrial Order*, 84–6.
53. John Melish, *Travels through the United States of America, in the Years 1806 & 1807, and 1809, 1810, & 1811; Including an Account of Passages Betwixt America and Britain, and Travels through Various Parts of Britain, Ireland, & Canada* (Philadelphia (printed for the author) and London: Reprinted for George Cowie and Co. In the Poultry, and John Cumming, Dublin, 1818), 84.
54. William Loughton Smith, *Journal of William Loughton Smith 1790–1791* (Cambridge: Cambridge University Press, 1917), 47.
55. Charles J. Taylor, *History of Great Barrington, (Berkshire County), Massachusetts* (Great Barrington: Clark W. Bryan & Co. Publishers, 1882), 101–34.
56. Taylor, *History of Great Barrington*, 357.
57. J.E.A. Smith, *The History of Pittsfield, (Berkshire County), Massachusetts, From the Year 1734 to the Year 1800* (Boston, MA: Lee and Shepard, 1869), 72.
58. Smith, *The History of Pittsfield*, 138.
59. Francis DeWitt, *Statistical Information Relating to Certain Branches of Industry in Massachusetts, For the Year Ending June 1, 1855* (Boston, MA: William White, Printer to the State, 1855), xiii.

60. Oliver Rink, "Before the English (1609–1664)," in *The Empire State: A History of New York*, ed. Klein Milton (Ithaca, NY: Cornell University Press, 2001), 12–13.
61. Japp Jacobs, *The Colony of New Netherland: A Dutch Settlement in Seventeenth Century America* (Ithaca, NY: Cornell University Press, 2009), 22–7.
62. Michael Kammen, *Colonial New York: A History* (New York: Scribner, 1975), 26.
63. Jacobs, *The Colony of New Netherland*, 30–1.
64. Rink, "Before the English," 27–8.
65. Jacobs, *The Colony of New Netherland*, 69–71.
66. Rink, "Before the English," 49.
67. Kammen, *Colonial New York*, 68.
68. Jaap Jacobs, *New Netherland: A Dutch Colony in Seventeenth-Century America* (Boston, MA: Brill, 2005), 383–4.
69. Jacobs, *The Colony of New Netherland*, 203–4.
70. Rink, "Before the English," 53.
71. Jacobs, *The Colony of New Netherland*, 37.
72. Immanuel Wallerstein, *The Modern World System II: Mercantilism and the Consolidation of the European World Economy. 1600–1750* (New York: Academic Press, 1980), 76–8.
73. Ronald Howard, "The English Providence (1664–1776)," in *The Empire State: A History of New York*, ed. Klein Milton (Ithaca, NY: Cornell University Press, 2001), 115.
74. Kammen, *Colonial New York*, 179–80.
75. Thomas E. Burke Jr., *Mohawk Frontier: The Dutch Community of Schenectady, New York, 1661–1710* (Ithaca, NY: Cornell University Press, 1991), 107.
76. Francis Whiting Halsey, *The Old Frontier: Its Wars with Indians and Tories, Its Missionary Schools, Pioneers and Land Titles* (New York: Charles Scribner's Sons, 1901), 99.
77. Ruth L. Higgins, *Expansion in New York with Especial Reference to the Eighteenth Century* (Philadelphia, PA: Porcupine Press, 1976), 98–9 (originally published in 1931); William Brewster, *The Pennsylvania and New York Frontier: History of from 1720 to the Close of the Revolution* (Philadelphia, PA: George S. MacManus Company, 1954), 194–7.
78. Staughton Lynd, *Class Conflict, Slavery, and the United States Constitution* (New York: Cambridge University Press, 2009). For an overview of feudalistic experiments in American history also see: Terence J. Byres, *Capitalism from Above and Capitalism from Below: An Essay in Comparative Political Economy* (New York: Palgrave Macmillan, 1996).
79. Lynd, *Class Conflict*, 66–7.
80. David Hamilton Grace, "Agricultural Gentility as a Revolutionary Social Vision: The Livingston Family and the New York Manor Class, 1660–1813," Dissertation, Department of History, University of Wisconsin, Madison, 2002. For what remains perhaps the definitive work on New

York manors, albeit with a slightly different perspective, also see: Sung Bok Kim, *Landlord and Tenant in Colonial New York: Manorial Society, 1664–1775* (Chapel Hill, NC: University of North Carolina Press, 1978).

81. Cynthia A. Kierner, *Traders and Gentlefolk: The Livingstons of New York, 1675–1790* (Ithaca, NY: Cornell University Press, 2011), 41–2. For a history of Robert Livingston's business career also see: Lawrence H. Leder and Vincent P. Carosso, "Robert Livingston (1654–1728): Businessman of Colonial New York," *The Business History Review* 30, no. 1 (1956): 18–45.
82. Martin Bruegel, *Farm, Shop, Landing: The Rise of a Market Society in the Hudson Valley, 1780–1860* (Durham, NC: Duke University Press, 2002), 44.
83. Charles W. McCurdy, *Anti-Rent Era in New York Law and Politics, 1839–1865* (Chapel Hill, NC: University of North Carolina Press, 2001).
84. Joseph S. Tiedemann and Eugene R. Fingerhut, eds., *The Other New York: The American Revolution Beyond New York City, 1763–1787* (Albany, NY: State University of New York Press, 2005).
85. Fred Anderson, *Crucible of War: The Seven Years' War and the Fate of Empire in British North America, 1754–1766* (New York: Vintage, 2000); Higgins, *Expansion in New York*, 87.
86. None of the towns in Alleghany, Broome, Cattaraugus, Cayuga, Chautauqua, Chemung, Chenango, Cortland, Erie, Franklin, Genesee, Hamilton, Jefferson, Lewis, Livingston, Madison, Monroe, Onondaga, Ontario, Orleans, St. Lawrence, Schuyler, Seneca, Steuben, Tioga, Tompkins, Wayne, Wyoming, and Yates counties were settled until the 1780s at the earliest. See: Higgins, *Expansion in New York*, 151–62.
87. Higgins, *Expansion in New York*, 117.
88. Edward Countryman, "From Revolution to Statehood (1776–1825)," in *The Empire State: A History of New York*, ed. Klein Milton (Ithaca, NY: Cornell University Press, 2001), 265.
89. William Chazanof, *Joseph Ellicott and the Holland Land Company* (New York: Syracuse University Press, 1970).
90. William Wyckoff, *The Developer's Frontier: The Making of the Western New York Landscape* (New Haven, CT: Yale University Press, 1988), 70–1.
91. Charles E. Brooks, *Frontier Settlement and the Market Revolution: The Holland Land Purchase* (Ithaca, NY: Cornell University Press, 1996), 24–6.
92. Brooks, *Frontier Settlement*, 76–92.
93. Brooks, *Frontier Settlement*, 48.
94. Clayton Mau, *The Development of Central and Western New York: From the Arrival of the White Man to the Eve of the Civil War as Portrayed Chronologically in Contemporary Accounts* (Rochester, NY: The Du Bois Press, 1944), 104–5.
95. Quoted in Mau, *The Development of Central and Western New York*, 174.
96. Quoted in Mau, *The Development of Central and Western New York*, 229.
97. Helen G. McMahon, *Chautauqua County: A History* (Buffalo, NY: Henry Stewart, 1964), 55.

98. McMahon, *Chautauqua County*, 84–117.
99. Andrew W. Young, *History of Chautauqua County, New York, from its First Settlement to the Present Time; with Numerous Biographical and Family Sketches* (Buffalo, NY: Printing House of Matthews & Warren, 1875), 101.
100. Brooks, *Frontier Settlement*, 64–5.
101. Chazanof, *Joseph Ellicott*, 54.
102. Alan Taylor, *William Cooper's Town: Power and Persuasion on the Frontier of the Early American Republic* (New York: Alfred A. Knopf, 1995), 97–110.
103. Diane Shaw, *City Building on the Eastern Frontier: Sorting the New Nineteenth-Century City* (Baltimore, MD: Johns Hopkins University Press, 2004), 30.
104. Carol Sheriff, *The Artificial River: The Erie Canal and the Paradox of Progress 1817–1862* (New York: Hill and Wang, 1996), 183.
105. Sheriff, *The Artificial River*, 40–5.
106. Susan Kleep, "Encounter and Experiment: The Colonial Period" in *Pennsylania: A History of the Commonwealth*, eds. Randall Millar and William Pencak (University Park, PA: Penn State University Press, 2002), 49–58.
107. Steven Craig Harper, *Promised Land: Penn's Holy Experiment, the Walking Purchase, and the Dispossession of the Delawares, 1600–1763* (Bethlehem, PA: Lehigh University Press, 2006), 28–9.
108. Edwin B. Bronner, *William Penn's "Holy Experiment": The Founding of Pennsylvania 1681–1701* (New York: Columbia University Press, 1963), 15.
109. Mary M. Schweitzer, *Custom and Contract: Household, Government, and the Economy in Colonial Pennsylvania* (New York: Columbia University Press, 1987), 89–96.
110. Bronner, *William Penn's "Holy Experiment,"* 64.
111. Gottfried Achenwall, *Achenwall's Obesrvations on North America, 1767* (Philadelphia, PA: Pennsylvania Magazine of History and Biography, 1903), 4.
112. Harper, *Promised Land*, 33.
113. Joseph E. Illick, *Colonial Pennsylvania: A History* (New York: Scribner, 1976), 30–6.
114. Gary B. Nash, *First City: Philadelphia and the Forging of Historical Memory* (Philadelphia, PA: University of Pennsylvania Press, 2002), 45–1.
115. Sharon V. Salinger, *"To Serve Well and Faithfully": Labor and Indentured Servants in Pennsylvania, 1682–1800* (New York: Cambridge University Press, 1987), 76.
116. Salinger, *"To Serve Well and Faithfully,"* 137–51.
117. Melish observed, "inquiry is then made what he can do; if he can work any trade, he is taken to the apartment where that branch is carried on, and has his task assigned to him … as a stimulus to industry, the convicts get credit in the books for the proceeds of their labour, and are debited with the expense of their board and clothing." Melish, *Travels through the United States*, 123.

118. John Smolenski, *Friends and Strangers the Making of a Creole Culture in Colonial Pennsylvania* (Philadelphia, PA: University of Pennsylvania Press, 2010).
119. Marianne Wokeck, "Pennsylvania: 'Hell for Preachers'?: Religion and the German Colonists," in *Backcountry Crucibles: The Lehigh Valley from Settlement to Steel*, eds. Jean R. Soderlund and Catherine S. Parzynski (Bethlehem, PA: Lehigh University Press, 2008), 26–37.
120. Arthur Cecil Bining, *Pennsylvania Iron Manufacture in the Eighteenth Century* (Harrisburg, PA: Pennsylvania Historical and Museum Commission, 1973), 20–7.
121. Bining, *Pennsylvania Iron Manufacture*, 96–153.
122. Beverly Prior Smaby, *The Transformation of Moravian Bethlehem: From Communal Mission to Family Economy* (Philadelphia, PA: University of Pennsylvania Press, 1988), 9.
123. Thomas Anburey, *Travels through the Interior Parts of America in a Series of Letters, Volume II* (Boston, MA: Houghton Mifflin Company, 1923), 298. Originally published in 1789.
124. Smaby, *The Transformation of Moravian Bethlehem*, 34–6.
125. Smaby, *The Transformation of Moravian Bethlehem*, 42–5.
126. Jerome H. Wood Jr., *Conestoga Crossroads: Lancaster, Pennsylvania 1730–1790* (Harrisburg, PA: Pennsylvania Historical and Museum Commission, 1979), 5.
127. Richard C. Wade, *The Urban Frontier: Pioneer Life in Early Pittsburgh, Cincinnati, Lexington, Louisville, and St. Louis* (Chicago, IL: University of Chicago Press, 1959). For a more recent discussion of cities and the development of the west see: Char Miller, *Cities and Nature in the American West* (Reno, NV: University of Nevada Press, 2010).
128. Wood Jr., *Conestoga Crossroads*, 9–11.
129. Rodger C. Henderson, *Community Development and the Revolutionary Transition in Eighteenth-Century Lancaster County, Pennsylvania* (New York: Garland Publishing, 1989), 49–56, 110–19.
130. Henderson, *Community Development*, 201.
131. Ella Chalfant, *A Goodly Heritage: Earliest Wills on an American Frontier* (Pittsburgh: University of Pittsburgh Press, 1955), 122.
132. Chalfant, *A Goodly Heritage*, 27.
133. For detailed discussions of conflicts over authority in Pennsylvania see: Daniel P. Barr, *A Colony Sprung from Hell: Pittsburgh and the Struggle for Authority on the Western Pennsylvania Frontier, 1744–1794* (Kent, OH: Kent State University Press, 2014); Patrick Spero, *Frontier Colony: The Politics of War in Early Pennsylvania* (Philadelphia, PA: University of Pennsylvania Press, 2016).
134. Kevin Kenny, *Peaceable Kingdom Lost the Paxton Boys and the Destruction of William Penn's Holy Experiment* (New York: Oxford University Press, 2009), 33.
135. Harper, *Promised Land*, 39.
136. Harper, *Promised Land*, 63–9.

137. Richard White, *"It's Your Misfortune and None of My Own": A History of the American West* (Norman, OK: University of Oklahoma Press, 1991).
138. David L. Preston, "Squatters, Indians, Proprietary Government, and Land in the Susquehanna Valley," in *Friends and Enemies in Penn's Woods: Indians, Colonists, and the Racial Construction of Pennsylvania*, eds. William Pencak and Daniel K. Richter (University Park, PA: University of Pennsylvania Press, 2004), 181.
139. Krista Camenzind, "Metonymy, Violence, Patriarchy, and the Paxton Boys," in *Friends and Enemies in Penn's Woods: Indians, Colonists, and the Racial Construction of Pennsylvania*, eds. William Pencak and Daniel K. Richter (University Park, PA: University of Pennsylvania Press, 2004), 202.
140. Camenzind, "Metonymy, Violence, Patriarchy, and the Paxton Boys," 204–6.
141. Paul Moyer, "'Real' Indians, 'White' Indians, and the Contest for the Wyoming Valley," in *Friends and Enemies in Penn's Woods: Indians, Colonists, and the Racial Construction of Pennsylvania*, eds. William Pencak and Daniel K. Richter (University Park, PA: University of Pennsylvania Press, 2004), 221.
142. Kenny, *Peaceable Kingdom Lost*, 51.
143. Kenny, *Peaceable Kingdom Lost*, 218.
144. Solon J. Buck and Elizabeth Hawthorn Buck, *The Planting of Civilization in Western Pennsylvania* (Pittsburgh, PA: University of Pittsburgh Press, 1939), 152.
145. Buck and Buck, *The Planting of Civilization*, 205.
146. Thomas P. Slaughter, *The Whiskey Rebellion: Frontier Epilogue to the American Revolution* (New York: Oxford University Press, 1986), 65.
147. Eugene Harper, *The Transformation of Western Pennsylvania, 1770–1800* (Pittsburgh, PA: University of Pittsburgh Press, 1991), 26.
148. Amphlett, *The Emigrant's Directory*, 74.
149. Anburey, *Travels through the Interior Parts of America*, 163.
150. Harper, *The Transformation of Western Pennsylvania*, 30–5.
151. Harper, *The Transformation of Western Pennsylvania*, 63.
152. Slaughter, *The Whiskey Rebellion*, 65.
153. Lynd, *Class Conflict, Slavery, and the United States Constitution.*
154. Leonard L. Richards, *Shays's Rebellion: The American Revolution's Final Battle* (Philadelphia, PA: University of Pennsylvania Press, 2002); Woody Holton, *Unruly Americans and the Origins of the Constitution* (New York: Hill and Wang, 2007).
155. Holton, *Unruly Americans*, 187.
156. For a broader discussion of the constitution in relation to American expansion see: Gary Lawson and Guy Seidman, *The Constitution of Empire* (New Haven, CT: Yale University Press, 2004); Sanford Levinson and Bartholomew H. Sparrow, eds., *The Louisiana Purchase and American Expansion, 1803–1898* (Oxford: Rowman & Littlefield Publishers, 2005).
157. Slaughter, *The Whiskey Rebellion*, 71–95.

158. H.M. Brackenridge, *History of the Western Insurrection, 1794* (New York: Arno Press, 1969), 22.
159. Slaughter, *The Whiskey Rebellion*, 115–86.
160. Charles Post, *The American Road to Capitalism: Studies in Class-Structure, Economic Development and Political Conflict, 1620–1877* (Chicago, IL: Haymarket Books, 2012), 77, 191.
161. John Florin, *The Advance of Frontier Settlement in Pennsylvania, 1638–1850: A Geographic Interpretation* (University Park, PA: University of Pennsylvania Press, 1977), 81.
162. Issac Craig to Samuel Hodgdon, August 5, 1803, *Issac Craig Letter Book*, Filson Historical Society.
163. Issac Craig to Robert Patterson, October 12, 1804, *Issac Craig Letter Book*, Filson Historical Society.
164. Issac Craig to James Kennedy, March 6, 1809, *Issac Craig Letter Book*, Filson Historical Society.

3. Kentucky and Ohio

1. Lyman Beecher, *A Plea for the West* (Cincinnati, OH: Truman and Smith, 1835), 11–12.
2. Frederick Jackson Turner, *The Frontier in American History* (New York: Holt, Rinehart and Winston, 1962), 2.
3. Turner, *The Frontier*, 30.
4. William Darby, *The Emigrant's Guide to the Western and Southwestern States and Territories* (New York: Kirk & Mercein, 1818), 3.
5. Frederick Jackson Turner, *Frontier and Section: Selected Essays of Frederick Jackson Turner* (Upper Saddle River, NJ: Prentice Hall, 1961), 63.
6. New western historians have tended to underemphasize the extent to which the "old" west was the west for those who lived through it. See: Patricia Limerick, *The Legacy of Conquest: The Unbroken Past of the American West* (New York: W.W. Norton & Co., 1987); Richard White, *"It's Your Misfortune and None of My Own": A History of the American West* (Norman, OK: University of Oklahoma Press, 1991); Richard White, *The Middle Ground: Indians, Empires, and Republics in the Great Lakes Region, 1650–1815* (New York: Cambridge University Press, 1991); William G. Robbins, *Colony and Empire: The Capitalist Transformation of the American West* (Lawrence, KA: University Press of Kansas, 1994); Robert V. Hine and John Mack Faragher, *The American West: A New Interpretive History* (New Haven, CT: Yale University Press, 2000); Anne F. Hyde, *Empires, Nations, and Families: A New History of the North American West, 1800–1860* (New York: HarperCollins, 2012).
7. Many scholars who acknowledge the west to be social rather than geographical still construct their narratives excluding much of the antebellum frontier, falling back on the geographical category they claim to criticize. For example, Richard White's well-known work *"It's Your Misfortune and None of My Own"* is one of the most comprehensive works on the topic.

And while he argues that the west is not just a geography, but a historical social construct, for White the west starts with the Dakotas, Nebraska, Kansas, Texas, and Oklahoma. States such as Missouri, Arkansas, Kentucky, and Ohio still appear too east to fit this problematic geographical concept of the west.

8. For a broader discussion of western conquest, including the role of the state, see: John R. van Atta, *Securing the West: Politics, Public Lands, and the State of the Old Republic, 1785–1850* (Baltimore, MD: Johns Hopkins University Press, 2014); Paul Frymer, *Building an American Empire: The Era of Territorial and Political Expansion* (Princeton, NJ: Princeton University Press, 2017).
9. Eric Hinderaker, *Elusive Empires: Constructing Colonialism in the Ohio Valley, 1673–1800* (New York: Cambridge University Press, 1997), 9.
10. Also see: Bethel Saler, *The Settlers' Empire: Colonialism and State Formation in America's Old Northwest* (Philadelphia, PA: University of Pennsylvania Press, 2015).
11. Fred Anderson, *Crucible of War: The Seven Years' War and the Fate of Empire in British North America, 1754–1766* (New York: Vintage, 2000), 22–3.
12. Anderson, *Crucible of War*, 25–53.
13. Pauline Maier, *From Resistance to Revolution: Colonial Radicals and the Development of American Opposition to Britain, 1765–1776* (New York: W.W. Norton & Co., 1991).
14. Otis Rice, *Frontier Kentucky* (Lexington, KY: University Press of Kentucky, 1993), 20–52.
15. Lowell Hayes Harrison and James Klotter, *A New History of Kentucky* (Lexington, KY: University Press of Kentucky, 1997), 19–20.
16. Rice, *Frontier Kentucky*, 62.
17. Harrison and Klotter, *A New History of Kentucky*, 25–6.
18. Stephen Aron, *How the West Was Lost: The Transformation of Kentucky from Daniel Boone to Henry Clay* (Baltimore, MD: Johns Hopkins University Press, 1996), 30.
19. Aron, *How the West Was Lost*, 70.
20. Aron, *How the West Was Lost*, 71–9.
21. Steven Channing, *Kentucky: A Bicentennial History (States and the Nation)* (New York: Norton & Co., 1977), 38, 59.
22. Christopher Waldrep, "Opportunity on the Frontier South of Green," in *The Buzzel about Kentucky: Settling the Promised Land*, ed. Craig Thompson Friend (Lexington, KY: University Press of Kentucky, 1999), 153.
23. Aron, *How the West Was Lost*, 58.
24. Craig Thompson Friend, "Merchants and Markethouses: Reflections on Moral Economy in Early Kentucky," *Journal of the Early Republic* 17, no. 4 (1997): 553–74; Craig Thompson Friend, "'Work & Be Rich' Economy and Culture on the Bluegrass Farm," in *The Buzzel about Kentucky:*

Settling the Promised Land, ed. Craig Thompson Friend (Lexington, KY: University Press of Kentucky, 1999), 143.

25. Harrison and Klotter, *A New History of Kentucky*, 99.
26. Aron, *How the West Was Lost*, 100; Friend, "'Work & Be Rich,'" 129.
27. Friend, "'Work & Be Rich,'" 130.
28. Friend, "'Work & Be Rich,'" 132.
29. John May to Samuel Beall, August 17, 1779, *Beall-Booth Family Papers*, Filson Historical Society.
30. John May to Samuel Beall, March, 1780, *Beall-Booth Family Papers*, Filson Historical Society.
31. John May to Samuel Beall, April 15, 1780, *Beall-Booth Family Papers*, Filson Historical Society.
32. John May to Samuel Beall, December 9, 1780, *Beall-Booth Family Papers*, Filson Historical Society.
33. William Henry to his brother, January 4, 1817, *Henry-Bacon Family Papers*, Filson Historical Society.
34. William Henry to his brother, January 4, 1817.
35. William Henry to John Henry, July 8, 1818, *Henry-Bacon Family Papers*, Filson Historical Society.
36. J. Donne to Colo. Wm. Christian, March 14, 1786, *Bullitt Family Papers/ William Christian Papers*, Filson Historical Society.
37. Robert Pryor to John Henry, July 8, 1818, *Henry-Bacon Family Papers*, Filson Historical Society.
38. See also: Honor Sachs, *Home Rule: Households, Manhood, and National Expansion on the Eighteenth-Century Kentucky Frontier* (New Haven, CT: Yale University Press, 2015), 41–70.
39. Annie Henry Christian to Patrick Henry, September 1786, *Bullitt Family Papers, Oxmoor Collection*, Filson Historical Society.
40. Annie Christian to Elizabeth Christian, January 2, 1788, *Bullitt Family Papers, Oxmoor Collection*, Filson Historical Society.
41. Annie to Elizabeth October 30, 1787, *Bullitt Family Papers, Oxmoor Collection*, Filson Historical Society.
42. Annie Christian to Mrs. Fleming, late 1780s (no date listed), *Bullitt Family Papers, Oxmoor Collection*, Filson Historical Society.
43. Will Trigg to Anne Fleming, March 26, 1806, *Fleming-Edmonds Family Papers*, Filson Historical Society
44. William Fleming to his wife (Nancy), December 26, 1779, *Fleming-Edmonds Family Papers*, Filson Historical Society.
45. Patricia Watlington, *The Partisan Spirit: Kentucky Politics, 1779–1792* (New York: Atheneum, 1972); Joan Wells Coward, *Kentucky in the New Republic: The Process of Constitution Making* (Lexington, KY: University Press of Kentucky, 1979); Lowell Hayes Harrison, *Kentucky's Road to Statehood* (Lexington, KY: University Press of Kentucky, 1992).
46. Nicos Poulantzas, *Political Power and Social Classes* (New York: Verso, 1975); Nicos Poulantzas, *State, Power, Socialism* (New York: Verso, 2014).

47. Watlington, *The Partisan Spirit*, 52; Coward, *Kentucky in the New Republic*, 7.
48. Watlington, *The Partisan Spirit*, 193–230.
49. Coward, *Kentucky in the New Republic*, 52–65.
50. These nepotistic relations were reflected in letters, to take one example, "I would advise you to survey off your tract say 400 acres of land including the place you live at—and let me execute a deed to my mother for the Same and I think it would be advisable to get two or three tenants (at least one on each of the tracts upon which you are not settled) to take leases from me for as many years as you think proper It will be adding to the value of the Land by getting it improved—Tell Frank I will make him a deed whenever he sends the survey and bonds." Richard Taylor Jr. to his father, December 14, 1822, *Taylor-Hay Family Papers*, Filson Historical Society.
51. Committee of Correspondence Circular, November 10, 1817, Filson Historical Society.
52. Adam Beatty, "An Essay on the Importance of Science to Agriculture," 1838, *Beatty Quisenberry/Adam Beatty Papers*, Filson Historical Society.
53. Watlington, *The Partisan Spirit*, 69.
54. James E. Wallace, "Let's Talk About the Weather: A Historiography of Antebellum Kentucky Agriculture," *The Register of the Kentucky Historical Society* 89, no. 2 (1991): 187.
55. Friend, "Merchants and Markethouses," 556.
56. Friend, "Merchants and Markethouses," 560.
57. Elizabeth A. Perkins, "The Consumer Frontier: Household Consumption in Early Kentucky," *Journal of American History* 78, no. 2 (1991): 489.
58. Perkins, "The Consumer Frontier, 499.
59. Perkins, "The Consumer Frontier, 508.
60. Thomas Clark, *A History of Kentucky* (Lexington, KY: J. Bradford Press, 1950), 171.
61. Harrison and Klotter, *A New History of Kentucky*, 141.
62. Wallace, "Let's Talk About the Weather," 190.
63. Richard Laverne Troutman, "Stock Raising in the Antebellum Bluegrass," *The Register of the Kentucky Historical Society* 55, no. 1 (1957): 15.
64. Wallace, "Let's Talk About the Weather," 197.
65. Troutman, "Stock Raising in the Antebellum Bluegrass," 20–1.
66. Harrison and Klotter, *A New History of Kentucky*, 125.
67. Karl Raitz and Nancy O'Malley, "Local-Scale Turnpike Roads in Nineteenth Century Kentucky," *Journal of Historical Geography* 33, no. 1 (2007): 6.
68. Raitz and O'Malley, "Local-Scale Turnpike Roads," 7.
69. Harrison and Klotter, *A New History of Kentucky*, 127.
70. J. Winston Coleman Jr., "Kentucky River Steamboats," *The Register of the Kentucky Historical Society* 63, no. 4 (1965): 300.
71. Coleman Jr., "Kentucky River Steamboats," 305.
72. Clark, *A History of Kentucky*, 183–4.

73. Harrison and Klotter, *A New History of Kentucky*, 133.
74. Ivan E. McDougle, *Slavery in Kentucky, 1792–1865* (Westport, CT: Negro Universities Press, 1970), 9–11.
75. Harrison and Klotter, *A New History of Kentucky*, 168.
76. McDougle, *Slavery in Kentucky*, 11.
77. J. Winston Coleman Jr., *Slave Times in Kentucky* (Chapel Hill, NC: University of North Carolina Press, 1940), 3.
78. Coleman Jr., *Slave Times in Kentucky*, 16.
79. Coleman Jr., *Slave Times in Kentucky*, 32–44.
80. McDougle, *Slavery in Kentucky*, 193.
81. Richard Sears, "Working Like a Slave: Views of Slavery and the Status of Women in Antebellum Kentucky," *The Register of the Kentucky Historical Society* 87, no. 1 (1989): 2.
82. Robert Weise, "Property, Gender, and the Sale of Mineral Rights in Pre-Industrial Eastern Kentucky," *Journal of the Appalachian Studies Association*, 7 (1995): 80; Margaret Ripley Wolfe, "Fallen Leaves and Missing Pages: Women in Kentucky History," *The Register of the Kentucky Historical Society* 90, no. 1 (1992): 82.
83. Sears, "Working Like a Slave," 14.
84. Wolfe, "Fallen Leaves and Missing Pages," 74.
85. Michael N. McConnell, *A Country between: The Upper Ohio Valley and Its Peoples, 1724–1774* (Lincoln, NE: University of Nebraska Press, 1992), 20–1.
86. Eugene Holloway Roseboom and Francis P. Weisenburger, *A History of Ohio* (New York: Prentice Hall, 1934), 25–8.
87. R. Douglas Hurt, *The Ohio Frontier: Crucible of the Old Northwest, 1720–1830* (Bloomington, IN: Indiana University Press, 1996), 55–9.
88. George W. Knepper, *Ohio and Its People* (Kent, OH: Kent State University Press, 1997), 38–40.
89. Walter T.K. Nugent, *Habits of Empire: A History of American Expansion* (New York: Vintage Books, 2009), 39.
90. Hurt, *The Ohio Frontier*, 2.
91. Jeremy Adelman and Stephen Aron, "From Borderlands to Borders: Empires, Nation-States, and the Peoples in between North American History," *American Historical Review* 104, no. 3 (1999): 814–41.
92. James Axtell, "The White Indians of Colonial America." *The William and Mary Quarterly* 32, no. 1 (1975): 55–88.
93. John Melish, *Travels through the United States of America, in the Years 1806 & 1807, and 1809, 1810, & 1811; Including an Account of Passages Betwixt America and Britain, and Travels through Various Parts of Britain, Ireland, & Canada* (Philadelphia (printed for the author) and London: Reprinted for George Cowie and Co. In the Poultry, and John Cumming, Dublin, 1818), 356 (emphasis in the original).
94. Melish, *Travels through the United States*, 447 (emphasis in the original).
95. As Andrew Cayton puts it, "these settlers had no legal right to occupy the land; technically, they were squatters. But their conception of property

ownership depended more upon actual possession than legal titles. Further, they had little respect for a distant national authority and felt no obligation to sacrifice their individual interests so that the national debt could be reduced. Their concern was with local custom and individual rights, not the aggrandizement of Congress." Andrew R.L Cayton, *The Frontier Republic: Ideology and Politics in the Ohio Country, 1780–1825* (Kent, OH: Kent State University Press, 1986), 3.

96. As the author continues, "for ordinary immigrants into the Northwest Territory, land was more than a commodity to be bought or sold, or a place to be leased from some distant landlord. It was the foundation of a family's independence, status, and future. To own land was to be free of all forms of slavery, whether in the form of semifeudal obligations to landlords or more impersonal debts or taxes." Cayton, *The Frontier Republic*, 4.
97. As Kees van der Pijl puts it, "like modes of production, modes of foreign relations combine, in a dynamic structure of determination, an evolving level of development of the productive forces with social relations—in this case, the relations involved in occupying a particular social and/or territorial space, protecting it, and organizing exchange with others." Kees van der Pijl, N*omads, Empires, States: Modes of Foreign Relations and Political Economy* (London: Pluto Press, 2007), ix.
98. Knepper, *Ohio and Its People*, 21.
99. Cayton, *The Frontier Republic*, 11.
100. Jonathan Hughes, "The Great Land Ordinances: Colonial America's Thumbprint on History," in *Essays on the Economy of the Old Northwest*, ed. David Klingaman and Richard K. Vedder (Columbus, OH: Ohio University Press, 1987), 1–18.
101. Roseboom and Weisenburger, *A History of Ohio*, 74.
102. Hughes, "The Great Land Ordinances," 8.
103. William Bergmann, "A 'Commercial View of This Unfortunate War': Economic Roots of an American National State in the Ohio Valley, 1775–1795," *Early American Studies* 6 (2008): 137–64.
104. Hurt, *The Ohio Frontier*, 110–39.
105. Bergmann, "A 'Commercial View of This Unfortunate War,'" 161.
106. William Bergmann, *The American National State and the Early West* (New York: Cambridge University Press, 2012), 66–9.
107. Knepper, *Ohio and Its People*, 56.
108. Roseboom and Weisenburger, *A History of Ohio*, 78.
109. Melish, *Travels through the United States*, 459.
110. Knepper, *Ohio and Its People*, 49–64.
111. Roseboom and Weisenburger, *A History of Ohio*, 92.
112. John Cleves Symmes, *The Correspondence of John Cleves Symmes, Founder of the Miami Purchase, Chiefly from the Collection of Peter G. Thomson* (New York: Pub. for the Historical and Philosophical Society of Ohio by the Macmillan Co., 1926), 17–24.
113. Cayton, *The Frontier Republic*, 69–77.

114. William Cooper Howells and William Dean Howells, *Recollections of Life in Ohio from 1813–1840* (Gainesville, FL: Scholars' Facsimiles & Reprints, 1963).
115. Virginia E. McCormick and Robert W. McCormick, *New Englanders on the Ohio Frontier: The Migration and Settlement of Worthington, Ohio* (Kent, OH: Kent State University Press, 1998), 119.
116. Emily Foster, *American Grit: A Woman's Letters from the Ohio Frontier* (Lexington, KY: University Press of Kentucky, 2002), 60.
117. Foster, *American Grit*, 40.
118. Tina Stewart Brakebill and Celestia Rice Colby, *"Circumstances are Destiny": An Antebellum Woman's Struggle to Define Sphere* (Kent, OH: Kent State University Press, 2006), 5.
119. Brakebill and Colby, *"Circumstances are Destiny,"* 47.
120. Brakebill and Colby, *"Circumstances are Destiny,"* 199.
121. Ginette Aley, "A Republic of Farm People: Women, Families, and Market-Minded Agrarianism in Ohio, 1820s–1830s," *Ohio History* 114 (2007): 28.
122. Robert Emmet Chaddock, *Ohio before 1850; a Study of the Early Influence of Pennsylvania and Southern Populations in Ohio* (New York: AMS Press, 1967), 22–3.
123. For instance, "In Ohio the market revolution belongs to the period after 1825. Admittedly, even before 1812 parts of the Ohio Valley had become involved in the downriver trade and some farmers in southern Ohio had driven cattle eastward for sale in seaboard markets, but such commercial activity was essentially limited. Moreover, as settlement proceeded into the interior of the state after 1815, so the area of cultivated country that was effectively cut off from outside markets increased. Initially concerned with survival, with meeting their own needs and those of new settlers, farmers in these districts served markets that were not only local but often protected by isolation." Donald J. Ratcliffe, "The Market Revolution and Party Alignments in Ohio, 1828–1840," in *The Pursuit of Public Power: Political Culture in Ohio, 1787–1861*, eds. Jeffrey Paul Brown and Andrew R.L. Cayton (Kent, OH: Kent State University Press, 1994), 99–100.
124. Ratcliffe, "The Market Revolution and Party Alignments," 101.
125. Andrew R.L Cayton, *Ohio: The History of a People* (Columbus, OH: Ohio State University Press, 2002), 53.
126. Knepper, *Ohio and Its People*, 148–60.
127. Daniel Aaron, *Cincinnati, Queen City of the West, 1819–1838* (Columbus, OH: Ohio State University Press, 1992), 26–7.
128. Hurt, *The Ohio Frontier*, 370.
129. Aaron, *Cincinnati, Queen City of the West*, 34–5.
130. Aaron, *Cincinnati, Queen City of the West*, 55.
131. Aaron, *Cincinnati, Queen City of the West*, 74.
132. Walter Glazer, *Cincinnati in 1840: The Social and Functional Organization of an Urban Community during the Pre-Civil War Period* (Columbus, OH: Ohio State University Press, 1999), 87.
133. Glazer, *Cincinnati in 1840*, 91–3.

134. Bruce Laurie, *Artisans into Workers: Labor in Nineteenth Century America* (New York: Hill and Wang, 1989).
135. Glazer, *Cincinnati in 1840*, 95.
136. Gurney, *A Journey in North America*, 30.
137. Hurt, *The Ohio Frontier*, 371.
138. Knepper, *Ohio and Its People*, 133.
139. Matthew Salafia, *Slavery's Borderland: Freedom and Bondage along the Ohio River* (Philadelphia, PA: University of Pennsylvania Press, 2013), 90–1.
140. Salafia, *Slavery's Borderland*, 109.
141. Salafia, *Slavery's Borderland*, 80.
142. Edgar F. Love, George C. Mendenhall, and C.F. Lowe, "Registration of Free Blacks in Ohio: The Slaves of George C. Mendenhall," *Journal of Negro History* 69, no. 1 (1984): 39.
143. Jill E. Rowe, "Mixing It Up," *Journal of Black Studies* 39, no. 6 (2009): 927.
144. Nikki Taylor, "Reconsidering the 'Forced' Exodus of 1829: Free Black Emigration from Cincinnati, Ohio to Wilberforce, Canada," *Journal of African American History* 87 (2002): 291.

4. Slavery and Capitalism

1. W.E.B. Du Bois, *Black Reconstruction in America* (New York: The Free Press, 1995), 16.
2. Eric Williams' famous work on capitalism and slavery also details the ways that slavery provided a foundation for British industrialism, although he focuses more on market relations than theorizing the ways that slave labor itself was a form of capitalism organized on the basis of unfree labor. Eric Williams, *Capitalism and Slavery* (Chapel Hill, NC: University of North Carolina Press, 1994). Originally published in 1944.
3. Du Bois, *Black Reconstruction*, 5.
4. Du Bois, *Black Reconstruction*, 5.
5. Du Bois, *Black Reconstruction*, 29.
6. William W. Freehling, *The Road to Disunion Volume I: Secessionists at Bay, 1776–1854* (New York: Oxford University Press, 1991).
7. Samuel C. Hyde Jr., "Plain Folk Reconsidered: Historiographical Ambiguity in Search of Definition," *Journal of Southern History* 71, no. 4 (2005): 803–30.
8. Eugene Genovese, *The Political Economy of Slavery; Studies in the Economy and Society of the Slave South* (New York: Pantheon Books, 1967), 31.
9. Neil Davidson, "The American Civil War Considered as a Bourgeois Revolution," *Historical Materialism* 19, no. 4 (2011): 80.
10. Robin Blackburn, *The American Crucible: Slavery, Emancipation and Human Rights* (New York: Verso, 2011), 68.
11. Stanley L. Engerman and Robert William Fogel, *Time on the Cross: The Economics of American Negro Slavery* (Boston, MA: Little, Brown, 1974), 71.

12. For an overview of these perspectives see: Sven Beckert and Seth Rockman, eds., *Slavery's Capitalism: A New History of American Economic Development* (Philadelphia, PA: University of Pennsylvania Press, 2016).
13. See Charles Post, "Slavery and the New History of Capitalism," *Catalyst* 1, no. 1 (2017): 173–92; John Clegg, "Capitalism and Slavery," *Critical Historical Studies* 2, no. 2 (2015): 281–304.
14. Charles Ball, "Slavery in the United States: A Narrative of the Life and Adventures of Charles Ball, A Black Man," in *I was Born a Slave Volume I*, ed. Yuval Taylor (Chicago, IL: Lawrence Hall Books, 1999), 351. Originally published in 1836.
15. Ralph Anderson and Robert Gallman, "Slaves as Fixed Capital: Slave Labor and Southern Economic Development," *Journal of American History* 64, no. 1 (1977): 24–46.
16. See David Harvey, *The Limits to Capital* (New York: Verso, 2006), 204–8.
17. Walter Johnson, *Soul by Soul Life Inside the Antebellum Slave Market* (Cambridge, MA: Harvard University Press, 1999), 48; Robert H. Gudmestad, *A Troublesome Commerce: The Transformation of the Interstate Slave Trade* (Baton Rouge, LA: Louisiana State University Press, 2003), 19.
18. Jonathan B. Pritchett, "Quantitative Estimates of the United States Interregional Slave Trade, 1820–1860," *Journal of Economic History* 61, no. 2 (2001): 467.
19. *The Daily Crescent*, New Orleans, vol. 1, no. 250, December 21, 1848.
20. Jonathan D. Martin, *Divided Mastery Slave Hiring in the American South* (Cambridge, MA: Harvard University Press, 2004), 8.
21. John J. Zaborney, *Slaves for Hire: Renting Enslaved Laborers in Antebellum Virginia* (Baton Rouge, LA: Louisiana State University Press, 2012), 5.
22. Frederick Law Olmstead, *A Journey in the Seaboard Slave States, with Remarks on their Economy* (New York: Mason Brothers, 1859), 14.
23. Olmstead, *A Journey in the Seaboard Slave States*, 10.
24. Olmstead, *A Journey in the Seaboard Slave States*, 47.
25. Olmstead, *A Journey in the Seaboard Slave States*, 75.
26. Olmstead, *A Journey in the Seaboard Slave States*, 83.
27. Olmstead, *A Journey in the Seaboard Slave States*, 91.
28. Olmstead, *A Journey in the Seaboard Slave States*, 551.
29. Olmstead, *A Journey in the Seaboard Slave States*, 371.
30. Martin, *Divided Mastery*, 178.
31. Linda Brent/Harriet Jacobs, "Incidents in the Life of a Slave Girl, Written by Herself," in *I was Born a Slave Volume II*, ed. Yuval Taylor (Chicago, IL: Lawrence Hall Books, 1999), 585. Originally published in 1861.
32. John Herbon Moore, "Simon Gray, Riverman: A Slave Who Was Almost Free," in *The Other Slaves: Mechanics, Artisans, and Craftsmen*, eds. James E. Newton and Ronald L. Lewis (Boston, MA: G.K. Hall & Co., 1978), 156–8.
33. Moore, "Simon Gray, Riverman," 158.

34. Robert William Fogel, *Without Consent or Contract: The Rise and Fall of American Slavery* (New York: Norton & Co., 1989), 103.
35. Robert S. Starobin, *Industrial Slavery in the Old South* (New York: Oxford University Press, 1975), 11.
36. Ronald L. Lewis, *Coal, Iron, and Slaves: Industrial Slavery in Maryland and Virginia, 1715–1865* (Westport, CT: Greenwood Press, 1979), 21.
37. Starobin, *Industrial Slavery*, 13.
38. Joseph John Gurney, *A Journey in North America, Described in Familiar Letters to Amelia Opie* (Norwich: Josiah Fletcher, 1841), 51.
39. William Loughton Smith, *Journal of William Loughton Smith 1790–1791* (Cambridge: Cambridge University Press, 1917), 65.
40. Richard Follett, "Slavery and Plantation Capitalism in Louisiana's Sugar Country," *American Nineteenth Century History* 1, no. 3 (2000): 4.
41. Mark M. Smith, *Mastered by the Clock: Time, Slavery, and Freedom in the American South* (Chapel Hill, NC: University of North Carolina Press, 1997).
42. Follett, "Slavery and Plantation Capitalism," 4.
43. Charles Dew, *Sam Williams, Forgeman: The Life of an Industrial Slave in the Old South* (Princeton, NJ: Princeton University Press, 1989), 411.
44. James Oakes, *Slavery and Freedom: An Interpretation of the Old South* (New York: W.W. Norton & Co., 1990), 129.
45. Francis J. Grund, *The Americans in their Moral, Social, and Political Relations Volume II* (London: Longman, Rees, Orme, Brown, Green, & Longman, 1837), 297.
46. Thomas Jefferson, *Notes on the State of Virginia* (Richmond, VA: J.W. Randolph, 1853), 150–1.
47. Grund, *The Americans*, 301.
48. T.R. Gray, "The Confessions of Nat Turner, the Leader of the Late Insurrection in Southampton, VA," in *I was Born a Slave Volume I*, ed. Yuval Taylor (Chicago, IL: Lawrence Hall Books, 1999), 242. Originally published in 1831.
49. The Marquis de Chastellux, *Travels in North-America, in the Years 1780–81–82* (New York, 1828), 286.
50. Linda Brent/Harriet Jacobs, "Incidents in the Life of a Slave Girl."
51. Milton Clarke, "Narratives of the Sufferings of Lewis and Milton Clarke," in *I was Born a Slave Volume I*, ed. Yuval Taylor (Chicago, IL: Lawrence Hall Books, 1999), 647. Originally published in 1846.
52. Olmstead, *A Journey in the Seaboard Slave States*, 583.
53. Daina Ramey Berry, *The Price for Their Pound of Flesh: The Value of the Enslaved, from Womb to Grave, in the Building of a Nation* (Boston, MA: Beacon Press, 2017), 19.
54. Sven Beckert, *Empire of Cotton: A Global History* (New York: Alfred A. Knopf, 2015).
55. Gurney, *A Journey in North America*, 67.
56. Ball, "Slavery in the United States," 281.
57. Harvey, *The Limits to Capital*, 415–38.

58. Martin, *Divided Mastery*, 35.
59. Fogel, *Without Consent or Contract*, 90.
60. Alan Olmstead and Paul Rhode, "Biological Innovation and Productivity Growth in the Antebellum Cotton Economy," *Journal of Economic History* 68, no. 4 (2008): 1155.
61. Craig Heinicke and Wayne A. Grove, "'Machinery has Completely Taken Over': The Diffusion of the Mechanical Cotton Picker, 1949–1964," *Journal of Interdisciplinary History* 39, no. 1 (2008): 65–96.
62. Olmstead and Rhode, "Biological Innovation," 1124.
63. Russell R. Menard, "Plantation Empire: How Sugar and Tobacco Planters Built Their Industries and Raised an Empire," *Agricultural History* 81, no. 3 (2007): 309.
64. Olmstead and Rhode, "Biological Innovation," 1129–35.
65. Edward Baptist recently argued that it was the systematic engineering of techniques of torture that was the main cause of productivity increases. He argues that "while some planters obsessively chased the latest fad for cotton-seed varieties ... others argued that new breeds added nothing to the 'picking qualities' of Petit Gulf. So something that cannot be explained by the seeds happened to produce a continuous increase in productivity." Organized violence, squeezing slaves harder, is the author's solution to this problem. But Baptist never clarifies who these "others" are, nor engages in a systematic analysis of southern capitalists who increased productivity *without* introducing new varieties of seeds or who did not expand west to more fertile soil. In other words, while Baptist goes on to explain a variety of torture techniques in detail, he never provides the proper empirical case to support his own argument. And, in fact, while it is likely impossible to precisely say how much of productivity was caused by, say, new varieties of seeds, given the evidence, it is hard to fathom whipping slaves harder and pushing them more could have increased cotton productivity nearly as much as it did rise. See: Edward Baptist, *The Half Has Never Been Told: Slavery and the Making of American Capitalism* (New York: Basic Books, 2016), 127. For further criticism also see: Post, "Slavery and the New History of Capitalism" and Clegg, "Capitalism and Slavery."
66. Fogel, *Without Consent or Contract*, 83.
67. Frank Lawrence Owsley, *Plain Folk of the Old South* (Baton Rouge, LA: Louisiana State University Press, 1949); also see: Hyde Jr., "Plain Folk Reconsidered."
68. Harold D. Woodman, *Slavery and the Southern Economy; Sources and Readings* (New York: Harcourt, Brace & World, 1966).
69. United States Census Bureau, "Census of Population and Housing 1860," accessed September 15, 2017 at www.census.gov/prod/www/decennial.html; Kenneth M. Stampp, *Peculiar Institution: Slavery in the Ante-Bellum South* (New York: Vintage, 1984), 30; David Williams, *The Old South: A Brief History with Documents* (Macon, GA: Mercer University Press, 2014); Charles Bolton, *Poor Whites of the Antebellum South: Tenants and*

Laborers in Central North Carolina and Northeast Mississippi (Durham, NC: Duke University Press, 1994), 5; Ira Berlin, *Slaves Without Masters: The Free Negro in the Antebellum South* (New York: Vintage Books, 1974), 136; Engerman and Fogel, *Time on the Cross*, 38; Ira Berlin and Herbert Gutman, "Natives and Immigrants, Free Men and Slaves: Urban Workingmen in the Antebellum American South," *American Historical Review* 88 (1983): 1175–200; Max Grivino, "'Chased Out on Slippery Ice': Rural Wages Laborers in Baltimore's Hinterlands, 1815–1860," in *Southern Society and Its Transformations, 1790–1860*, eds. Michelle Gillespie, Susan Delfino, and Lous Kyriakoudes (Columbia, MO: University of Missouri Press, 2011), 121–2.

70. Oakes, *Slavery and Freedom*, 80–103; Gavin Wright, *The Political Economy of the Cotton South: Households, Markets, and Wealth in the Nineteenth Century* (New York: Norton & Co., 1978), 33.
71. Chastellux, *Travels in North America*, 291.
72. John Melish, *Travels through the United States of America, in the Years 1806 & 1807, and 1809, 1810, & 1811; Including an Account of Passages Betwixt America and Britain, and Travels through Various Parts of Britain, Ireland, & Canada* (Philadelphia (printed for the author) and London: Reprinted for George Cowie and Co. In the Poultry, and John Cumming, Dublin, 1818), 189.
73. Ball, "Slavery in the United States," 386.
74. Olmstead, *A Journey in the Seaboard Slave States*, 84.
75. Owsley, *Plain Folk*, 135.
76. Olmstead, *A Journey in the Seaboard Slave States*, 348.
77. Steven Hahn, *The Roots of Southern Populism: Yeoman Farmers and the Transformation of the Georgia Upcountry, 1850–1890* (New York: Oxford University Press, 2006), 4.
78. Hahn, *The Roots of Southern Populism*, 18.
79. Stephanie McCurry, *Masters of Small Worlds: Yeoman Households, Gender Relations, and the Political Culture of the Antebellum South Carolina Low Country* (New York: Oxford University Press, 1995).
80. William Harris, "The Organization of Work on a Yeoman Slaveholder's Farm," *Agricultural History* 64, no. 1 (1990): 41.
81. Harris, "The Organization of Work, 50.
82. Steven Sarson, "Yeoman Farmers in a Planters' Republic: Socioeconomic Conditions and Relations in Early National Prince George's County, Maryland," *Journal of the Early Republic* 29, no. 1 (2009): 70.
83. Bradley Bond, "Herders, Farmers, and Markets on the Inner Frontier: The Mississippi Piney Woods, 1850–1860," *Plain Folk of the South Revisited*, eds. Samuel Hyde Jr. (Baton Rouge, LA: Louisiana State University Press, 1997), 97.
84. Richard Lyman Bushman, "Markets and Composite Farms in Early America," *The William and Mary Quarterly* 55, no. 3 (1998): 364.
85. Jeff Bremer, "Frontier Capitalism: Market Migration to Rural Central Missouri, 1815–1860," in *Southern Society and Its Transformations*,

1790–1860, eds. Michelle Gillespie, Susan Delfino, and Lous Kyriakoudes (Columbia, MO: University of Missouri Press, 2011), 89.

86. Bolton, *Poor Whites of the Antebellum South*, 74–92.

5. The Progress of Empire

1. Henry Rowe Schoolcraft, *Journal of a Tour into the Interior of Missouri and Arkansaw* (London: Sir Richard Phillips and Co., 1821), 102.
2. L.U. Reavis, *Saint Louis; the Future Great City of the World* (St. Louis, MO: St. Louis County Court, 1870), 31.
3. This chapter focuses mainly on the western expansion of slavery in the post-1815 era. For a discussion of the ways in which slavery in North American emerged out of the broader contours of world market formation and the Caribbean slave order itself see: John Craig Hammond, "Slavery, Settlement, and Empire: The Expansion and Growth of Slavery in the Interior of the North American Continent, 1770–1820," *Journal of the Early Republic* 32, no. 2 (2012): 175–206.
4. Thomas Hart Benton, cited in James Neal Primm, *Lion of the Valley, St. Louis, Missouri* (Boulder, CO: Pruett Publishing Co., 1981), 113.
5. J.M. Peck, *A New Guide for Emigrants to the West* (Boston, MA: Gould, Kendall & Lincoln, 1837), 115.
6. Peck, *A New Guide for Emigrants*, 121.
7. Eric Wolf, *Europe and the People Without History* (Berkeley and Los Angeles, CA: University of California Press, 1997), 158.
8. William E. Foley, *A History of Missouri: Volume 1, 1673–1820* (Columbia, MO: University of Missouri Press, 1971), 1.
9. Stephen Aron, *American Confluence: The Missouri Frontier from Borderland to Border State. History of the Trans-Appalachian Frontier* (Bloomington, IN: Indiana University Press, 2006), 18; William E. Foley, *The Genesis of Missouri: From Wilderness Outpost to Statehood* (Columbia, MO: University of Missouri Press, 1989), 5.
10. Foley, *The Genesis of Missouri*, 12.
11. Aron, *American Confluence*, 30.
12. Henry R. Schoolcraft, *A View of the Lead Mines* (New York: Charles Wiley & Co., 1819), 13.
13. Foley, *The Genesis of Missouri*, 23–34.
14. Jeff Bremer, *A Store Almost in Sight: The Economic Transformation of Missouri from the Louisiana Purchase to the Civil War* (Iowa City: University of Iowa Press, 2014), 9–10.
15. Robin Blackburn, *The American Crucible: Slavery, Emancipation and Human Rights* (New York: Verso, 2011), 173.
16. Walter T.K. Nugent, *Habits of Empire: A History of American Expansion* (New York: Vintage Books, 2009), 41.
17. Schoolcraft, *Journal of a Tour*, 6.
18. Schoolcraft, *Journal of a Tour*, 6.
19. Schoolcraft, *Journal of a Tour*, 32.

20. Schoolcraft, *Journal of a Tour*, 50.
21. Schoolcraft, *Journal of a Tour*, 40.
22. Malcom J. Rohrbough, *The Trans-Appalachian Frontier: People, Societies, and Institutions, 1775–1850* (New York: Oxford University Press, 1978), 94.
23. H.M. Brackenridge, *Views of Louisiana; Together with a Journal of a Voyage up the Missouri River, in 1811* (Pittsburgh, PA: Cranes, Spear, and Eichbaum, 1814), 136.
24. Peck, *A New Guide for Emigrants*, 93.
25. Foley, *The Genesis of Missouri*, 82.
26. Bremer, *A Store Almost in Sight*, 33–6.
27. Stafford Poole and Douglas Slawson, *Church and Slave in Perry County, Missouri, 1818–1865* (Lewiston, NY: Edwin Mellen Press, 1986), 13.
28. Walter A. Schroeder, *Opening the Ozarks: A Historical Geography of Missouri's Ste. Genevieve District, 1760–1830* (Columbia, MO: University of Missouri Press, 2002), 346.
29. Bremer, *A Store Almost in Sight*, 31.
30. James R. Wettstaed, "Perspectives on the Early-Nineteenth century Frontier Occupations of the Missouri Ozarks," *Historical Archaeology* 37, no. 4 (2003): 99.
31. Schroeder, *Opening the Ozarks*, 435.
32. Schoolcraft, *A View of the Lead Mines*, 5–45.
33. Foley, *The Genesis of Missouri*, 9–10.
34. Foley, *The Genesis of Missouri*, 89.
35. *Prospectus of the Missouri Iron Company and Missouri and Iron Mountain Cities Together with a Map of the State of Missouri and Plans of the Cities* (Boston, MA: Marden & Kimball, Printers, 1837), 5.
36. Perry McCandless, *A History of Missouri: Volume II, 1820–1860* (Columbia, MO: University of Missouri Press, 1972), 44.
37. Bremer, *A Store Almost in Sight*, 45–50.
38. Aron, *American Confluence*, 166. For the history of merchants and capital in St. Louis also see: Jay Gitlin, *The Bourgeois Frontier: French Towns, French Traders, and American Expansion* (New Haven, CT: Yale University Press, 2010), 68–82.
39. Schroeder, *Opening the Ozarks*, 128–46.
40. Douglas R. Hurt, *The Ohio Frontier: Crucible of the Old Northwest, 1720–1830* (Bloomington, IN: Indiana University Press, 1996), x–7.
41. Henry King, *Report of a Geological Reconnoisance of that Part of the State of Missouri Adjacent to the Osage River, made to Wulliam H. Morell, Chief Internal Improvement, by Order of the Board of Internal Improvement* (Missouri, 1840), 505.
42. Andrew C. Isenberg, "The Market Revolution in the Borderlands: George Champlin Sibley in Missouri and New Mexico, 1808–1826," *Journal of the Early Republic* 21, no. 3 (2001): 449.
43. Aron, *American Confluence*, 201.
44. Isenberg, "The Market Revolution in the Borderlands," 464.

45. William W. Freehling, *The Road to Disunion Volume I: Secessionists at Bay, 1776–1854* (New York: Oxford University Press, 1991), 146–56.
46. Jason Combs, "The South's Slave Culture Transplanted to the Western Frontier," *The Professional Geographer* 56, no. 3 (2004): 365.
47. Douglas R. Hurt, *The Ohio Frontier*, 217–19.
48. Diane Mutti Burke, *On Slavery's Border: Missouri's Small-Slaveholding Households, 1815–1865* (Athens, GA: University of Georgia Press, 2010), 27.
49. Burke, *On Slavery's Border*, 28.
50. Burke, *On Slavery's Border*, 56.
51. Burke, *On Slavery's Border*, 94–102.
52. Daniel Walker Howe, *What Hath God Wrought: The Transformation of America, 1815–1848* (New York: Oxford University Press, 2007).
53. David Harvey, *The Condition of Postmodernity* (Oxford: Blackwell, 1990), 240.
54. Walter Johnson, *River of Dark Dreams: Slavery and Empire in the Cotton Kingdom* (Cambridge, MA: Harvard University Press, 2013), 98.
55. Bremer, *A Store Almost in Sight*, 126.
56. Primm, *Lion of the Valley*, 201.
57. Bremer, *A Store Almost in Sight*, 146–52.
58. Jeanne M. Whayne, *Arkansas: A Narrative History* (Fayetteville, AK: University of Arkansas Press, 2002), 20.
59. Arnold S. Morris, *Colonial Arkansas, 1686–1804: A Social and Cultural History* (Fayetteville, AK: University of Arkansas Press, 1991), 9.
60. Morris, *Colonial Arkansas*, 17.
61. Whayne, *Arkansas: A Narrative History*, 93.
62. Robert Bean and Jacob Barkman, "Memorial to the President by the Territorial Assembly," cited in *The Territorial Papers of the United States Volume XX* (Washington, DC: Government Printing Office, 1954), 127. Quote from 1825.
63. Schoolcraft, cited in Charles Bolton, *Arkansas, 1800–1860: Remote and Restless. Histories of Arkansas* (Fayetteville, AK: University of Arkansas Press, 1998), 6.
64. James M. Woods, *Rebellion and Realignment: Arkansas's Road to Secession* (Fayetteville, AK: University of Arkansas Press, 1987), 13.
65. Jeannie M. Whayne, Thomas A. Deblack, George Sabo III, and Morris S. Arnold, *Arkansas: A Narrative History* (Fayetteville, AK: University of Arkansas Press, 2013), 113.
66. Charles Bolton, *Arkansas, 1800–1860: Remote and Restless. Histories of Arkansas* (Fayetteville, AK: University of Arkansas Press, 1998), 49; Charles Grier Sellers, *The Market Revolution: Jacksonian America, 1815–1846* (New York: Oxford University Press, 1991), 16.
67. Donald McNeilly, *The Old South Frontier: Cotton Plantations and the Formation of Arkansas Society, 1819–1861* (Fayetteville, AK: University of Arkansas Press, 2000), 85.

68. Richard Slotkin, *Regeneration through Violence: The Mythology of the American Frontier, 1600–1860* (Middletown, CT: Wesleyan University Press, 1973), 85–7.
69. G.W. Featherstonhaugh, *Excursion through the Slave States Vol. II* (London: John Murray, 1844), 42 (emphases in the original).
70. Alex Cummings, Letter to Samuel C. Roane, *The Territorial Papers of the United States Volume XX* (Washington, DC: Government Printing Office, 1954), 33. Originally published in 1825.
71. Whayne, *Arkansas: A Narrative History*, 97–8.
72. Harry Ashmore, *Arkansas, a Bicentennial History* (New York: Norton & Co., 1978), 33.
73. Bolton, *Arkansas, 1800–1860*, 75–86; Whayne, *Arkansas: A Narrative History*, 79.
74. Woods, *Rebellion and Realignment*, 18.
75. Woods, *Rebellion and Realignment*, 21.
76. Featherstonhaugh, *Excursion through the Slave States*, 7.
77. Featherstonhaugh, *Excursion through the Slave States*, 8.
78. Featherstonhaugh, *Excursion through the Slave States*, 31.
79. Featherstonhaugh, *Excursion through the Slave States*, 137.
80. Featherstonhaugh, *Excursion through the Slave States*, 17.
81. Featherstonhaugh, *Excursion through the Slave States*, 86.
82. Featherstonhaugh, *Excursion through the Slave States*, 27.
83. Brooks Blevins, *Hill Folks: A History of Arkansas Ozarkers & Their Image* (Chapel Hill, NC: University of North Carolina Press, 2002), 18.
84. Featherstonhaugh, *Excursion through the Slave States*, 170.
85. Blevins, *Hill Folks*, 22–7.
86. Bolton, *Arkansas, 1800–1860*, 98–9.
87. Whayne et al., *Arkansas: A Narrative History*, 119.
88. Bolton, *Arkansas, 1800–1860*, 125–7.
89. C.F. Williams, S.C. Bolton, Carl H. Moneyhon, and LeRoy T. Williams, eds., *A Documentary History of Arkansas* (Fayetteville, AK: University of Arkansas Press, 1984), 69.
90. McNeilly, *The Old South Frontier*, 153.
91. McNeilly, *The Old South Frontier*, 143–51.
92. Whayne et al., *Arkansas: A Narrative History*, 143.
93. Bolton, *Arkansas, 1800–1860*, 129.
94. Woods, *Rebellion and Realignment*, 25.
95. McNeilly, *The Old South Frontier*, 134–6.
96. Whayne et al., *Arkansas: A Narrative History*, 111–13.
97. David Dale Owen, *First Report of a Geological Reconnaissance of the Northern Counties of Arkansas* (Little Rock: Johnson & Yerkes, 1858), 11–12.
98. Bolton, *Arkansas, 1800–1860*, 176–7.
99. Houston, cited in D.W. Meinig, *Imperial Texas: An Interpretive Essay in Cultural Geography* (Austin, TX: University of Texas Press, 1969), 7.
100. Cushing, cited in Meinig, *Imperial Texas*, 7.

101. Donald Chipman, *Spanish Texas: 1519–1821* (Austin, TX: University of Texas Press, 1992), 11.
102. Chipman, *Spanish Texas*, 241.
103. Gary Clayton Anderson, *The Conquest of Texas: Ethnic Cleansing in the Promised Land, 1820–1875* (Norman, OK: University of Oklahoma Press, 2005), 20.
104. Sellers, *The Market Revolution*, 6.
105. Anderson, *The Conquest of Texas*, 20–2.
106. Anderson, *The Conquest of Texas*, 31–2.
107. John Edward Weems, *Dream of Empire; a Human History of the Republic of Texas, 1836–1846* (New York: Simon and Schuster, 1971), 23.
108. T.R. Fehrenback, *Lone Star: A History of Texas and the Texans* (Cambridge: Da Capo Press, 1968), 114.
109. Fehrenback, *Lone Star*, 134–5.
110. Fehrenback, *Lone Star*, 142–3.
111. Andreas Reichstein, *Rise of the Lone Star: The Making of Texas* (College Station, TX: Texas A&M University Press, 1989), 37.
112. Reichstein, *Rise of the Lone Star*, 40.
113. Randolph B. Campbell, *An Empire for Slavery: The Peculiar Institution in Texas, 1821–1865* (Baton Rouge, LA: Louisiana State University Press, 1989), 15.
114. Stephen F. Austin, *Laws, Orders, and Contract on Colonization, 1821–1829* (Saltillo, 1829), 568.
115. Campbell, *An Empire for Slavery*, 17–23.
116. Campbell, *An Empire for Slavery*, 40.
117. David Montejano, *Anglos and Mexicans in the Making of Texas, 1836–1986* (Austin, TX: University of Texas Press, 1987), 21–52.
118. Theodore Sedgwick, *Thoughts on the Proposed Annexation of Texas to the United States* (New York: D. Fanshaw, 1844), 39 (emphasis in the original).
119. Sedgwick, *Thoughts on the Proposed Annexation*, 32.
120. Robert J. Walker, *Letter of Mr. Walker, of Mississippi, Relative to the Annexation of Texas* (Washington, DC: The Globe Office, 1844), 9.
121. Benjamin Lundy, "Texas and Mexico," in *The Anti-Texass Legion, Protest of some Free Men, States and Presses Against the Texass Rebellion, Against the Law of Nature and of Nations* (Albany, NY: The Patriot Office, 1845), 3 (emphases in the original).
122. Sedgwick, *Thoughts on the Proposed Annexation of Texas*, 54.
123. Orville Dewey, *A Discourse on Slavery and the Annexation of Texas* (New York: Charles S. Francis and Company, 1844), 7.
124. Brantz Mayer, *History of the War Between Mexico and the United States, with a Preliminary View of its Origin Vol. I* (New York: Wiley and Putnam, 1847), 6.
125. Mayer, *History of the War Between Mexico and the United States*, 44.
126. Anson Jones, *Letters Relating to the History of Annexation* (Philadelphia, 1852), 26.

127. Junius, "Annexation of Texas," *The Junius Tracts No. IX* (New York: Greeley & McElrath, 1844), 40 (emphasis in the original).
128. Anderson, *The Conquest of Texas*, 3–7.
129. Richard G. Lowe and Randolph B. Campbell, *Planters and Plain Folk: Agriculture in Antebellum Texas* (Dallas, TX: Southern Methodist University Press, 1987), 27.
130. Lowe and Campbell, *Planters and Plain Folk*, 118–19.
131. Elizabeth Silverthorne, *Plantation Life in Texas* (College Station, TX: Texas A&M University Press, 1986), 32.
132. Silverthorne, *Plantation Life in Texas*, 40.
133. Silverthorne, *Plantation Life in Texas*, 49.
134. Campbell, *An Empire for Slavery*, 56–75.
135. Lowe and Campbell, *Planters and Plain Folk*, 162–3.
136. J. De Cordova, *Lecture on Texas* (Philadelphia, PA: Ernest Crozet, 1858), 26.
137. Fehrenback, *Lone Star*, 297.
138. W.B. Dewees, *Letters from an Early Settler of Texas* (Louisville, KY: Norton & Griswold, 1852), 80.
139. Dewees, *Letters from an Early Settler*, 31.
140. De Cordova, *Lecture on Texas*, 8.
141. Melinda Rankin, *Texas in 1850* (Boston, MA: Damrell & Moore, 1850), 23.
142. Mary Austin Holley, *Texas* (Lexington, KY: J. Clarke & Co., 1836), 134 (emphases in the original).
143. Jo Ella Powell Exley, *Texas Tears and Texas Sunshine: Voices of Frontier Women* (College Station, TX: Texas A&M University Press, 1985), 5–14.
144. Exley, *Texas Tears and Texas Sunshine*, 24.
145. Exley, *Texas Tears and Texas Sunshine*, 112–15. For a broader discussion of certain aspects of gender and frontier life in Texas see: Adrienne Caughfield, *True Women and Westward Expansion* (College Station, TX: Texas A&M University Press, 2005).
146. Lowe and Campbell, *Planters and Plain Folk*, 134–5.
147. See: John Ashworth, *Slavery, Capitalism, and Politics in the Antebellum Republic Volume I: Commerce and Compromise 1820–1850* (New York: Cambridge University Press, 1995); John Ashworth, *Slavery, Capitalism, and Politics in the Antebellum Republic Volume II: The Coming of the Civil War 1850–1861* (New York: Cambridge University Press, 2007).

6. The Consolidation of the American Capitalism

1. For an overview of politics and territorial struggles relating to slavery in the run up to the Civil War also see: Michael A. Morrison, *Slavery and the American West: The Eclipse of Manifest Destiny* (Chapel Hill, NC: University of North Carolina Press, 1997).
2. John Ashworth, *Slavery, Capitalism, and Politics in the Antebellum Republic Volume I: Commerce and Compromise 1820–1850* (New York:

Cambridge University Press, 1995); Stanley Lebergott, "Labor Force and Employment, 1800–1960," in *Output, Employment, and Productivity in the United States after 1800*, ed. Dorothy Brady (National Bureau of Economic Research, 1966), accessed January 10, 2018 at www.nber.org/chapters/c1567.pdf.

3. Thomas Weiss, "U.S. Labor Force Estimates and Economic Growth, 1800–1860," in *American Economic Growth and Standards of Living before the Civil War*, eds. Robert E. Gallman and John Joseph Wallis (Chicago, IL: University of Chicago Press, 1992), 22.
4. David Gordon, Richard Edwards, and Michael Reich, *Segmented Work, Divided Workers: The Historical Transformation of Labor in the United States* (Cambridge: Cambridge University Press, 1983), 48.
5. David Montgomery, *Beyond Equality; Labor and the Radical Republicans, 1862–1872* (New York: Knopf, 1967), 30.
6. Norman Ware, *The Industrial Worker, 1840–1860: The Reaction of American Industrial Society to the Advance of the Industrial Revolution* (Chicago, IL: I.R. Dee, 1990).
7. Ware, *The Industrial Worker*, xx.
8. Bruce Laurie, *Artisans into Workers: Labor in Nineteenth Century America* (New York: Hill and Wang, 1989), 57.
9. Joseph Rayback, *A History of American Labor* (New York: Free Press, 1966), 54.
10. Melvyn Dubofsky and Foster Rhea Dulles, *Labor in America: A History* (Wheeling, IL: Harlan Davidson, 1999), 23–31.
11. Dubofsky and Dulles, *Labor in America*, 32.
12. Thomas Skidmore, "The Rights of Man to Property!" in *Socialism in America: From the Shakers to the Third International: A Documentary History*, ed. Albert Fried (New York: Columbia University Press, 1992), 126.
13. Skidmore, "The Rights of Man to Property!" 124.
14. David Montgomery, *Workers' Control in America: Studies in the History of Work, Technology, and Labor Struggles* (Cambridge: Cambridge University Press, 1981), 13.
15. Herbert Gutman, *Work, Culture, and Society in Industrializing America: Essays in American Working-Class and Social History* (New York: Vintage Books, 1977).
16. David Brody, *In Labor's Cause: Main Themes on the History of the American Worker* (New York: Oxford University Press, 1993), 28.
17. Rolla M. Tryon, *Household Manufactures in the United States, 1640–1860* (New York: A.M. Kelley, 1966).
18. Lorena Walsh, "Consumer Behavior, Diet, and the Standard of Living in Late Colonial and Early Antebellum America, 1770–1840," in *American Economic Growth and Standards of Living before the Civil War*, eds. Robert Gallman and John Joseph Wallis (Chicago, IL: University of Chicago Press, 1992), 228.

19. John Lauritz Larson, *The Market Revolution in America: Liberty, Ambition, and the Eclipse of the Common Good* (New York: Cambridge University Press, 2010), 125.
20. David Roediger, *The Wages of Whiteness: Race and the Making of the American Working Class* (New York: Verso, 1999), 134.
21. Gordon, Edwards, and Reich, *Segmented Work*, 75.
22. Laurie, *Artisans into Workers*.
23. Charles Post, *The American Road to Capitalism: Studies in Class-Structure, Economic Development and Political Conflict, 1620–1877* (Chicago, IL: Haymarket Books, 2012), 73.
24. Post, *The American Road*, 81.
25. Post, *The American Road*, 92.
26. Elizabeth Blackmar, "Inheriting Property and Debt: From Family Security to Corporate Accumulation," in *Capitalism Takes Command: The Social Transformation of Nineteenth Century America*, eds. Michael Zakim and Gary John Kornblith (Chicago, IL: University of Chicago Press, 2012), 96.
27. Blackmar, "Inheriting Property and Debt," 102.
28. Blackmar, "Inheriting Property and Debt," 109.
29. Thomas Dublin, *Women at Work: The Transformation of Work and Community in Lowell, Massachusetts, 1826–1860* (New York: Columbia University Press, 1979); Naomi Lamoreaux, Daniel Raff, and Peter Temin, "Beyond Markets and Hierarchies: Toward a New Synthesis of American Business History," *American Historical Review* 108 (2003): 412.
30. Thomas Cochran, *Frontiers of Change: Early Industrialism in America* (New York: Oxford University Press, 1981), 121.
31. Robert Wright, "Capitalism and the Rise of the Corporation Nation," in *Capitalism Takes Command: The Social Transformation of Nineteenth Century America*, eds. Michael Zakim and Gary John Kornblith (Chicago, IL: University of Chicago Press, 2012), 148–9.
32. Wright, "Capitalism and the Rise of the Corporation Nation," 165.
33. George Rogers Taylor, *The Transportation Revolution, 1815–1860* (New York: Rinehart, 1951), 85.
34. Alfred Chandler Jr., *The Visible Hand: The Managerial Revolution in American Business* (Cambridge, MA: Belknap Press of Harvard University, 1977), 94–108.
35. Chandler Jr., *The Visible Hand*, 110.
36. See, for example: Kenneth Stampp, *The Causes of the Civil War* (Upper Saddle River, NJ: Prentice-Hall, 1961); David Potter, *The Impending Crisis, 1848–1861* (New York: Harper & Row, 1976); Bruce Collins, *The Origins of America's Civil War* (New York: Holmes & Meier, 1981); James McPherson, *Battle Cry of Freedom: The Civil War Era* (New York: Oxford University Press, 1988); Bruce Levine, *Half Slave and Half Free: The Roots of Civil War* (New York: Hill and Wang, 1992); Michael Perman, *The Coming of the American Civil War* (Lexington, MA: D.C. Heath, 1993); Ashworth, *Slavery, Capitalism, and Politics Volume I*; John Ashworth, *Slavery, Capitalism, and Politics in the Antebellum Republic*

Volume II: The Coming of the Civil War 1850–1861 (New York: Cambridge University Press, 2007); William Freehling, *The Road to Disunion Volume I: Secessionists at Bay, 1776–1854* (New York: Oxford University Press, 1991); William Freehling, *The Road to Disunion Volume II: Secessionists Triumphant 1854–1861* (New York: Oxford University Press, 2007); Robert Broadwater, *Did Lincoln and the Republican Party Create the Civil War: An Argument* (Jefferson, NC: McFarland & Co., 2008); Marc Egnal, *Clash of Extremes: The Economic Origins of the Civil War* (New York: Hill and Wang, 2009; Post, *The American Road.*

37. Eric Foner, "The Civil War and Slavery: A Response," *Historical Materialism* 19, no. 4 (2011): 95.
38. Diane Barnes, Brian Schoen, and Frank Towers, eds., *The Old South's Modern Worlds: Slavery, Region, and Nation in the Age of Progress* (New York: Oxford University Press, 2011), 5.
39. Brian Schoen, "The Burdens and Opportunities of Interdependence: The Political Economies of the Planter Class," in *The Old South's Modern Worlds: Slavery, Region, and Nation in the Age of Progress*, eds. L. Diane Barnes, Brian Schoen, and Frank Towers (New York: Oxford University Press, 2011), 67.
40. Schoen, "The Burdens and Opportunities of Interdependence," 73.
41. John Majewski, *Modernizing a Slave Economy: The Economic Vision of the Confederate Nation* (Chapel Hill, NC: University of North Carolina Press, 2009), 23–4.
42. Majewski, *Modernizing a Slave Economy*, 25.
43. Majewski, *Modernizing a Slave Economy*, 54.
44. William Thomas, "'Swerve Me?': The South, Railroads, and the Rush to Modernity," in *The Old South's Modern Worlds: Slavery, Region, and Nation in the Age of Progress*, eds. L. Diane Barnes, Brian Schoen, and Frank Towers (New York: Oxford University Press, 2011), 175–6.
45. Thomas, "'Swerve Me?'" 169–73.
46. Majewski, *Modernizing a Slave Economy*, 81.
47. Freehling, *The Road to Disunion Volume I*, 144–9.
48. Ashworth, *Slavery, Capitalism, and Politics Volume I*, 69–70.
49. Freehling, *The Road to Disunion Volume I*, 255–85.
50. Freehling, *The Road to Disunion Volume I*, 310–36.
51. Collins, *The Origins of America's Civil War*, 67.
52. Ashworth, *Slavery, Capitalism, and Politics Volume I*, 419.
53. Freehling, *The Road to Disunion Volume I*, 367.
54. Collins, *The Origins of America's Civil War*, 72.
55. Freehling, *The Road to Disunion Volume I*, 369–70; Ashworth, *Slavery, Capitalism, and Politics Volume I*, 418–20.
56. Walter T.K. Nugent, *Habits of Empire: A History of American Expansion* (New York: Vintage Books, 2009), 154–5.
57. Ashworth, *Slavery, Capitalism, and Politics Volume I*, 431.
58. Nugent, *Habits of Empire*, 155–6.
59. Potter, *The Impending Crisis*, 18–22.

60. Potter, *The Impending Crisis*, 109.
61. Potter, *The Impending Crisis*, 112.
62. Potter, *The Impending Crisis*, 199–201.
63. Freehling, *The Road to Disunion Volume II*, 75.
64. Ashworth, *Slavery, Capitalism, and Politics Volume II*, 64.
65. Potter, *The Impending Crisis*, 212.
66. Freehling, *The Road to Disunion Volume II*, 80.
67. Freehling, *The Road to Disunion Volume II*, 109–22.
68. Freehling, *The Road to Disunion Volume II*, 205–21.
69. Philip Sheldon Foner, *Business & Slavery: The New York Merchants & the Irrepressible Conflict* (New York: Russell & Russell, 1968).
70. Calvin Schermerhorn, *The Business of Slavery and the Rise of American Capitalism, 1815–1860* (New Haven, CT: Yale University Press, 2015), 204.
71. Egnal, *Clash of Extremes*, 101–5.
72. Egnal, *Clash of Extremes*, 192, 239.
73. Robert Francis Engs and Randall Miller, eds., *The Birth of the Grand Old Party: The Republicans' First Generation* (Philadelphia, PA: University of Pennsylvania Press, 2002), 2.
74. George Mayer, *The Republican Party, 1854–1966* (New York: Oxford University Press, 1967), 25–30.
75. Michael Holt, "Making and Mobilizing the Republican Party, 1854–1860," in *The Birth of the Grand Old Party: The Republicans' First Generation*, eds. Robert Francis Engs and Randall Miller (Philadelphia, PA: University of Pennsylvania Press, 2002), 34.
76. Holt, "Making and Mobilizing the Republican Party," 40.
77. Mayer, *The Republican Party*, 65.
78. Eric Foner, *Free Soil, Free Labor, Free Men: The Ideology of the Republican Party before the Civil War* (New York: Oxford University Press, 1988); Jonathan Glickstein, *Concepts of Free Labor in Antebellum America* (New Haven, CT: Yale University Press, 1991).
79. Foner, *Free Soil*, 17.
80. Ashworth, *Slavery, Capitalism, and Politics Volume II*, 267.
81. Freehling, *The Road to Disunion Volume II*, 99.
82. Freehling, *The Road to Disunion Volume II*, 97–100.
83. Buchanan, cited in Frederick Moore Binder, *James Buchanan and the American Empire* (Selinsgrove, PA, London, and Cranbury, NJ: Susquehanna University Press, 1994), 234.
84. Binder, *Buchanan and the American Empire*, 245–70.
85. Robert May, *The Southern Dream of a Caribbean Empire, 1854–1861* (Baton Rouge, LA: Louisiana State University Press, 1973), 25–9.
86. May, *The Southern Dream*, 47.
87. May, *The Southern Dream*, 46–71.
88. May, *The Southern Dream*, 85–106.
89. McPherson, *Battle Cry of Freedom*, 236.

90. Freehling, *The Road to Disunion Volume II*, 147; Nugent, *Habits of Empire*, 218.
91. David Hacker, "A Census-Based Count of the Civil War Dead," *Civil War History* 57, no. 4 (2011): 307–48.
92. Heather Cox Richardson, *The Greatest Nation of the Earth: Republican Economic Policies during the Civil War* (Cambridge, MA: Harvard University Press, 1997), 27.
93. Ralph Andreano, *The Economic Impact of the American Civil War* (Cambridge, MA: Schenkman Publishing Co., 1962); David T. Gilchrist and W. David Lewis, eds., *Economic Change in the Civil War Era; Proceedings* (Greenville, SC: Eleutherian Mills-Hagley Foundation, 1965).
94. Thomas C. Cochran, "The War and National Economic Growth. Did the Civil War Retard Industrialization?" in *The Economic Impact of the American Civil War*, ed. Ralph L. Andreano (Cambridge, MA: Schenkman Publishing Co., 1962), 152.
95. Saul Engelbourg, "The Economic Impact of the Civil War on Manufacturing Enterprise," *Business History* 21, no. 2 (1979): 150–4.
96. Paul W. Gates, *Agriculture and the Civil War* (New York: Knopf, 1965), 134–239.
97. Montgomery, *Beyond Equality*, 91–6.
98. Montgomery, *Beyond Equality*, 98–105.
99. Phillip Shaw Paludan, "War is the Health of the Party: Republicans in the American Civil War," in *The Birth of the Grand Old Party: The Republicans' First Generation*, eds. Robert Francis Engs and Randall M. Miller (Philadelphia, PA: University of Pennsylvania Press, 2002), 66.
100. Richardson, *The Greatest Nation of the Earth*, 59–60.
101. Richardson, *The Greatest Nation of the Earth*, 86–139.
102. Fred A. Shannon, *The Farmer's Last Frontier: Agriculture, 1860–1897* (New York: Holt, 1961), 55.
103. Shannon, *The Farmer's Last Frontier*, 64.
104. James McPherson, "Afterword," in *The Birth of the Grand Old Party: The Republicans' First Generation*, eds. Robert Francis Engs and Randall M. Miller (Philadelphia, PA: University of Pennsylvania Press, 2002), 170.
105. Eric Foner, *Reconstruction: America's Unfinished Revolution, 1863–1877* (New York: HarperCollins, 1989), 446.
106. C. Vann Woodward, *Origins of the New South, 1877–1913* (Baton Rouge, LA: Louisiana State University Press, 1951).
107. William Gillette, *Retreat from Reconstruction, 1869–1879* (Baton Rouge, LA: Louisiana State University Press, 1979).
108. Foner, *Reconstruction*, 54.
109. Foner, *Reconstruction*, 51.
110. Foner, *Reconstruction*, 58.
111. Michael W. Fitzgerald, *Splendid Failure: Postwar Reconstruction in the American South* (Chicago, IL: Ivan R. Dee, 2007), 31.
112. Foner, *Reconstruction*, 153–61.

113. The literature on sharecropping and the post-war south is huge. Some of the works I found useful for writing this section in particular include: Edward L. Ayers, *The Promise of the New South: Life after Reconstruction* (New York: Oxford University Press, 1992); Foner, *Reconstruction*, 404; Fitzgerald, *Splendid Failure*, 61; Charles Aiken, *The Cotton Plantation South since the Civil War* (Baltimore, MD: Johns Hopkins University Press, 1998); Roger Ransom and Richard Sutch, "Capitalists Without Capital: The Burden of Slavery and the Impact of Emancipation," *Agricultural History* 62, no. 3 (1988): 133–60; Jay R. Mandle, "Continuity and Change: The Use of Black Labor after the Civil War," *Journal of Black Studies* 21, no. 4 (1991): 414–27; Sean Kelley, "A Texas Peasantry? Black Smallholders in the Texas Sugar Bowl, 1865–1890," *Slavery and Abolition* 28, no. 2 (2007): 193–209; Martin Ruef, "The Demise of an Organization Form: Emancipation and Plantation Agriculture in the American South, 1860–1880," *American Journal of Sociology* 109, no. 6 (2004): 1365–410; Brian Kelly, "Jubilee and the Limits of African American Freedom after Emancipation," *Race & Class* 57 no. 3 (2016): 59–70; Susan A. Mann, "Sharecropping in the Cotton South: A Case of Uneven Development in Agriculture," *Rural Sociology* 49, no. 3 (1984): 412–29; Ronald L.F. Davis, "The U.S. Army and the Origins of Sharecropping in the Natchez District—a Case Study," *Journal of Negro History* 62, no. 1 (1977): 60–80; Donald L. Winters, "Postbellum Reorganization of Southern Agriculture: The Economics of Sharecropping in Tennessee," *Agricultural History* 62, no. 4 (1988): 1–19; Louis Ferleger, "Sharecropping Contracts in the Late-Nineteenth-Century South," *Agricultural History* 67, no. 3 (1993): 31–46; Alex Lichtenstein, "Was the Emancipated Slave a Proletarian?" *Reviews in American History* 26, no. 1 (1988): 124–45; James R. Irwin and Anthony Patrick O'Brian, "Where Have All the Sharecroppers Gone? Black Occupations in Postbellum Mississippi," *Agricultural History* 72, no. 2 (1998): 280–97; Adam Wolkoff, "Every Man His Own Avenger: Landlord Remedies and the Antebellum Roots of the Crop Lien and Chattel Mortgage in the United States," *Law and History Review* 35, no. 1 (2017): 131–54; Susan A. Mann, "Slavery, Sharecropping, and Sexual Inequality," *Signs* 14, no. 4 (1989): 774–98; Erin Stewart Mauldin, "Freedom, Economic Autonomy, and Ecological Change in the Cotton South, 1865–1880," *Journal of the Civil War Era* 7, no. 3 (2017): 401–24; Shirley A. Hollis, "Neither Slave nor Free: The Ideology of Capitalism and the Failure of Radical Reform in the American South," *Critical Sociology* 35, no. 1 (2009): 9–27; Edward L. Ayres, *The Promise of the New South* (New York: Oxford University Press, 2007).

114. Edward Royce, *The Origins of Southern Sharecropping* (Philadelphia, PA: Temple University Press, 1993), 185; R. Pearce, "Sharecropping: Towards a Marxist View," in *Sharecropping and Sharecroppers*, ed. T.J. Byres (London: Frank Cass and Company, 1983), 54.

115. Royce, *The Origins of Southern Sharecropping*, 185.

116. Royce, *The Origins of Southern Sharecropping*, 186.

117. Irwin and O'Brian, "Where Have all the Sharecroppers Gone?"
118. Aiken, *The Cotton Plantation South*, 23.
119. Martin Ruef, *Between Slavery and Capitalism: The Legacy of Emancipation in the American South* (Princeton, NJ: Princeton University Press, 2014), 131–55.
120. Gillette, *Retreat from Reconstruction*, 363–80.
121. W.E.B. Du Bois, *Black Reconstruction in America* (New York: The Free Press, 1995), 584.
122. Heather Cox Richardson, *The Death of Reconstruction: Race, Labor, and Politics in the Post-Civil War North, 1865–1901* (Cambridge, MA: Harvard University Press, 2001), 25.
123. Woodward, *Origins of the New South*, 116–17.
124. Pedro Camejo, *Racism, Revolution, Reaction, 1861–1877: The Rise and Fall of Radical Reconstruction* (New York: Monad Press. 1976), 117.
125. James L. Roark, *Masters Without Slaves: Southern Planters in the Civil War and Reconstruction* (New York: Norton & Co., 1977); Howard N. Rabinowitz, *The First New South, 1865–1920* (Arlington Heights, IL: Harlan Davidson, 1992), 19.
126. Camejo, *Racism, Revolution, Reaction*, 117.
127. Camejo, *Racism, Revolution, Reaction*, 115–26.

Conclusion: Capital and the Conquest of Space

1. David Harvey, *The New Imperialism* (New York: Oxford University Press, 2005), 26.
2. For a discussion of the role of the state in securing capitalist development for agribusiness also see: Brad Bauerly, *The Agrarian Seeds of Empire: The Political Economy of Agriculture in US State Building* (Chicago, IL: Haymarket, 2018). For an example of how railway companies viewed the west as a space of potential profit also see: Claire Strom, *Profiting from the Plains: The Great Northern Railway and the Corporate Development of the America West* (Seattle, WA: University of Washington Press, 2003). And for an exploration of industrialization and the west see: David Igler, *Industrial Cowboys: Miller & Lux and the Transformation of the Far West, 1850–1920* (Berkeley and Los Angeles, CA: University of California Press, 2001).
3. William G. Robbins, *Colony and Empire: The Capitalist Transformation of the American West* (Lawrence, KA: University Press of Kansas, 1994), 88–9.
4. William Cronon, *Nature's Metropolis: Chicago and the Great West* (New York: W.W. Norton & Co., 1991), 29.
5. J.M. Peck, *A Gazetteer of Illinois* (Philadelphia, PA: Grigg & Elliot, 1837), 52–61; J.M. Peck, *The Traveler's Directory for Illinois* (New York: J.H. Colton, 1939), 62–87.

6. William Bross, ed., *History of Chicago: Historical and Commercial Statistics, Sketches, Facts and Figures, Republished from the "Daily Democratic Press"* (Chicago, IL: Jansen, McClurg & Co., 1876), 5.
7. Bross, *History of Chicago*, 69.
8. Robbins, *Colony and Empire*, 66–8.
9. Rossiter W. Raymond, *Statistics of Mines and Mining in the States and Territories West of the Rocky Mountains* (Washington, DC: Government Printing Office, 1873), 7.
10. Thomas Antisell, *On the Relations of Physical Geography to Agriculture (Address at the Seventh Annual Meeting of the U.S. Agricultural Society)*, 1859.
11. "Colorado," from *Appleton's Hand-book of American Travel*, in *Colorado: Its Resources, Parks, and Prospects as a New Field for Emigration*, ed. William Blackmore (London: Sampson Low, Son, and Marston, 1869), 15.
12. Rovert E. Strahorn, *To the Rockies and Beyond, or a Summer on the Union Pacific Railroad and Branches* (Omaha, NE: The New West Publishing Company, 1879), 34.
13. Denver Board of Trade, *Colorado* (Denver, CO: Daily Colorado Tribune Print, 1868); William Blackmore, *Colorado: Its Resources, Parks, and Prospects as a New Field for Emigration* (London: Sampson Low, Son, and Marston, 1869), 6.
14. Frank W. Warner, *Montana and the Northwest Territory* (Chicago, IL: Blakely, Brown & Marsh, 1879), 20.
15. Louis Janin, *Report on Some of the Lead Mining Claims of the Whitewood Mining District, in the Black Hills, Lawerence County, Dakota* (San Francisco, CA: Spaulding & Williams, Steam Book, Card and Job Printers, 1879), 34–47.
16. L.D. Burch, *Nebraska as it is: A Comprehensive Summary of the Resources, Advantages and Drawbacks, of the Great Prairie State* (Chicago, IL: C.S. Burch & Co., 1878), 12.
17. Burch, *Nebraska as it is*, 64.
18. Burch, *Nebraska as it is*, 66.
19. Burch, *Nebraska as it is*, 69.
20. Burch, *Nebraska as it is*, 73.
21. Alfred Sorenson, *Early History of Omaha* (Omaha, NE: Office of the Daily Bee, 1876), 19.
22. Sorenson, *Early History of Omaha*, 32.
23. C.C. Spalding, *Annals of the City of Kansas and the Great Western Plains* (Kansas City, MO: Van Horn & Abeel's Printing House, 1858), 13.
24. Spalding, *Annals of the City of Kansas*, 14.
25. Spalding, *Annals of the City of Kansas*, 101.
26. Data compiled from the report of the commissioner of agriculture estimates the dollar amounts of Indian corn, wheat, rye, oats, barley, buckwheat, potatoes, tobacco, and hay. For the data the northeastern states chosen were Maine, New Hampshire, Vermont, Massachusetts, Rhode Island, Connecticut, New York. New Jersey, Pennsylvania, Delaware, and

Maryland. Western states chosen are Ohio, Indiana, Illinois, Wisconsin, Minnesota, Iowa, Missouri, Kansas, Nebraska, California, Oregon, and Nevada. Fred K. Watts, *Report of the Commissioner of Agriculture for the Year 1875* (Washington, DC: Government Printing Office, 1876), 23–7.

27. Bruce Cumings, *Dominion from Sea to Sea: Pacific Ascendency and American Power* (New Haven, CT: Yale University Press, 2009), 100.
28. John Frost, *History of the State of California* (New York: Millar, Orton & Co., 1857), 40.
29. Frost, *History of the State of California*, 55, 90, 100.
30. Ernest Seyd, *California and its Resources: A Work for the Merchant, the Capitalist, and the Emigrant* (London: Trubner and Co., 1858), 121.
31. As of 2016–17, California produced 51 percent of the country's citrus, above Florida's 45 percent. United States Department of Agriculture, *Citrus Fruits 2017 Summary* (National Agricultural Statistics Service, 2017), accessed January 28, 2018 at http://usda.mannlib.cornell.edu/usda/current/CitrFrui/CitrFrui-08-31-2017.pdf.
32. Cumings, *Dominion from Sea to Sea*, 225.
33. Niall McCarthy, "California Dreamin'? Only 5 Countries Have a Bigger GDP than the Golden State," *Forbes*, November 16, 2016, accessed January 28, 2018 at www.forbes.com/sites/niallmccarthy/2016/11/16/california-dreamin-only-5-countries-have-a-bigger-gdp-than-the-golden-state-infographic/#5905af81468d.
34. Paul Neff Garber, *The Gadsden Treaty* (Philadelphia, PA: University of Pennsylvania Press, 1923), 18.
35. Garber, *The Gadsden Treaty*, 139.
36. Robbins, *Colony and Empire*, 72–87.
37. Megan Kate Nelson, "Death in the Distance: Confederate Manifest Destiny and the Campaign for New Mexico, 1861–1862," in *Civil War Wests: Testing the Limits of the United States*, eds. Adam Arenson and Andrew R. Graybill (Oakland, CA: University of California Press, 2015), 34–41.
38. Lance Blyth, "Kit Carson and the War for the Southwest: Separation and Survival along the Rio Grande, 1862–1868," in *Civil War Wests: Testing the Limits of the United States*, eds. Adam Arenson and Andrew R. Graybill (Oakland, CA: University of California Press, 2015), 64–5.
39. Richard White, *"It's Your Misfortune and None of My Own": A History of the American West* (Norman, OK: University of Oklahoma Press, 1991), 95–7.
40. Pedro Camejo, *Racism, Revolution, Reaction, 1861–1877: The Rise and Fall of Radical Reconstruction* (New York: Monad Press. 1976), 30; Sidney Lens, *The Forging of the American Empire* (London: Pluto Press, 2003), 138.
41. *Lens, The Forging of the American Empire*, 136–7.
42. For a discussion of the culture of empire in these regards also see: Janne Lahti, *Cultural Construction of Empire: The U.S. Army in Arizona and New Mexico* (Lincoln, NE: University of Nebraska Press, 2012).

43. White, "*It's Your Misfortune and None of My Own,*" 104–15.
44. Sven Beckert, "American Danger: United States Empire, Eurafrica, and the Territorialization of Industrial Capitalism, 1870–1950," *American Historical Review* 122, no. 4 (2017): 1137–70.
45. See: Alfred McCoy, *In the Shadows of the American Century: The Rise and Decline of US Global Power* (Chicago, IL: Dispatch Books, 2017).

Index

The Pluto Press Newsletter

Hello friend of Pluto!

Want to stay on top of the best radical books we publish?

Then sign up to be the first to hear about our new books, as well as special events, podcasts and videos.

You'll also get 50% off your first order with us when you sign up.

Come and join us!

Go to bit.ly/PlutoNewsletter